CROCKETT'S FLOWER GARDEN

PHOTOGRAPHY BY
RUSSELL MORASH

LITTLE, BROWN
AND COMPANY
BOSTON/TORONTO

CROCKETT'S FLOWER GARDEN

BY
JAMES UNDERWOOD CROCKETT

WITH THE ASSISTANCE OF
MARJORIE WATERS

Seventh Printing
Designed by
Dianne Smith Schaefer/Designworks

Drawings by
George Ulrich
WAK
Published simultaneously in Canada
by Little, Brown & Company
(Canada) Limited

Printed in the United States of
America

To my children
Carol, Bob, Jean,
and Mary

CONTENTS

INTRODUCTION

Jim Crockett wrote three books of gardening advice based on his popular and much-loved PBS television series, "Crockett's Victory Garden." The first, also called *Crockett's Victory Garden*, deals mostly with vegetables. The second, *Crockett's Indoor Garden*, is Jim's guide to the care of houseplants. This third book, *Crockett's Flower Garden*, is devoted entirely to outdoor flowers. Of the three, it is the book Jim was most eager to write, for outdoor flowers were his first horticultural love, an affection dating back to his boyhood, to summer days at his grandmother's, and the first gladiolus he planted. It wasn't that Jim played favorites among plants; every growing thing fascinated and delighted him (although he could dispatch a superfluous weak seedling without a qualm). But flowers are beautiful when beauty is not required of them, and this gift to the world pleased Jim to no end.

Jim did not live to complete this book himself. He had been at work on it for over a year when he died of cancer. During this time he had outlined the book, chosen the flowers to be included, designed the features, and, with his longtime collaborator, Marjorie Waters, was in the process of writing the manuscript from his shelves of notebooks and the transcripts of his television shows. As his illness progressed, work on the book became increasingly important to him, and he continued to labor on this project even when he was forced to cut back on many of his other professional obligations.

After Jim's death, Marjorie Waters put the manuscript into final shape, and to assist her, two new people were added to the team that had worked with Jim on the first two books in the series. John Pelrine, the full-time gardener who tends the Victory Garden at WGBH-TV in Boston, contributed his thorough and intimate knowledge of Jim's gardening procedures. Thurston Handley, an old friend of Jim's and horticulturalist at the Middlesex (Massachusetts) County Extension Service, read the finished text for horticultural accuracy.

The rest of the people who worked on this book were able to contribute an understanding of Jim's way of doing things gained from their long and happy association with him. Russell Morash, the producer who created "Crockett's Victory Garden" for WGBH-TV, took the photographs. The procedural illustrations were drawn by George Ulrich. Dianne Smith Schaefer of Designworks was the book's designer and art director. At Little, Brown, Mike Mattil copyedited the manuscript, editorial assistant Laura Evans checked the text for consistency, and Peter Carr, General Manager of Manufacturing, supervised the book through production. As Jim's editor, I kept watch over the project.

Jim was greatly pleased with two distinctive features that characterize all three books in this series. The first is that they are based on the day-to-day experience of a real garden, where actual horticultural events take place. As Jim said again and again, he was interested in teaching only what was practical for the average home gardener, and he felt that the real-world setting gave a substance, a specific usefulness to gardening advice that he found lacking in other books. Second, the books are organized chronologically, in monthly chapters that give the reader a timetable for managing the many tasks of the gardening year.

Like its predecessors, *Crockett's Flower Garden* is based on the month-to-month sequence of events in the Victory Garden in Boston, but in addition it incorporates many of the flower-gardening projects undertaken by Jim at a more expansive suburban garden, west of the city. The book was designed to be used by the novice planning a first garden as well as by experienced gardeners who have been digging in the soil all their lives. Jim was thorough and meticulous both as a gardener and teacher, and he felt an obligation to demonstrate the simplest task for the beginner to make sure it was done right. At the same time, he took special joy in sharing the experts' tricks, techniques, and shortcuts with all his readers. Thus, by mixing basic advice with more complex projects, he structured *Crockett's Flower Garden* to keep pace with any gardener as he or she gained in experience and skill.

The book consists of nine monthly chapters, February through October, and a tenth entitled "After Frost." Each of the monthly chapters contains a series of entries in alphabetical order, covering individual plants that need attention during the month. From the bewildering number of plants and plant varieties, Jim chose some one hundred flowers for inclusion in this book. These are his favorites, in part because of their special beauty and dependability, and in part because they grow well in many different parts of the country. They come from the four major categories of flowers, and are identified by marginal symbols next to the entry title: Ⓐ annuals, Ⓟ perennials, Ⓑ biennials, and Ⓑ bulbs. Tubers and corms that can be saved for years if dug in the fall are labeled as annuals.

For some plants, such as chrysanthemums and hollyhocks, there are both annual and perennial versions, and a clarifying word has been added in parentheses after the entry title to avoid confusion.

As with the first two books, there is an essay-length feature at the end of each monthly chapter. Three of these (May, September, and October) are general discussions of annuals, perennials and biennials, and bulbs, and it's a good idea to read this background information first, before turning to the individual entries. The other features cover important gardening procedures and general information applicable throughout the gardening year, although the features are located in the month when they will be most needed.

The calendar of gardening events on which this book is structured comes from climate conditions in Zone 5, where the Victory Garden is located. In this area, February brings the first hint of springlike conditions — longer day length, brighter sunlight — and October brings the first frost. There is a great deal of weather variation across the country, so

before you use this book, you should determine in which zone you are located (see the map in the Appendix) as well as the expected dates of your last spring and first fall frosts. Your county agricultural agent will be able to provide this information for your general area, and neighbors who garden will probably have even more accurate predictions for your site. When you have this information, you can compare it to the Victory Garden weather schedule and make adjustments as necessary. Most of these adjustments will occur in the spring. For instance, if your last expected spring frost date is in mid-March, a month ahead of the Victory Garden's, you will be able to do the spring chores a month ahead of the book schedule.

You should read the individual entries in the book before buying plants or seeds for your garden, because Jim took particular care to include a great deal of advice on which varieties have done unusually well, and which have special qualities worth noting. Jim always recommended that people start plants from seeds whenever possible because it is cheaper and there is a much greater selection available. Yet he knew that for many gardeners, buying plants from garden centers is the only option. In this book you will find information on both.

Readers familiar with *Crockett's Victory Garden* and *Crockett's Indoor Garden* will probably notice a few changes in gardening procedures and information in this book. In some cases, Jim thought it necessary to clarify a point, but most of the changes occurred because Jim simply changed his mind about the best way to do something. As with all great teachers, Jim was always eager to continue learning. He never ceased trying out new ideas, or unfamiliar approaches to gardening, whether they were based on the latest technology or the long-forgotten methods of old-timers. This lively curiosity of Jim's, this energetic pursuit of knowledge, this zest for sharing what he learned, made the experience of working on these books with him unforgettable for all of us. We were his students as well as his collaborators, and we are better gardeners thanks to Jim. But he gave us much more than this. He was fired by a deep spiritual understanding and awe of the natural world, and it was impossible to be near him and not feel the glow. He often said that he considered himself a lucky man because he had spent his life doing what he loved most. Because he shared this love so willingly, we, his friends, readers, and students, are lucky too.

William D. Phillips
Little, Brown & Company

Monthly Checklist

Browallia
Coleus
Dusty Miller
Geranium
Gloriosa Daisy
Impatiens
Lobelia
Pinks
Vinca
Wax Begonia

Marmelade, a variety of gloriosa daisy (see page 23)

FEBRUARY

February can be one of the wintriest months in the Victory Garden, bringing cold weather and some of the season's heaviest snows. But fierce as the weather may be, the days are longer and the sun noticeably brighter. So this is the month when work begins in earnest on the flowers for the Victory Garden. We can move ahead quickly at this stage because we have spent the winter preparing and making plans for the next season's garden, poring over catalogues, ordering seeds, designing the individual gardens.

Most of this month is devoted to seed-sowing. We can set annuals outdoors in the Victory Garden on the first of May, so this is the month we sow the plants that require a rather long growing period, from 8 to 12 weeks, before they are large enough to be set into the garden. There are only a few plants requiring such a long period of growing on, but they are among the most popular of all garden flowers: petunias, impatiens, wax begonias, and geraniums are among them.

Because we have greenhouse facilities, we often sow perennial and biennial seeds this month, too. Alyssum, bee balm, Carpathian harebells, delphiniums, English daisies, forget-me-nots, gaillardias, gloriosa daisies, lupines, Maltese cross plants, pansies, and shasta daisies can all be sown now for flowering plants this year. This isn't a routine I recommend to gardeners without a greenhouse, however, as it is unlikely that you have enough sunny windowsills to keep all these plants growing well. My advice is to sow perennials during the summer and winter them over outdoors (see the September feature), leaving your sunny spots indoors free for the slow-growing annuals.

While most of our work is indoors this month, we also have the first outdoor work of the season. The very early spring-flowering minor bulbs, such as chionodoxa and squill, that were mulched for the winter should be uncovered 2 to 3 weeks before their expected flowering time. I always do this in two stages — first the top half of the layer and then, about a week later, the rest — so that the emerging tips of green aren't damaged by sudden exposure to bright light. (In ground-level bulb beds, there's no need to mulch. See After Frost.)

Browallia This is a modest, gentle-looking plant that blooms beautifully through the early part of the season; while it prefers half-day sunlight, it grows well in full or filtered sun. Best of all, its different varieties present a range of lovely blue flowers — always the prized color in the flower garden — from pale powder blue through deeper shades of violet and purple. There's a white-flowered variety, too, but I haven't grown it in the Victory Garden, because our choice for a trailing white-flowered plant would be sweet alyssum. Such handsome blues, on the other hand, are hard to come by. Browallias are available in trailing and upright varieties, so there are choices both for containers and for the garden bed.

Browallias are very slow growing from seed, but aside from their pace, they are no trouble at all for the home gardener, so long as they are sown indoors 8 to 10 weeks before the garden date. Our garden date is May 1, which moves browallia sowing back to the third or fourth week of February. This produces sturdy, good-sized plants by the

One of several available varieties of blue-flowered browallia

set-out date. (In order to produce nearly full-grown plants, ready to burst into flower when they're set into the garden, we have sometimes given browallias more than 8 to 10 weeks of growing time in the Victory Garden, which commits us to moving the plants into larger pots as they grow. This is an effort we're willing to make because we have a greenhouse in which to keep plants vigorous all along, but for the home gardener, it's not practical.) Browallia seeds are easy to find in garden catalogues; the botanical name is *Browallia speciosa.*

Because browallia seeds are extremely fine, and because they need light to germinate, the seeds should not be covered after sowing. Otherwise, I follow our normal sowing routine (see the August feature), giving them 5 to 7 days in the cold frame before setting them into the garden.

A **Coleus** Coleus are grown not for their flowers, but for their colored foliage. While they're more commonly found growing in pots indoors, they're a fine garden plant. Best in

Seedlings of several varieties of coleus, grown from a mix

half-day or filtered sunlight, they tend to flower in full sun, which simply drains their energies. There are many types of coleus available, each with its own distinctive coloration — in patterns of red, white, pink, and green — and sometimes an unusual leaf shape as well. We've grown beds of coleus at our suburban Victory Garden, massing plants of one variety together. We've also used coleus in window boxes as a change of pace from more commonplace window-box plants. We've had particularly good results with the dwarf varieties, both in a window box and in a bed; at less than 1 foot tall, the dwarf scale is suitable to our garden, and the shorter types have the added merit of being self-branching. The dwarf varieties have a spread of 6 to 9 inches.

In the past, these tender perennials were grown only from cuttings, because seeds did not produce true-to-type seedlings. In the newer varieties, this problem has been solved; they can be started from seed, and then propagated in late summer by cuttings of the mature plant. So although seedlings are widely available from garden centers later in the spring, we start our own crop indoors in February, 8 to 12 weeks before our May 1 garden date. Seed houses carry several varieties. *Coleus x hybridus* is the botanical name.

The seeds should not be covered after sowing. (For the sowing procedure, see the August feature.) The seeds of the dwarf varieties sprout quickly, but the seedlings grow slowly: there's an ugly-duckling quality to coleus, as it's often the case that the brightest-colored mature plants were the slowest-growing seedlings. It's important to know that when they're very small, all coleus seedlings are green — the color doesn't develop until the first true leaves approach maturity, when the plants are about 2 inches tall.

Before setting them out, I move the seedlings to the cold frame for 5 to 7 days.

A **Dusty Miller** The best flower gardens are studies in variety, with different textures, colors, and sizes combined in a way that is both interesting and graceful. It's not only flowering plants that contribute to this picture. There are a few plants whose foliage is appealing enough to earn them places in the flower garden. Of these, dusty miller is among my favorites, as it is one of the few foliage plants that thrive in full sun. (It also grows well in half-day or filtered sunlight.) Its soft pale leaves show the bright colors of flowering plants to their best advantage. A tender perennial, dusty miller has much the same function as artemisia has in the perennial border. I'm particularly taken with dusty miller as a companion plant to geraniums in sunny window boxes (see the June feature).

Diamond, a variety of dusty miller

Dusty miller seedlings are fairly commonplace in garden centers in the spring, but they grow easily from seed, too. The main problems facing the gardener when ordering seeds is that there are several plants, from several genera, sold as dusty miller. You may find them labeled as *Senecio* or *Cineraria* or *Centaurea*. The important point is that all plants sold as dusty miller are essentially alike. Some will be taller than others, some have a heavier look, but all are grown as annuals and produce silvery-gray leaves. We've grown the varieties Diamond and Silver Feather; the latter is particularly fine-foliaged.

Young dusty millers are slow growing, so we give them a head start by sowing them indoors toward the end of February, 8 to 10 weeks before the garden date. The seeds should not be covered, as light is necessary for germination (see the August feature). Before they're transplanted to the garden, dusty millers need up to a week in the cold frame to harden off.

A **Geranium** Though geraniums are increasingly popular as bedding plants, we've been traditionalists as far as these plants are concerned, growing them almost exclusively as window-box and outdoor pot plants in the Victory Garden. I'm especially partial to red or pink geraniums combined with dusty miller (see this month's entry), and I rarely let a year go by without setting them together into our window boxes. At our suburban site, we've also planted geraniums in large tubs to dress up the area around the house. Geraniums are tender perennials that grow to shrub size in warm climates, but in the Victory Garden, where we treat

Opposite: Geraniums in the window box along the Victory Garden greenhouse

these plants as annuals, they reach heights of 15 to 20 inches. Their spread is about equal to their height. Geraniums need full sun, dry air, warm days, and cool nights. With the exception of the dry air, we can meet most of these needs, and keep geraniums in blossom from May until frost.

The most popular way to start a geranium collection is to buy plants in the spring. If you do not need many plants, if you are interested in double-flowered types (or those with variegated foliage), or if you do not have the indoor conditions geraniums need, this is probably still your best route. However, there have been dramatic improvements in the germination of geranium seeds since the 1960s, and this is an alternative worth considering. There are no double-flowered or variegated plants available from seed — these have to be propagated by cutting — but there are many excellent varieties on the market. All are *Pelargonium x hortorum*. The seeds are expensive, but this route is still far cheaper than buying potted plants in the spring.

Seed-grown geraniums, growing on in the greenhouse

In the Victory Garden, where we can provide greenhouse conditions, we grow all our geraniums from seed, sowing them between mid-January and early February, 12 to 16 weeks before our set-out date. However, for the gardener without a greenhouse or hotbed equipment or an unusually sunny spot indoors, keeping the seedlings growing well until spring may be very difficult. As an alternative, I suggest sowing the seeds a little later, giving them only 8 to 10 weeks before set-out. By waiting just those few weeks, you give the plants the advantage of longer days and warmer, brighter light, and they will nearly catch up with plants started earlier.

Geranium seeds have a tough outer surface. If something isn't done to crack or soften this shell, germination is difficult. Most seed houses sell scarified seeds, which have been scraped to give the seeds a better chance to sprout. If you don't buy scarified seeds, it's a good idea to soak them for 24 hours in warm water. (For the complete seed-sowing procedure, see the August feature.)

The germination of geranium seeds takes place over a span of 2 or 3 weeks. If they were sown in a communal pot, as is our general practice, the emerging seedlings would be disturbed when the larger ones were transplanted, so we sow the seeds directly into six-packs. We put just 1 seed to a compartment rather than our usual 2, since the seeds are costly. Because they are sown so far in advance of the set-out date — a necessity if the plants are to be far enough along by warm weather — they will need to be transplanted into larger containers later in the spring. As a rule, we have the seedlings in individual 4-inch pots when we set them into the cold frame for a week or so of conditioning.

[A]   **Gloriosa Daisy** Gloriosa daisies are the cultured offspring of one of the best-known wildflowers in America, the black-eyed Susan. The wild plant is very free-flowering on its own, so most of the breeders' efforts have been directed toward expanding the color range and making the flowers larger and more substantial. There are excellent varieties that have large single flowers with dark centers and yellow petals. In the Victory Garden we've grown a dark-centered (black-eyed) All-America Winner called Double Gold. Its flowers are much fuller, but otherwise it resembles the wildflowers more than some of the other available varieties. Like most of the full-size gloriosa daisies, Double Gold grows to be about 3 feet tall and 2 feet across. There are also dwarf varieties that are about a foot shorter. All produce very good cut flowers. All need full sun to do their best, but will grow and flower on half-day sunlight, too.

Gloriosa daisies are usually advertised as very versatile plants, so tolerant of harsh winters that they can be treated as perennials, so free-flowering the first year that they can be grown as annuals. It is true that the plants will live through a cold winter — they would survive in the Victory Garden without trouble — but they do not produce a good crop year after year unless they are divided every spring. In horticultural circles it's generally agreed that it is better to treat them as annuals or biennials, and pull the plants after one flowering season. Here, we treat them as annuals; we sow the seeds around the middle of this month, set out the seedlings with the other annuals on the first of

May, and pull out the plants after fall frost. The seeds are widely available from seed houses; the botanical name is *Rudbeckia*.

The seed-sowing routine for gloriosa daisies is the standard one (see the August feature), but because the plants need such a long lead time indoors, they outgrow their six-packs before the set-out date. When this happens, we move them to individual 4-inch pots. (Gloriosa daisies should *not* be pinched. See the August feature.) These are cool-weather plants, so we put them into the cold frame for 2 to 4 weeks before they go into the open garden on May 1. They are actually so frost-tolerant that they could be transplanted to the garden a week or two ahead of the other annuals, especially if they've been hardened off in the cold frame.

Ⓐ   Impatiens These plants have been popular garden flowers for generations, but in the past few years they have gained even more of a following, out of appreciation for their

Futura, a mixed variety of impatiens

ease of culture and their free-flowering, modest good looks. Our grandparents knew these plants by their long-time common names, Patient Lucy and Busy Lizzy, but the botanical name is *Impatiens*.

There are many varieties of impatiens available to the gardener, including an impressive assortment of colors, from pale pastel to vivid hots. Some are bicolored, and some have variegated foliage. They are all about a foot tall, with a spread of 12 to 15 inches. They flower all summer long. I've grown the upright types either lined up along the front edge of the garden, or massed together in a large, shady area. I've also potted three young trailing-type impatiens together in a hanging pot to grow in a shaded area outdoors.

I start new crops of impatiens from seed early every spring. It is possible to grow plants indoors over winter and take cuttings for the upcoming season's outdoor crop (see the August entry), but I don't have enough room in the greenhouse to devote to so many plants. The seeds are inexpensive, and while germination is slow, seed-grown plants will be ready for the garden if they're sown indoors 8 to 12 weeks in advance of the set-out date. In the Victory Garden, where our annuals go into the garden the first of May, we sow impatiens seeds in February. The seeds need light to germinate, so they are not covered after sowing; otherwise, the sowing technique is the standard one, described in the August feature. Five or 6 days before set-out, the seedlings go into the cold frame for conditioning.

Ⓐ **Lobelia** The beauty of this plant is in its short growth, never taller than 6 inches, and in the great quantity of delicate flowers. The plant seems to explode into bloom. We've grown mostly trailing varieties in hanging baskets and window boxes, where a single plant will trail 9 to 12 inches, but the upright varieties make fine edging or rock garden plants. There are rose- and white-flowered varieties, in addition to the blues; as usual, I choose the blues. All lobelias prefer half-day or filtered sunlight; if they're kept well watered, full sun is okay, too. They bloom from early summer through frost. In the Victory Garden, flower production often drops off in hot midsummer; when this happens, I cut them back by about half their height and they usually come back into bloom in 3 or 4 weeks.

Unlike many of the other flowers started from seed in the Victory Garden this month, lobelia is a true annual that dies at the end of its single growing season, so new crops must be started fresh from seed every year. The seeds are easily available in garden catalogues by the botanical name *Lobelia erinus*.

Sapphire, a variety of trailing lobelia

Lobelias require about 10 weeks to grow from seed to garden-size plants, so we sow them in pots indoors about the middle of this month, following the normal sowing procedure (see the August feature). Because lobelia seeds need light in order to germinate, they should not be covered after sowing. During the last week of April I set the seedlings into a cold frame to harden off for at least 5 days, and they're ready for the great outdoors the first of May.

A **Pinks** There are many species of *Dianthus* that are grown in garden culture. Some are perennials, some biennials, and some annuals. Among the annuals, the most common are varieties of *Dianthus chinensis*, called China pinks, or simply pinks, in honor of the once-dominant flower color. In the Victory Garden, we have had good luck with a variety called Snowfire, which is 10 to 12 inches tall at maturity. This variety is not pink; it has white flowers with red centers. Snowfire is a relatively new introduction and very free-flowering. We've also grown Magic Charms, usually sold as a mixture of orange, pink, red, and white; they're shorter than Snowfire, peaking at 6 to 8 inches. All varieties are about as wide as they are tall and all produce nice cut flowers.

Pinks are better in cool weather than in hot. The new varieties, including Snowfire, are bred for heat resistance and bloom all summer, right up to frost, dropping off only a little during midsummer. All do best in half-day sunlight, but can take full sun in areas where summers are cool. Our routine is to start them indoors toward the end of this month, 8 to 10 weeks before the garden date (see the August feature). Before set-out, pinks are given at least two weeks in the cold frame, where chilly temperatures help them develop into sturdy plants.

A **Vinca** Vinca, also known as Madagascar periwinkle, is one of the Victory Garden standouts. A tender perennial, it is grown here as an annual bedding plant in summer, and indoors through the winter. The foliage is rich and shiny, handsome even when the plant is not in bloom, and the flowers have a long vase life when cut for bouquets. The pink varieties are best, but whites are available too. It's a good plant for a sunny, warm location; as a matter of fact, it won't flower in areas where night temperatures fall below 60°F. It's more tolerant where light is concerned, blossoming in half-day or filtered light, as well as the full sun that it prefers. It's rarely affected by either diseases or pests. There are upright varieties as tall as 12 inches or so, but there is also a short, creeping variety called Polka Dot. All vincas bloom from early summer to frost.

Opposite: China pinks, the variety Snowfire

Vincas are gaining in popularity, but gardeners may have trouble finding seedlings in garden centers in the spring. The seeds are easy to come by through garden catalogues, though. They're usually known simply as Vinca after the original botanical name, *Vinca rosea*, or may be listed by their common name, Madagascar periwinkle. Their current botanical name is *Catharanthus roseus*, but they are rarely sold as such.

Sowing them during February, we give the plants 8 to 12 weeks to grow indoors before they go into the garden.

Little Pinkie, a Madagascar periwinkle variety

Toward the end of April, we set them into the cold frame for up to a week of hardening-off before they go into the open ground in early May. (For complete sowing information, see the August feature.)

Ⓐ **Wax Begonia** Wax begonias have a very useful trait in the flower garden: they blossom until frost either in fairly heavy shade or, if kept watered and shaded through midday, in bright sunshine. This makes them an excellent bedding plant for an area that crosses the sun/shade lines in the garden. We've grown them in every imaginable location in the Victory Garden. There are nice white varieties, several shades of pink, and some good, bright reds. The series we've grown is called Thousand Wonders. Wax begonias range in height from 6 to 12 inches, with a roughly equal spread.

The seedlings are easy to find in garden centers in the spring, but we start the Victory Garden crop indoors in February, 8 to 12 weeks before set-out in early May. This

Thousand Wonders Rose, a wax begonia

long advance time is needed because wax begonia seeds are among plantlife's smallest, and because growth from seed is slow. Most seedlings are transplanted to six-packs when the first true leaves develop, but wax begonias are so tiny and so shallow-rooted at this point that they can be left in shared quarters until the second or third set of true leaves develops. Even then, they're often only an inch tall and have to be picked out carefully with the tip of a knife or label. Before setting them into the garden, we give them 5 days or so in the cold frame to harden off.

Wax begonias are related to, but quite different from, tuberous-rooted begonias (see the March entry). Often seed houses use the term "fibrous-rooted" to identify wax begonias and distinguish them from their relatives. The botanical name is *Begonia semperflorens-cultorum*.

GARDEN DESIGN

The original site for Crockett's Victory Garden is a square of land directly outside the television studios of WGBH-TV in Boston. It's a wonderful spot for a garden, but it is not the kind of site that most gardeners face, open, sunny, rectangular, and flat as it is. Home gardeners have slopes to contend with, and trees, and buildings, and odd corners. So about two seasons into our series, we began taping many of our shows at a home garden site in one of the suburbs northwest of Boston, a site that offered us more room, a real garden setting, and a chance to experiment in ways that were impossible in the Victory Garden itself.

Our first glimpse of the site staggered us. The lawn was enormous, stretching up a hill and out of sight. The house had been recently bought by a new owner after having been on the market, unoccupied, for most of the summer. During that time, and I suspect for several years before, nothing much had been done to the grounds. The grass tickled our knees as we tromped around. In places, the vegetation was a near jungle of daylilies, giant lilacs, grape vines. It was clear that at one time the garden had been cared for, but that was long ago. We went to work immediately, evaluating, identifying ancient treasures, marking some plants for uprooting by the crowbar crew, and planting new gardens. By the time the owners had been in the house a couple of years, their yard was a showplace. Which proves how

much can be done, whether your yard is overgrown, or naked as a baby, or simply planned according to a previous owner's taste. Success is not a matter of magic, just a good plan, a love of gardening, and, I admit, some hard work.

Whether you've moved to a new house or have recently decided to try flower gardening in a place you've had for years, the first step is to take a good, hard look at what you have growing already. You may want to ask an experienced gardener to join you for this, as it is extremely hard for the novice to identify old, overgrown plants, especially when they are not in flower.

The next step is to draw up a plan of the entire yard, to scale. This doesn't have to look like it was done by a landscape architect, but it should be as accurate as you can possibly make it. The dimensions and proportions are critical. Put everything in your drawing that will have an impact on the garden, that is, will affect either sunlight or air circulation or root spread. The usual elements are trees and large shrubs, buildings (don't forget the house), driveways and sidewalks, walls or fences. Also include any oddities of the landscape that will play a role, such as deep slopes, outcroppings of rock, or low, wet spots. Mark the northerly orientation so you can tell where the sunny sections of the yard will be.

Sunlight is one of the most important factors in garden planning. It's also one of the hardest to plan for, especially if you are working out your garden plan in the winter. There are two things to keep in mind. One is that deciduous trees cast much more shade in summer than you might suspect as

you look at winter's naked branches. Another is that the arc of the sun's passage changes slightly every day; the part of the yard that is sunny in April may be in deep shade in August. It may take you a year of careful watching before you're sure of the way the sunlight will fall on your garden at different times of the season.

If you want to grow vegetables, select this site first. Vegetables need at least 6 hours of sunlight a day, whereas many flowers will tolerate less. When you've picked a spot for your vegetable garden, mark it on the drawing. Once this is done, you can begin to think about where to put your flowers.

Many gardeners have a tendency at this point to look for spots for their favorite flowers, rather than looking for flowers that fit the site. If possible, try not to set your sights on particular flowers yet: it can limit your thinking to a few plants when in fact there are hundreds of flowers from which to choose. While you're planning your garden, keep your mind open to the possibilities.

Think about how you use the yard, and how you would like to, about the sections of the yard that you see most from inside the house, about how the house looks to passersby. You don't have to confine yourself to the garden bed; remember that containerized plants, in pots, window boxes, or hanging baskets, are part of this picture, too. It's a good idea at this point to sketch out a few different plans on separate sheets of tracing paper, overlaid on your garden drawing. You're still thinking only of the areas where you would like to see flowers, not of the actual shapes of the sites, or the particular flowers.

You may find that you

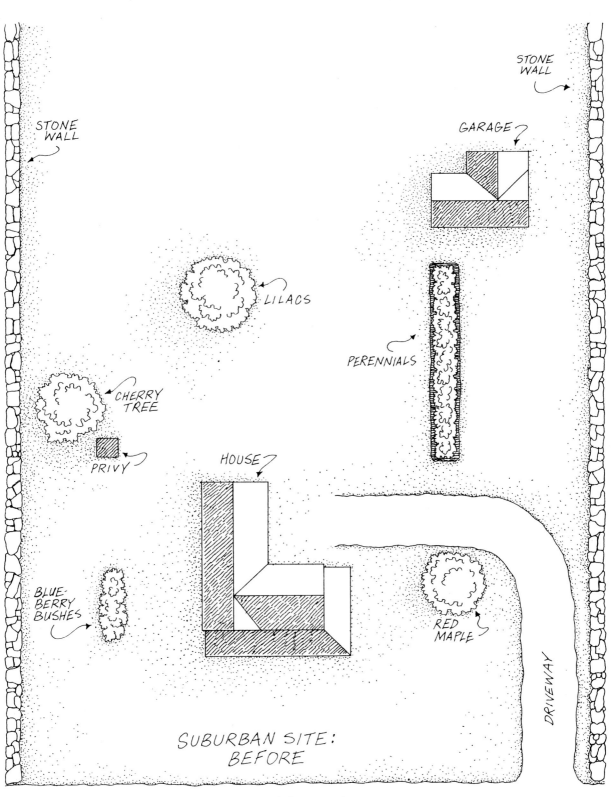

STONE WALL

STONE WALL

GARAGE

LILACS

PERENNIALS

CHERRY TREE

PRIVY

HOUSE

BLUE-BERRY BUSHES

RED MAPLE

DRIVEWAY

SUBURBAN SITE: BEFORE

STREET

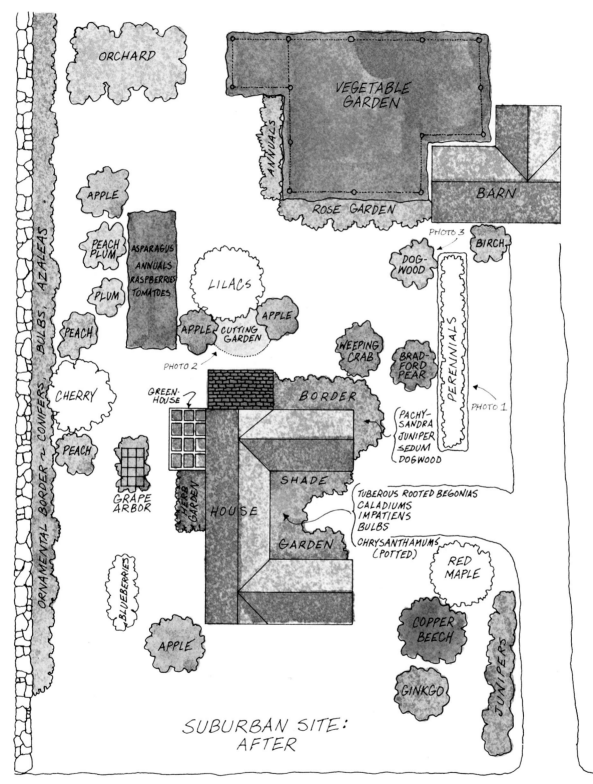

SUBURBAN SITE:
AFTER

want one garden to cover a multitude of purposes, one section of prepared soil for vegetables and flowers. Combination gardens can be spectacular; in fact, it's a lifelong habit of mine to plant flowers among vegetables. And it may be your only practical choice. Or you may decide on several smaller gardens, which usually produce a more graceful effect.

If you decide on a number of small gardens, aim for a casual look. Give the gardens a rounded shape, rather than square or rectangular. This is especially recommended in a completely rectilinear site; irregular shapes can help to break up square property lines. (Perennial gardens that follow the classic model are usually long rectangles, which show the plants to best advantage. For more, see the September feature.) And locate the gardens so they have a visual anchor of some sort — either a tree, or the wall of the house, or a driveway. If the garden is not placed along or around some large object, it tends to look stranded, as if it had been dropped from the sky.

One of the best arguments for the many-small-gardens approach is that it draws the eye to several parts of the yard and makes the whole area seem more interesting. This effect is even more pronounced if the plantings include bulbs, annuals, perennials — a range of plants that will flower at different times of the season. In our suburban site, the perennial border has center stage during the spring and fall, the rose garden in early summer, and the annual garden through the hot midsummer months. Throughout the season, the house itself is in flower with potted geraniums and a window box filled with marigolds. In a smaller yard, the size of

the plantings would probably be scaled down, but the overall effect is one of moving color, and it's very appealing.

During the planning stage, I encourage you to think in the long range, so you have a sense of what you want the yard to look like five or six years into the future. You don't have to do the work all at once; as a matter of fact, unless the site is quite small, you'd be unwise to do so. Set a first-year goal, and be modest about it. Do a little more each year, but give yourself several seasons to pull things into shape. I don't use the word finished because in my book gardens are never finished. They're always open to changes, to new ideas, new designs.

Finally, when you have decided on the placement of your garden, and know which site you would like to begin with, you can turn to the catalogues. For me, this is where the fun is. I send for current catalogues around Christmastime, when most of the major seed houses are advertising in newspapers and magazines, so I can spend January nights making decisions about summer flowers. There are some plants that

will be listed in all catalogues, others that are offered by only one house, and prices vary; it makes sense to shop around.

My first step is to make a list of the plants I would like to grow, and I include both old favorites and new varieties. My gardens are different every year, and for me, this change is an important part of the pleasure gardening gives me. Every season has its own character, every year its own distinct look. Plant breeders are always at work, improving the looks and tolerance of flowering plants; many times, the experiments of one year become the old favorites of years to come.

Here's one rather specific piece of advice as you begin. In the first year or two, rely on annuals for color and an immediate payoff for your efforts. Perennial plants are expensive, they require more in the way of soil preparation than annuals, and it takes them a couple of seasons to reach their peak. Perennials are the royalty of the flower world, but they are not the shortcut to the

Photo 1: Perennials at the suburban site, with roses and annuals in the background

1

2

self-maintaining garden. If you have a site that you would like to see eventually devoted to perennials, start with a plant or two the first year — whatever your budget of time and money can afford — and fill in the rest of the bed with annuals. Gradually, year by year, you can introduce more perennials. (And you can save yourself some time by sowing them from seed yourself. See the September feature.)

Once I know which plants I want to grow, I diagram the individual gardens and give the plants specific locations. This must be done in late winter, if

Photo 2: The cutting garden, in the company of a dwarf apple tree
Photo 3: Sunrise at the suburban site, early fall

seeds are to be ordered and plants begun on schedule. Decisions about placement are based on one's own taste, but there are a few rules worth following. In general, aim for variety unless you're planting a mass of one kind of annual or bulb for a carpet effect. By variety I mean not only flower color, though that is certainly important. The plants themselves must contribute to the varied look of the garden. Some are tall and willowy, others low-to-the-ground creepers. Some are ferny, others bold and glossy. Some have deep green foliage while others are nearly gray. The point is that from a distance, it is mass and scale and overall color that you will notice in your garden, as much if not more than individ-

ual flowers. This is the reason that we usually plant clusters of plants, unless one specimen is quite large; the clusters should contain uneven numbers of plants, because even-numbered plantings tend to look boxy, no matter how you arrange them. (For more about planning annual, perennial, and bulb gardens, see the May, September, and October features.)

Finally, I hope you will keep records of your gardens from year to year. This is the only way to know for sure which varieties you have grown, which have done well, which you have found to be less than satisfying. The memory alone can't be trusted when there is so much material involved.

3

Monthly Checklist

Ageratum
Aster (Annual)
Caladium
Calendula
Celosia
Chrysanthemum (Annual)
Cornflower
Cosmos
Dahlia
Gazania
Globe Amaranth
Hollyhock (Annual)
Marigold
Nasturtium
Nicotiana
Nierembergia
Petunia
Phlox (Annual)
Portulaca
Salvia
Scabiosa
Snapdragon
Statice
Strawflower
Swan River Daisy
Sweet Alyssum
Sweet Pea
Tuberous-Rooted Begonia
Verbena
Zinnia

An annual chrysanthemum, the variety Rainbow (see page 45)

MARCH

In this area, March brings the first days that feel like spring, when the sun is warm and bright and the world comes awake. This is the kind of weather that makes gardeners itch to get outside and start digging. I understand this urge all too well, but it must be fought until the ground has dried out sufficiently, which takes several weeks of warm, bright days. If the soil is worked prematurely, when it is still wet, it becomes compacted, so dense that air and water can't circulate properly, and this can result in permanent damage to the soil structure. There is a simple test to determine if the soil is ready to work. Pick up a handful of soil and squeeze it into a ball; then flick your finger into the soil ball a couple of times. If the mass of soil remains intact or falls apart in heavy clumps, it's too wet to work; if it crumbles like chocolate cake, it's ready.

If we have a fairly snowless winter or an early spring, we can sometimes work our soil in March, but frequently we must postpone digging until April and confine our outdoor activities this month to the partial removal of the winter mulch that covers our perennials, biennials, and late spring-flowering bulbs. I usually remove the top half of the mulch layer during the last week of March, wait a week, and then remove the rest on the first of April.

Aside from this minimal outdoor effort, the primary work of this month is to continue sowing the seeds indoors for annuals. In fact, this is one of the busiest seed-sowing months in the garden because so many annuals — certainly the bulk of our collection — require 4 to 8 weeks of growing time before they are of garden size. If the seeds are sown now, the plants will have filled out their six-pack compartments when they are moved to the garden on the first of May. This is also the time to unpack some of the tender tubers that have spent the winter in storage; caladiums, dahlias, and tuberous-rooted begonias are all started into growth this month in the Victory Garden so they have a head start on the season when they go into the ground along with the other annuals on the first of May.

Ⓐ **Ageratum** It's not often that a plant offers a selection of blue flowers from which to choose, but this one does. All the blues, whether pale or deep, have a pinkish tint to them, particularly in the bud stage. Blue is not the only flower color in ageratums — there are also pinks and whites. But the pink varieties are dull-colored and sparse-flowered on rank-growing plants. The white-flowered varieties are better than the pink ones, but there are always old, brown flowers that cling to the plants, detracting noticeably from their looks. Color aside, there are some varieties that are nearly a foot tall, but the more popular varieties are 6 inches tall and 6 to 12 inches across. They'll do well in full or half-day sunlight.

Most varieties on the market today are hybrids of *Ageratum houstonianum*. Sometimes seeds of the old species types are available at less cost — hybridizing is an expensive process — but the hybrids are preferable. Our old standby has been the hybrid Blue Blazer.

Blue Blazer ageratum

Blue Blazer ageratum seedlings growing on in the greenhouse

We sow the seeds of these annuals between early and mid-March to give the plants 6 to 8 weeks of growth before they go into the garden. (For the process, see the August feature.) Ageratums do not transplant well when they're very young, so I let two or three sets of true leaves develop before I move them to individual compartments in six-packs. Because the plants are allowed to stay in their common territory longer than average, the seeds should be sown thinly so the developing seedlings have room enough to grow in good health. By the time they are ready for transplanting, they should be standing 1 inch apart in the pot; this may require thinning the seedlings as they grow. A few days before set-out, the seedlings go into the cold frame to become conditioned.

A   **Aster (Annual)** Aster is a widely used garden term, applied to both annual and perennial plants. Most of the perennial asters are true asters (see the New England aster in the April chapter); most of the annuals, commonly called China asters, are not true asters but are varieties of *Callistephus chinensis*.

Traditionally, China asters have been grown in cutting gardens, where the tall-growing plants yield some of the loveliest pale pink and blue flowers available to the gardener. Gardeners have faced fairly serious disease problems with old-time asters, especially with wilt and aster-yellows. Thanks to the work of the plant breeders, there are now dwarf varieties available, bringing the plants into prominence in the display garden as well as in the cutting garden. The breeders have also developed varieties more able to withstand disease. Some varieties are wilt-resistant, all but eliminating that troublesome visitor. Yellows is far more serious, and while some varieties have been bred that are yellows-tolerant, none can actually be rated resistant. (In horticultural terminology, resistance is stronger than tolerance.)

In the Victory Garden we have concentrated on a variety known as Red Mound, which forms a compact plant 12 inches in all directions and is therefore short enough to grow unstaked. It blooms through July and August. It is wilt-resistant and yellows-tolerant, and in all a low-maintenance, dependable annual. It is not the plant that comes to most people's minds when they think of asters, though.

Among the more familiar types of asters, with pastel-colored flowers, there are both dwarf and intermediate varieties. The dwarf asters are 12 to 18 inches tall and the same dimension across; many of the dwarf varieties are not able to bloom continuously all summer, and the flowers, while good for cutting, are shorter-stemmed than their traditional, tall counterparts. The intermediates offer the best of both worlds. Their blossom period is more reliable, they're short enough to grow unstaked, except in exposed, windy areas, and they provide long-stemmed cut flowers.

The intermediate varieties of annual asters need about 1 month to grow from seed to garden-size plants, so they can be sown indoors at the end of this month or the beginning of April. The dwarf plants, including Red Mound, need a little longer, so we sow them in mid-March, giving them up to 6 weeks to grow before they go into the garden on May 1. The sowing procedure for all varieties is the standard one (see the August feature). A week or so before the set-out date, I put all the seedlings into the cold frame for conditioning.

Pink Magic, a variety of annual aster

A   **Caladium** Caladiums do what few other plants can: bring color to deep shade. There are several varieties available. Some have bigger leaves than others, but all have variously colored foliage. Some varieties are two-toned, with shades of green and cream, but it's more common to find red or pink incorporated into the color scheme as well. Caladiums crave shade, and I think they look their best in a natural, woody setting; they aren't quite trim enough for the garden bed. We usually grow the dwarf varieties, which are about 12 inches tall, with a 12- to 18-inch spread. The botanical name is *Caladium hortulanum*.

In the spring, caladium tubers are available from seed houses and garden centers. With the right attention, the tubers can also be held over from year to year (see the October entry). We start the tubers into growth in March so they have a chance to develop some foliage before they go into the garden in mid-May. We give each tuber its own 6-inch pot filled with potting soil or soilless mix; if you plan to set the tubers in the ground pots and all (see the May

Caladium, the variety Candidum

entry), it's better to start with an 8- or 10-inch pot. Each tuber should be covered by 1 inch of soil. At this stage, caladiums need both warmth and moisture to initiate growth, so I keep the soil moist — not soaked — and the pots sitting on bottom heat until the growth starts. They need bright indirect light while they are growing indoors. Just before they are transplanted to the garden, we give them 5 or 6 days in the cold frame, even though this subjects them to full sun. The spring sun isn't strong enough to harm them.

Caladiums can be propagated now, too, by dividing the tubers. Because the eyes are not visible in the dormant tuber, the routine is to set the tubers uncovered on a flat of moist peat moss. As soon as growth breaks from the eyes, lift the tubers and cut them into sections, making sure there's at least one eye to each section. Dust the cut edges with sulfur, then pot them up as usual.

[A] **Calendula** This is a good plant for cool but sunny weather. Deprived of these conditions, it doesn't have as

Yellow Coronet calendulas

long a season, or produce as many flowers, as some other annuals, but the flowers it does send up, either yellow or orange, are held well on stiff, tall stems, making them excellent for cutting. In fact, we grow them in the cool section of our greenhouse in the winter, just for the cut flowers. Outdoors, it's traditional to plant calendulas in the herb garden; the yellow varieties are best for this, as the orange flowers are too bright against the muted colors of the herb garden. The taller varieties are 18 to 24 inches tall, with a spread of 12 to 15 inches. The dwarf varieties stand about 12 inches tall and 6 to 9 inches across.

Seedlings may not be widely available from garden centers, but most of the catalogues list calendula seeds. They're usually labeled as calendulas, though "pot-marigold" is sometimes mentioned too. The correct botanical name is *Calendula officinalis*. Calendulas come very easily from seed. We sow them in early March, 6 to 8 weeks before set-out on the first of May. (See the August feature for complete sowing directions.) These cool-weather plants are given at least 2 weeks in the cold frame before they're set out.

[A] **Celosia** The plumed celosia (*Celosia argentea plumosa*) is one of the most unusual plants available to the flower gardener. For most of the summer, this annual bears feathery red, orange, or yellow plumes, which are the plant's flowers. In the Victory Garden we've grown mostly the dwarf red varieties, which are about 1 foot tall with 6-inch plumes; a single plant will spread 9 to 12 inches. The combination of rich color and grassy foliage makes them seem a little improbable, but they have their role in the garden. They command attention. They're beautiful in a breeze. And the plumes can be dried for winter flower arrangements. Celosias are best in full sun, but they will tolerate half-day sunlight. Celosia seeds are sold by many seed houses. The plants are sometimes identified as feathered or plumed celosia, or as woolflowers.

In the Victory Garden, we give celosias a 4- to 6-week head start on the growing season by sowing them indoors toward the end of March. (Don't pinch out the tips of these plants, as this will ruin their shape. For more, see the August feature.) Before they're set into the garden in early May, we give them a few days in the cold frame.

Red Fox, a variety of plumed celosia

A   **Chrysanthemum (Annual)** The most familiar chrysanthemums in the flower garden are perennials (see the April entry), but there is a fine annual chrysanthemum that deserves more attention. Like some of its relatives, the annual is a tidy plant with daisylike flowers. Its leaves are similar to those of perennial chrysanthemums, but smaller and coarser. In contrast to perennials, annuals have a long blooming season — from summer to fall. The plants are about a foot tall, with an equal spread. There are varieties that bear white or yellow flowers resembling ordinary daisies, but the one I'm partial to is a variety called Rainbow (*Chrysanthemum carinatum*), which bears flowers with multicolored concentric rings. (I've seen this plant referred to as painted daisy but that name is better reserved for a daisy-flowered perennial of another genus. See the July entry.) Rainbow's warm gold or orange flowers are excellent for cutting. We've grown them in the annual border, and in 8- to 10-inch pots. They are best in half-day sun.

Annual chrysanthemum seedlings are not easy to find; they're unavailable in all but the very largest garden centers. But some seed houses carry the seeds. Rainbow is available only as a mix.

We sow annual chrysanthemum seeds in late March, giving them 4 to 6 weeks to grow before we put them into the garden with the other annuals on the first of May. (For the seed-sowing routine, see the August feature.) Toward the end of April we move the seedlings to the cold frame for 5 or 6 days.

A   **Cornflower** Also known as bachelor's buttons, cornflowers are quick-growing annuals that are covered with cheerful flowers. The flowers are handsome both on the plant and in the vase. At one time they were available only in blue, but now there are pink, red, and white varieties; the best are the pale blues and pale pinks. The botanical name is *Centaurea Cyanus.* The standard-size plants are over 2 feet tall; we usually grow the dwarf strains, which peak at 12 to 15 inches, with an approximately equal spread. Among the dwarfs is a nice mixture called Polka Dot. No cornflower is an especially long-bloomer, lasting, on the average, for a month or so; if we deadhead them religiously, we can keep them in bloom from mid-June into August.

Cornflowers are airy, light plants that look graceful in a breeze. And they are healthier for breezes as well. They are vulnerable to mildews — there are no resistant varieties — so they are not good candidates for a protected area. They require sun and openness so the air can circulate freely and keep mildew at bay.

Blue Boy, a variety of cornflower

Sown 4 to 6 weeks before the set-out date, cornflowers go into the garden as seedlings nearly of blossoming size. In the Victory Garden, where our set-out date is May 1, we sow the seeds indoors toward the end of March, following the sowing routine described in the August feature. To help them harden off, we set the seedlings into the cold frame for a few days before set-out.

🅐 **Cosmos** Some varieties of cosmos are up to 4 feet tall; most dwarf varieties are about half that height. We have grown both types in the Victory Garden. Among the taller cosmos is a handsome mix called Early Sensation, a plant that is about 4 feet tall, with a 12- to 18-inch spread. We've also grown and very much liked a dwarf orange-flowered All-America Winner called Diablo, which is a more modest 18 inches tall, with a spread of 12 to 15 inches. We've used Diablo both in the garden and as a pot plant for an 8- to 10-inch pot. Most cosmos come in shades of pink, orange, and red. There are white-flowered varieties, and

Cosmos, the variety Diablo

some lovely yellows, too. Diablo is a hybrid with semidouble flowers, but there are few other hybrids available. Most of the nonhybrid varieties produce single flowers; this may detract some from the plant's effect as a cut flower — though personally I still consider it a beauty — but it gives the plants an old-fashioned grace that heavier, double-flowered plants can't match. All cosmos have in their favor a tolerance for neglect and for relatively dry, minimally fertilized soil, but they do beautifully in the Victory Garden's prepared soil. They do well in full or half-day sun. If the old, faded flowers are diligently picked off, cosmos bloom until frost.

The taller cosmos are usually sold as seedlings in garden centers in the spring, but Diablo may be harder to find. The botanical name of the older types is *Cosmos bipinnatus*; Diablo is *Cosmos sulphureus*. However, cosmos are so quick from seed that many gardeners sow them directly in garden soil in April and have flowers by the end of June. In the Victory Garden, we give them a 4- to 6-week handicap on the season, sowing them indoors from mid- to late March for our May 1 garden date. (See the August feature.) We give them a few days in the cold frame before setting them into the garden.

[A]   **Dahlia** Dahlias are available in a wide range of blossom colors and formations. Most of the plants are tall (3 to 5 feet), and the flowers themselves are dramatic in size, shape, and color. Some dahlia flowers dwarf the span of my hand; others are only 2 inches or so across. They're among the best cut flowers around. Most of the dahlias we grow in the Victory Garden are planted in a corner of the perennial border and treated as tender perennials: when cool fall weather comes, we dig up the tubers and store them over winter (see the October entry). Then in March, we start single tubers into growth again, and by the end of the season each has multiplied and produced a clump of several tubers. New tubers are also on the market in the early spring.

Whether you store dahlia clumps yourself, or order them from a seed house, the first spring job is to divide each clump into individual tubers. (If you divide your dahlia tubers in the fall and then treat them with melted paraffin — see the October entry — you are ready to plant; the paraffin does not have to be removed.) The tubers are all joined at the main stem of the plant, where there will be buds visible just above the tubers. To divide, I take a sharp knife and separate the tubers so that each has a section of crown and buds. Then I plant each tuber vertically in a 6- to 8-inch pot filled with potting soil. The crown should be covered with 1 to 2 inches of soil. After planting, I water the soil well, and

The flower of a tuberous dahlia

then set the pot out of the sun until growth starts. It probably won't need watering again until the shoots appear in 10 days or so. The important thing is not to drown the tuber at this stage, when it has very little root system with which to absorb moisture. (When the first shoots have grown larger, they can be taken for stem cuttings, a thrifty and simple way to propagate these often expensive plants. For a description of the procedure, see the April entry.)

There is a second type of dahlia that is also available from seed catalogues; it is referred to either as the annual dahlia, or as seed-grown dahlia. In truth, the annual dahlia is not genetically different from the more familiar dahlias that are labeled tender perennials. Both blossom from early summer to frost and produce clumps of tubers by the end of a single growing season. The primary difference between them is the ease with which the plants grow from seed. Dahlias identified as tuberous-rooted or tender perennials do not come true from seed, so the only practical way to treat them is to plant single tubers in the spring, lift the clumps in the fall, and start them back into growth after winter storage.

The so-called annual dahlias will also produce clumps of tubers by the end of the first growing season, but they come so easily from seed that the tuber-storage routine, while workable, is unnecessary. They can simply be treated as annuals and grown from seed every year. In addition, the annuals are more readily available in dwarf varieties, some barely more than a foot tall with flowers still 2 or 3 inches across. For many gardens, certainly for the Victory Garden, this reduced scale is a major plus.

There are several varieties of annual dahlias available, including Border Jewels, Rigoletto, Unwin's Dwarfs, and Redskin. At maturity, they are all around 15 inches tall, and 12 to 15 inches across. They produce flowers in white, yellow, and shades of pink and red. The seeds for all the annual dahlias should be sown 6 to 8 weeks before set-out, so we start them early in March (see the August feature) to bring the plants to set-out size by May.

As helpful as the annual dahlias are in the garden, the prestige of the tender perennials is not seriously threatened. There are many more varieties available as tubers, and for size and intricacy of flower, they are unquestionably superior. The tubers of some varieties are expensive, sometimes very expensive, but each tuber multiplies within a single growing season, so for the price of one tuber in the spring the gardener willing to store them has half a dozen the following year.

Gazania Hot weather is very hard on most annuals, but this is one that stands up to summer sun and dryness beautifully. Old varieties are such sun-lovers that their flowers close at night and on cloudy days, so they are most at home in the deserts of the Southwest. However, in the Victory Garden, where summers are hot and humid, gazanias do very well. The new hybrids are excellent; they don't flower quite as abundantly as some other annuals, but they keep going from early summer to frost. The daisylike blossoms are beautifully colored in shades of yellow, red, bronze, and orange. The flowers themselves are usually multicolored. The variety we've grown in the Victory Garden is a mix called Sunshine. Under the right conditions, this variety is almost all flower; its blooms are 4 or 5 inches across on 8- to 12-inch stems, hovering over foliage only 6 inches tall. Like most gazanias on the market for the gardener, Sunshine is a variety of *Gazania linearis*. There are other varieties available that are both taller and smaller-flowered. Gazanias are tender perennials that we grow as annuals.

Gazanias grow from seed to garden size in 4 to 6 weeks, so we sow the seeds indoors during the second half of

Special Mix, one of the older mixed varieties of gazania

Gazania seedlings ready for transplant

Buddy, a variety of globe amaranth

March. These are plants that should not be pinched back, as it will ruin their shape. (See the August feature.) They need a few days in the cold frame before they're moved to the garden.

A **Globe Amaranth** I've grown globe amaranths in the Victory Garden since the beginning. They're a free-flowering true annual, producing cloverlike rounded flowers in pink, reddish-purple, or white all summer long. The blossoms are good for cut flowers and for drying. In fact, because the blossoms hold their color and shape almost indefinitely, this is one of the best dried-flower varieties for the home gardener. Though it's usually grown for the harvest of its flowers, globe amaranth is a handsome flowering plant for the garden, too. Most varieties on the market today are dwarfs, in the height range of 12 to 15 inches. All will begin flowering before they reach their full height. The mixes are the most popular among dried-flower enthusiasts, but in the Victory Garden we've grown a handsome magenta variety known as Buddy.

Globe amaranth is best in sunny, open areas where humidity and moisture do not accumulate. We've grown it as a bedding plant in full sun in the Victory Garden, and while our summers are more humid than globe amaranth would like, it has always done well. The botanical name is *Gomphrena globosa*, and the plant is sometimes known simply as gomphrena. It's fairly rare to find seedlings in the spring, but the seeds are available through most seed catalogues, generally as a mixture.

In the Victory Garden, we start globe amaranths 6 to 8 weeks before set-out, sowing them in early March. The seeds are tough, so we soak them in warm water for a day before planting. Do not pinch the tips of these seedlings, as this will interfere with the plants' natural shape. Globe amaranth seedlings spend a few days in the cold frames before they're transplanted to the garden on May first. (For more about starting seeds, see the August feature.)

Hollyhock (Annual) Annual hollyhocks and perennial hollyhocks (see the July entry) are the same species, *Alcea rosea* (sometimes *Althaea rosea*). They come in the same color range: white, shades of red, yellow, pink, and rose. Both do well in full or half-day sun. They have the same flower and leaf shape. The difference between them is that some varieties will blossom from seed sown the same year; these are treated as annuals and can be pulled at the end of one season. And some varieties blossom the second year and beyond; these are the perennials. The two blossom for about the same length of time, but the annuals bloom later, coming in in August from seeds sown indoors the first of April and lasting nearly until frost. The perennials come into bloom late in June and continue into August. The perennials are more common, but the annuals have one major feature in their favor: with only a single-season life span, they are not so susceptible to damage from rust, the worst problem the perennials face.

An annual hollyhock, the variety Majorette

The two most common annual hollyhock varieties are both All-America Winners. Summer Carnival is about 5 feet tall at maturity, Majorette about half that height. We've grown both in the Victory Garden. They're available only as mixes; Summer Carnival has no yellow, but otherwise both mixtures will produce the range of hollyhock colors.

Hollyhock seedlings become very large very quickly, so they need only 4 to 6 weeks to grow indoors before they're set out. In the Victory Garden, this timing puts the sowing around the middle of this month. The sowing procedure is the standard one (see the August feature); however, these are plants that should not be pinched back, as this will cause them to lose their characteristic shape. About a week before planting time, the seedlings go into the cold frame for conditioning.

Marigold Most garden centers carry some varieties of marigold seedlings in the spring, to supply the enormous market for these popular bedding-plant annuals that bloom from early summer until frost. But no nursery could possibly offer the range of marigolds available from seed houses. The problem with ordering from catalogues is that, for the uninitiated, the terms used to classify the various marigolds are

Opposite: Planting seedlings of Orange Nugget marigolds in sites marked by lime

Yellow Galore, an intermediate-height marigold, in the annual border along the Victory Garden greenhouse

fearsomely confusing. To simplify: most marigolds in culture today are labeled either French or African; the African is sometimes known as American. (The terms have nothing to do with the marigold's native land, which is Mexico.) The two species are very different, with different habits of growth. The French are shorter plants (1 foot tall at most) with smaller flowers; they have a spread of 6 to 12 inches. African marigolds are tall (up to 3 feet or more), bushy plants that bear larger flowers in greater quantity. They have a spread of 18 to 36 inches. The Africans are available in several flower shapes, some labeled chrysanthemum-flowered or carnation-flowered.

Though the terms French, African, and American are still found in most seed catalogues, hybridization of marigolds has progressed so far that these old classifications are rapidly breaking down. There are now several new strains on the market, all varieties of the genus *Tagetes*, that derive from these older plants and incorporate their best characteristics. One of my favorites is the Nugget series, which is nearly as short as the French, but bushier (spreading 9 to 12 inches) and more free-flowering, like its African parent. The Nugget marigolds are sterile — they do not produce viable seed — and for this reason they are labeled "mule" marigolds. There are other mules on the market, too; they are noteworthy because they do not need to be deadheaded, except for the sake of appearance. They lack the genetic urge to set seed, so they stay fresh all season with very little attention from the gardener.

The tall African marigolds would make a good annual hedge, but in the rectangular confines of the Victory Garden their size works against them. We concentrate on the smaller French varieties, and on the Nuggets. Each has its strong points. The French offer more color selection, with more bicolors, but the mules have ease of culture on their side. We've grown marigolds in every location possible — in window boxes, in beds, in pots, and in the greenhouse. Goldie, a variety of French marigold, is almost the flower symbol of the Victory Garden, we use it so frequently. As bedding plants, they are particularly handsome next to blue ageratum (see the entry this month). They are very adaptable plants, growing well in full or half-day sunlight, and in less-than-perfect soil conditions.

The shorter marigolds, both the French and the Nugget mules, need 6 to 8 weeks growing indoors before they're ready for the garden (the taller African strains require only 4 to 6 weeks). So we sow ours early in March, and give the seedlings 5 or 6 days in the cold frame before putting them into the garden. (For seed-sowing, see the August feature.)

Whirlybird nasturtiums

 **Nasturtium** Nasturtiums are enjoying something of a renaissance, thanks to the introduction of dwarf strains that have all but replaced the unwieldy 8-foot-long trailers that were once the gardener's only choice. There are dwarf types available as uprights, usually around 12 inches in all directions, and semitrailers with stems 24 inches long. The uprights are excellent for the garden bed, and the semitrailers for hanging pots and window boxes. In the Victory Garden we've grown Jewel and the Whirlybird series, which are uprights, and Gleam, a strain of semitrailer. All three are available as mixes, as well as by separate colors; the nasturtium's color range is all within the red-yellow-gold end of the spectrum, with many shades between. All varieties have the unique leaf shape — roundish with a wavy edge — that distinguishes nasturtiums. All blossom from spring until frost. All are true annuals of the genus *Tropaeolum*.

The common wisdom is that nasturtiums resent transplant and should be sown directly in the spot where they are to flower. I have found that what they resent is root disturbance; as young seedlings they suffer if they are pricked out of their germinating medium and moved to other quarters. So I do start them indoors in early March, 6 to 8 weeks before our set-out date of May 1, but I take their preferences into consideration and sow them either in peat pots or six-packs, 2 seeds in a pot or compartment. When the seedlings are 1 to 2 inches tall, I snip off the weaker seedling at the soil line and leave the stronger to grow on. Upright varieties do not need pinching back; the trailing types will actually be harmed by pinching. After a few days hardening off in the cold frame, the seedlings are ready for transplant. (For more details, see the August feature.)

A   **Nicotiana**   Though the plants are lovely to look at, nicotiana is grown primarily because it gives off one of the sweetest fragrances known. (I recommend planting them where the fragrance can be enjoyed.) Older varieties of nicotiana — also called flowering tobacco — closed their flowers during daylight, but the newer ones on the market have open flowers day and night. These are good cut flowers, with colors including white, vivid reds, and an excellent pink. All nicotianas bloom summer to frost in full or half-day sun. The standard varieties are full-foliaged plants that stand some 30 inches tall, but we generally grow a free-flowering strain called Nicki hybrids, which are 18 to 24 inches tall, and 12 to

A cutting garden of Nicki White nicotianas, Peter Pan Scarlet zinnias, and pink Lilliput zinnias

15 inches across. The taller varieties are usually sold as a mix, while the several varieties of the Nicki strain are generally sold individually; the red-flowered Nicki is an All-America Winner. Most seed houses sell the seeds of these true annuals. The botanical name is *Nicotiana alata*. Garden centers may sell seedlings of the Nicki mixture, but it will probably be hard to find color-separated seedlings in all but the largest nurseries.

Because nicotianas will grow to garden size in 4 to 6 weeks, we sow the seeds indoors during the latter part of March. The seeds need light to germinate, so they shouldn't be covered. And the seedlings, as they develop, should not be pinched back. After a few days in the cold frame, the seedlings are ready for the open garden on the first of May. (See the August feature for complete sowing information.)

Nierembergia, the variety Purple Robe

A **Nierembergia** If you are looking for a tidy violet-blue edging or window-box plant to combine with other annuals, the blue-flowered nierembergia (*N. hippomanica*) is the prime choice. The most available variety is Purple Robe. At maturity, it is only 6 to 9 inches tall, spreading an equal distance with a dense show of color. The blooms are somewhat similar to African violet flowers, but smaller; they have a slightly bowled shape that has earned the plant the name blue cup flower. They're half-hardy perennials that we treat as annuals. Given both full or half-day sun and moisture, they blossom from spring to frost.

The seeds of nierembergia are sold through most garden catalogues; the seedlings are not so commonplace in garden centers in the spring. They need 6 to 8 weeks indoors to be garden size by May first, so we sow the seeds indoors early in March (see the August feature). Before setting them out, we put the seedlings into the cold frame for 5 or 6 days.

A **Petunia** For many years petunias have been the top-selling flowers in the country, and with good reason. They are among only a handful of annuals that come in every possible flower color, including some lovely, even fragrant, blues. They are also easy to care for and long-flowering. They look like the garden optimists with their plentiful, open, brightly colored flowers. And they're versatile, doing well in the flower bed, in window boxes, and in hanging baskets. Most petunias are uprights, and stand about 12 inches tall, with an equal or slightly greater spread. A few have more trailing habits and are sold as balcony or cascading petunias. All are at their best in full sun, but they'll grow and flower on half-day or filtered sunlight; they'll be leggy in filtered light. Though they must be grown as annuals in cold-

Old Glory Red petunias

winter areas, petunias are tender perennials in warm climates. Properly treated (see the May entry), they'll blossom almost continuously from early summer through light frost.

Petunias are the mainstay of the commercial bedding industry, and widely sold in the spring. But they're very easy to start from seed, and the seeds are very easy to find. (The botanical name is *Petunia hybrida*.) Garden catalogues devote pages and pages to petunias, which means the gardener has many more choices in buying seeds than in buying seedlings. Most of the varieties sold today are hybrids developed since the early 1960s; these new introductions are far superior to the species that previously dominated the market. Even the problem of yellow petunias — always the poorest petunia color — has been nearly conquered; the yellows are still a bit lifeless, but Summer Sun, the best one so far, is fairly good.

Most seed houses categorize petunias according to flower size, the common categories being grandiflora, multiflora, and doubles of different types. Of these, the standard doubles have the fullest flower, but they are the most susceptible to weather damage, a common petunia problem; we grow them only within the safety of the greenhouse. The grandifloras, as their name suggests, have the largest flowers of the three types. But it's the multifloras — either singles or doubles — that we grow almost exclusively in the Victory Garden; their flowers are smaller, relatively, but

Planting petunias among cosmos Diablo and yellow marigolds

there are more flowers per plant, and they are more able to withstand rain and wind than many others.

For a head start on the season, petunias should be sown 6 to 8 weeks before the garden date. In the Victory Garden, we sow the seeds early this month to have garden-size plants by our set-out date. The seeds are fine as dust, and should not be covered after sowing (see the August feature). Petunia seedlings spend at least the last 2 weeks of April in the cold frame before they're set into the garden.

A **Phlox (Annual)** Annual phlox are one of my favorite bedding plants. They're a good compact size; the dwarf varieties, which I grow in the Victory Garden, are only 6 to 8 inches tall, with a 6- to 12-inch spread. Most varieties are good in a range of temperatures, cold and hot. Like all phlox, they're best in full sun but can take half-day sun and still blossom until fall. The flower heads of most dwarf annual phlox, including Crimson Beauty, are rounded clusters that resemble the flower heads of perennial phlox, but there is also a star-flowered plant, called Twinkle; it's a fascinating-looking plant but not quite so durable in hot, dry weather as some of the others on the market.

Annual phlox seedlings are found in some garden centers in the spring, but the seeds are sold by most of the seed

houses (botanical name, *P. drummondii*) and are easy to
sow. Twinkle seeds are available only as a mixture. They
need 6 to 8 weeks of development before set-out, so I start
the seeds in early March (see the August feature). These are
plants that are best in cool weather, so we give them at
least 2 weeks in the cold frame before we transplant them to
the garden.

Beauty, a mixed variety of annual phlox

Ⓐ   **Portulaca**   This is one of the few annuals that thrive
in hot, sunny, dry weather. Six to 9 inches tall, with a
spread twice that distance, portulaca (*P. grandiflora*) is
a perfect edging plant for sunny locations. The foliage is unusual, with its almost fernlike look. The plentiful flowers, in
hot colors and pale pastels, are carried from early summer
until frost. The older varieties were so sun-hungry that they
closed their flowers in the shade, but new hybrids stay open
in most weather. Afternoon Delight, a mix and a relatively
new introduction, stays open all day, regardless of light and
heat conditions. Sunglo isn't quite so commendable on this

Sunglo, a variety of portulaca

score, but it is available in separate colors. All portulaca are at their best when grown in dry heat, but they have been very satisfactory in the hot, humid Victory Garden.

To grow to good size by the set-out date, portulaca must be sown indoors 6 to 8 weeks in advance; we do this early in March. The plants need a few days in the cold frame before transplant. (For complete information on sowing seeds, see the August feature.)

Ⓐ **Salvia** There is quite an array of salvia available for garden culture. We've grown two of the most popular, blue salvia and scarlet sage. Both do well in full, half-day, or filtered sun.

Blue salvia (*S. farinacea*) is a tender perennial with delicate spikes of flowers; in the Victory Garden we grow it as an annual. It is sometimes known as mealycup sage. Depending on the variety, it stands 18 to 24 inches tall with a 15- to 18-inch spread. We've grown a blue-flowered version called Victoria, which blossoms early summer to frost. It's probably the nicest of the salvia we've grown. It's good both in the garden and in the vase.

The annual scarlet sage (S. *splendens*) is the better known of the two salvia. Heights vary with the variety, from as short as 8 inches to more than 2 feet, but most produce astonishing red spikes — probably the hottest reds available for the flower garden. We've grown both Red Blazer and Blaze of Fire; both are a little more than a foot tall, and an equal dimension across. They blossom from early summer to fall.

We sow the seeds for both types of salvia indoors late this month, 4 to 6 weeks before our set-out date of May 1.

Red Blazer, a variety of scarlet sage

The red-flowered varieties of S. *splendens* need light to germinate, so these seeds are not covered. (For propagation directions, see the August feature.) Blue salvia needs no further attention until transplant in May, but I usually pinch the tips of standard-size scarlet sage seedlings when they're 3 or 4 inches tall, which delays flowering about 3 weeks. This step can be skipped for the dwarf varieties, which branch fairly well on their own. All salvia need a few days in the cold frame before transplant to the garden early in May.

Scabiosa Since my childhood, I have loved the flowers of the annual scabiosa; since my childhood, I have disliked its name, which sounds painful. The common name is pincushion flower, a reference to the dotlike pistils that are visible above the flower head. The plant is a sun-lover (full or half-day) that blossoms from spring to frost, producing wiry-stemmed flowers that are good for cutting. Some scabiosa are nearly 3 feet tall; the dwarf plants are about 18 inches tall, and about 12 inches across. I usually grow the

Imperial Giants Mixed, a tall variety of scabiosa, particularly good for the cutting garden

dwarf plants in the Victory Garden. The seeds are sold as mixed colors, which include white, pale pink, and shades of red, some so deep they are nearly black. The botanical name is *Scabiosa atropurpurea*.

Scabiosa is an easy plant to start indoors following the normal sowing routine (see the August feature). Plants need 4 to 6 weeks to grow before they're set out, so I start them late this month. I don't pinch back the tips of these plants, as this would damage their shape. After a few days in the cold frame, they're ready for the garden by May 1.

🅰 **Snapdragon** The simple reason that snapdragons are such familiar garden flowers is that they have so much to recommend them. They're a spectacular cut flower, with their distinctive flower spikes, their clear, bright colors, their light, spicy fragrance. They like nearly full sun, benefiting from shade through the hot midday. They're available in a range of sizes, from tall (3 to 4 feet), to intermediate (12 to 24 inches), to dwarf (8 to 12 inches). We've grown both the dwarf and the intermediate sizes in the Victory Garden. The intermediate are particularly good because they're tall enough to provide long-stemmed cut flowers, yet not so tall that they take over the garden; they have a 12- to 18-inch spread. The dwarfs will spread 6 to 12 inches, and are a good scale for the front of the garden; I particularly like Little Darling, an All-America Winner.

The main drawback to snapdragons is that when the temperatures go too high, they don't flower so freely. In the Victory Garden, they do well in the cool spring and, if the faded flowers are picked regularly, they come back into flower in the fall, but they take most of the summer months off. The new hybrids are improved on this score, but even they won't stay in full flower all summer long.

Seed houses sell several varieties of snapdragons; the botanical name is *Antirrhinum majus*. Older varieties of snapdragons had problems with rust, but the newer hybrids are bred for rust-resistance. Among the full-size snapdragons, it may make sense to order the doubles, as their flowers are larger and longer-lasting than the singles. However, the process of doubling the flowers has dramatically changed their looks; they no longer have the little "snapping" petal formation that gave these plants their name. For the nostalgic among us, that is a loss.

A few seed houses sell pelleted snapdragon seeds, which have been coated to make the tiny seeds easier to handle. If the variety you select is available in pelleted form, it's a good idea to order them. With their increased bulk, pelleted seeds are easier to sow thinly, and a thin sowing improves both the chances of germination and the health of the seedlings. As an alternative, unpelleted seeds can be mixed with sand before sowing (see the August feature).

Because snapdragons are so sensitive to high temperatures, it is especially important to start them indoors. I sow the seeds toward the beginning of March, giving the plants 6 to 8 weeks of growth before I set them into the open garden. Snapdragon seeds need light to germinate, so they are not covered after sowing. Before planting, the seedlings go into the cold frame for up to 2 weeks to increase their sturdiness. (For the complete seed-sowing procedure, see the August feature.)

Rocket Yellow, a long-spiked variety of snapdragon

A **Statice** Most seed catalogues sell more than one variety of statice. The one I've grown in the Victory Garden is an annual known primarily as a dried flower because it holds its color and shape well. The correct botanical name is *Limonium sinuatum*, but statice is sometimes sold as *Statice sinuata*. It is also known by the common name notchleaf statice. Its foliage tends to lie fairly flat along the ground, spreading from 12 to 18 inches. The flower stems grow straight up to a height of about 18 inches. Statice is best in full sun, but grows in half-day sunlight, too, especially if the shady hours are early in the morning or late in the afternoon. It blooms from summer to fall, producing a range of flower colors, of which the blue-purple is the most popular.

When the seed clusters form on statice plants, each seed is encased in a hull. Some seed houses will hull the seeds before shipping; others will send the seed clusters. It's better to buy the hulled seeds if possible; otherwise, you must pick the clusters apart and sow the sections on their sides. If the catalogue specifies "seeds," they are probably hulled.

Purple statice, excellent flowers for a dry bouquet

Notchleaf statice plants need 4 to 6 weeks growing indoors before setting out, so we get them started toward the end of March. We follow the standard sowing procedure, except that these are plants that should *not* be pinched back (see the August feature). Before setting the seedlings into the garden on May 1, I give them up to a week in the cold frame to harden off.

Ⓐ   **Strawflower** Strawflowers are one of a number of plants, called everlastings, that are grown expressly to be dried and arranged for long-lived winter bouquets. In the Victory Garden, I've grown a mix called Bright Bikinis, which produces a compact plant about 18 inches tall, and 9 to 15 inches across, with very intense red, yellow, or orange flowers all summer long. The brightness of the colors is the major selling point, because it means brighter colors after the flowers are dried.

One of the flower colors available in Bright Bikinis, a strawflower mix

Strawflowers are sun-loving annuals — they'll take half-day sunlight, too — that are sold by seed through most garden catalogues. The botanical name is *Helichrysum bracteatum*. The plants need a head start of 4 to 6 weeks before they are large enough to go into the garden, so we sow them indoors toward the end of March. The seeds should not be covered; nor should the emerging seedlings be pinched back. (For complete sowing information, see the August feature.) We put the seedlings into the cold frame for 5 days or so before planting them in the garden.

Ⓐ **Swan River Daisy** Several plants share the name daisy because they have long narrow petals that radiate out from a central section. Some of these daisy-flowered plants are annuals, and some perennials. The Swan River daisy is a very free-flowering annual bearing 1-inch blossoms on somewhat weak stems. It grows in mounds, about 12 inches all

This is the dominant color in the commonly available mix of Swan River daisies

around. The flowers are either lavender, blue or white; as a rule, the seeds are sold as a mixture. Because of their size and dense display of flowers, Swan River daisies make very good rock garden plants. Though the stems are not stiffly upright, the plants produce good cut flowers.

Swan River daisies (*Brachycome iberidifolia*) are happiest in a cool, sunny spot, but they've been a very successful plant in the Victory Garden, even when grown in window boxes in full sun. They will blossom all summer if the temperatures stay cool; otherwise, they quit.

As seedlings, Swan River daisies are hard to come by, but the seeds are sold by most of the catalogue houses. We sow the seeds indoors in early March to give the seedlings 6 to 8 weeks to grow before they're set into the garden. We use the standard sowing procedure (see the August feature). The seedlings take their turn in the cold frame for 5 or 6 days just before they're transplanted to the garden.

A **Sweet Alyssum** This is one of the most frequently grown annuals in the Victory Garden. It blossoms early, and it's a wonderful edging plant, dense with flowers and only 4 to 6 inches tall; it has a creeping habit of growth that will give it a spread of 9 to 15 inches by maturity. We've used

Sweet alyssum seedlings, including the purple-flowered Rosie O'Day and the white Carpet of Snow

sweet alyssum as an edging plant along the garden walk, and we've grown it in window boxes, allowing the trailing growth to cascade over the side. I've also put it into the rock garden behind my home. Mostly, I've grown the white-flowered varieties, especially Carpet of Snow; there are shades of violet-pink available, too, but they aren't as free-flowering as the whites. All sweet alyssum do well in full or half-day sun, blossoming through most of the spring and summer with the right treatment (see the May entry).

Given 6 to 8 weeks to grow indoors, sweet alyssum is ready for our garden set-out date of May 1. We sow the seeds indoors in early March, following the standard sowing procedure (see the August feature), and giving these cold-tolerant seedlings at least 2 weeks in the cold frame before setting them out. The seedlings are also widely available in garden centers in the spring.

Sweet alyssum is a tender perennial that is usually grown as an annual; its botanical name is *Lobularia maritima*.

Rosie O'Day sweet alyssum

A **Sweet Pea** This flower is one of my personal all-time favorites. It presents the most delightful picture, with its gentle colors and fluttery petals, and it has fragrance as a bonus. To my thinking, a vaseful of sweet peas is absolutely unbeatable, and there are many who agree with me.

But sweet peas are not easy plants to grow. They require a combination of sunlight and cool temperatures that is very difficult for most gardeners in most parts of the country to manage for more than a few weeks of the year. During hot weather, sweet peas must be mulched to keep the soil moist and cool. They are weak-stemmed, and even the short varieties must be staked with brush or netting. Sweet peas have a flowering season that lasts only as long as there are cool days and cool nights. When the daytime temperatures begin to climb above 65°F, the plants collapse. So for the longest season possible, gardeners in hot-summer areas want to put out the largest seedlings they can, just as soon as the danger of hard frost has passed. The problem here is that sweet peas do not tolerate root disturbance, which makes them difficult to transplant. Many garden experts advise against sowing them indoors for this reason.

That is quite a string of negatives. Nevertheless, I haven't let a season pass in the Victory Garden without growing sweet peas. I make adjustments where I can, offer them the best conditions possible, and live with the fact that their blossom period is brief. One reason I can do this is that sweet peas can in fact be started indoors if they are sown directly into six-packs or individual pots; what they resent is

Sweet peas, the variety White Leamington

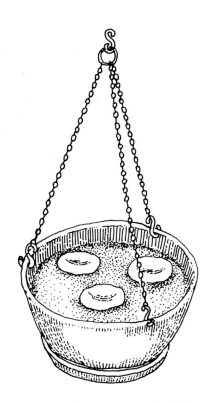

TUBEROUS-ROOTED BEGONIAS

being pulled by the roots from the germinating medium. Sown in six-packs or pots, they are transplanted only once — to the garden — and they are never abruptly separated from their soil. I put 2 seeds to a compartment or pot; as the seedlings develop 2 inches or so of growth, I cut off the weaker at the soil line and leave the stronger to grow on. Like all legumes, sweet peas have the ability to feed on the nitrogen in the air. To help them in this regard, I treat the seeds before sowing with nitrogen-inoculant, a powder available from most garden centers. By sowing the seeds the first of March, I have seedlings ready for the cold frame in early April and the garden 2 weeks later (see the April entry).

Sweet pea seeds are easy to find in garden catalogues; the botanical name for these true annuals is *Lathyrus odoratus*. Most of the varieties available today are weak-stemmed climbers that mature at 3 to 5 feet tall. Some varieties are labeled as heat-resistant, but in practice there doesn't seem to be a significant difference in heat tolerance from variety to variety.

A   **Tuberous-Rooted Begonia**   Here's a lush, even exotic-looking, plant for an area that is shaded from all but the day's gentlest sun. Tuberous-rooted begonias bloom from early summer until frost in a wide range of flower shapes and colors. There are three kinds available for garden culture: the standard, upright varieties, which are 12 to 18 inches tall; the multifloras, which are a little shorter than the standards, with smaller but far more numerous flowers; and the pendulous, hanging-basket types. All are selections of *Begonia tuberhybrida*. We have grown the hanging varieties almost exclusively in the Victory Garden, usually three tubers of the same variety together to an 8- or 10-inch pot. The standard and multiflora varieties do very well planted in the garden itself, but they have a tropical look that some may think out of place. By comparison to the two upright-growing types, the choice among hanging varieties of tuberous-rooted begonias is very limited, but the ones available are beautiful.

Most garden catalogues sell the tubers in the spring; in the Victory Garden, we store our tubers from year to year, and start them back into growth early in March. The first step is always to inspect the tubers for insects or soft, bruised spots; if the tubers aren't firm and clean, they should be discarded. Then I fill an 8- or 10-inch hanging pot with a moistened soil specially blended for container gardening (see the June feature). For fullness, I plant 3 tubers of the same variety to one pot of this size. The tubers are easily damaged at this stage, so I scoop out small spaces for them in the soil, and just set them on, pressing them very lightly to establish contact with the medium. They should be sitting, rounded side down, about ½-inch deep. They should not be covered with soil, nor should the tubers touch one another. After planting, I move the containers into a bright spot out of direct sunlight and keep the soil barely moist for about a week while the tubers become established. At that point they're put on their regular growing-season diet: constantly moist soil and a once-monthly light dose of houseplant fertilizer, mixed with water. When the weather is warm enough, in early May, I move the pots outdoors to a spot where they're in half-day or filtered sunlight, and they bloom all summer long.

   The best way to propagate tuberous-rooted begonias is by dividing the tubers. If you decide to do this, you will have to allow the tubers to begin growing in order to see where the buds, or eyes, are. I usually pot them in a shallow flat in my standard soil mix for container gardening (see the June feature). I plant the tubers as if I were planting them for the whole season, as described above. But when the

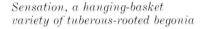

Sensation, a hanging-basket variety of tuberous-rooted begonia

growth starts, I pry them up from the soil, working gently with a fork, and divide the tubers into one-eyed sections. Then I dust the cut surfaces of the sections with sulfur, and give them a day or two in a dry place out of the sun. When they're dry, I plant each division, eyes up, as above.

Tuberous-rooted begonia seeds are sold by some of the seed houses, but as of now, seed culture is too long-term for the home gardener unless the indoor light is very good. As a rule, tubers are very modestly priced, and because they can be saved and stored year to year (see the October entry), they're actually bargains.

Sangria, a bright-centered variety of verbena

Ⓐ   **Verbena**   The interesting aspect of this plant is its small, vividly colored flowers borne in large, rounded clusters. Most varieties grow in tidy mounds 8 or 10 inches tall, with nearly the same dimension horizontally. In the Victory Garden, we've grown a red-flowered All-America Winner called Blaze, as well as some mixed varieties. Sangria, another All-America Winner, has deep red flowers on 8- to 10-inch plants; unlike other varieties, Sangria has a spread of 12 to 18 inches, making it especially good as an edging or window-box plant.

Verbenas are tender perennials that we treat as annuals. They are happiest when they are sunny, dry, and cool. The Victory Garden qualifies as neither dry nor cool, but we've been pleased with our success nonetheless; the varieties we've grown have blossomed right up until frost. They do struggle some through the hottest part of the summer, but it's not enough to complain about. Sangria is particularly tolerant to hot weather.

Seedlings of some varieties of verbena are easy to find in garden centers in the spring, though the choice is apt to be limited. Most catalogues offer a range of varieties by seed, in white and shades of red and blue. The botanical name is *Verbena x hybrida*. In the Victory Garden, we sow the seeds early in March to give them 6 to 8 weeks to grow before they're transplanted to the garden. The sowing procedure is the standard one described in the August feature. Because these are cool-weather plants by nature, I move them to the cold frame for at least 2 weeks prior to transplanting.

Ⓐ   **Zinnia**   Zinnias come in a wide range of colors, from subtle to sharp. In fact, they are one of the few annuals that offer the complete color spectrum. There is even a surprising green-flowered variety, called Envy. Zinnias blossom all season long, right up to frost, if they're grown in full or half-day sun in a well-ventilated spot. They're susceptible to mildew, which stagnant air encourages. Older varieties of zinnias suffered with prematurely aging flowers, but the newer hybrids on the market are much better on this score. Still, it makes good sense to keep the garden looking fresh by removing faded blossoms.

As a glance at a garden catalogue will show, there are several varieties of zinnia available. The bulk of them are tall, reaching heights of 18 to 36 inches. These are particularly good choices if you're interested in long-stemmed cut flowers, but the tall plants often need to be staked. The tall varieties are also apt to go to seed unless they're rigorously deadheaded.

In the Victory Garden, where small plants are best, we grow the dwarf varieties of zinnia, 18 inches tall or less. They require no staking, and the range of flower colors is comparable to the taller varieties. They also produce good cut flowers, though of course the stems are shorter. There are several dwarf types on the market, but the best is a strain of hybrids called Peter Pan (*Z. elegans*). They stand about 12 inches tall and 9 to 12 inches across. There are many colors from which to choose; notably, every color of Peter Pan zinnia has been voted an All-America Winner. Old Mexico (*Z. Haageana*), a bronze-yellow bicolor variety, is another fine choice; it has the advantage of being a little taller than the Peter Pans, at 14 inches, but it is still short enough to grow unstaked. Both types have flowers in the 2- to 3-inch range, which is smaller than some varieties on the market.

Zinnia seedlings are easily found in garden centers in the spring, but the range of choice is, by necessity, relatively small. In the Victory Garden, we start our own. Dwarf varieties need 6 to 8 weeks growing indoors before the set-out date, so we sow the seeds (see the August feature) during the first part of March. (The taller-growing varieties need only 4 to 6 weeks to grow inside.) Zinnias grow quickly, and they do not like having their pace checked by poor growing conditions, like lack of moisture or overcrowding; so we keep a watch over them, make sure the soil is kept just moist, and transplant the tiny seedlings right on schedule when the true leaves appear. The dwarf varieties will branch well on their own, but the taller zinnias are best if they're pinched back once, when the seedlings have 2 or 3 sets of true leaves. All zinnias need a few days in the cold frame before they're set into the garden.

Old Mexico zinnia

THE COLD FRAME

The cold frame is one of the simplest and most ancient of gardening tools. It is nothing more than a four-sided wooden box with a clear or translucent top that opens and closes. Its function is to provide temperature control and wind protection for the plants within the frame; it does this by intensifying and holding the sun's heat. Ideally, cold frames should always be oriented toward the sun's highest point in the sky, but because the sun's position changes with the seasons, this is possible only by moving the frame regularly to follow the light. The most practical solution is simply to aim the opening of the frame due south.

We have half a dozen cold frames in the Victory Garden, in all but constant use. In the summer, we use them uncovered as nursery space for young seedlings; with a lath cover (see below) to provide shading, they become an excellent summering spot for houseplants. In the fall and winter, they offer a protected, cold-weather environment for forcing spring-flowering bulbs or wintering over the hardy chrysanthemums (see the August entry). We also use them in the spring for cold-tolerant annuals like sweet peas and gloriosa

daisies; two weeks or more in the cold frame provides them with the low temperatures that they need for the best development. But the primary use of our cold frames is in conditioning seedlings before they're set into the garden itself (see the August feature). Well-conditioned seedlings can mean the difference between a thriving, vigorous garden and one that is merely struggling along. The cold frame isn't the only way to provide this conditioning, but it is the best. For all its age, it has yet to be improved on in this regard.

When our grandparents needed a cold frame, they propped an old storm window on top of a crate. This is still a workable arrangement, but the storm window is usually heavy, and the glass is apt to break. A better cold frame is easy to build with only basic carpentry tools, and there are also pre-assembled frames available both from garden centers and through mail-order catalogues. Whether you build or buy a frame, there are several issues worth considering.

Size The traditional dimensions of a cold frame are 3 feet by 6 feet. The Victory Garden cold frame is smaller, at roughly 4 feet square, but you may not want or need frames this large. There are smaller ones on the market, preassembled, that may be more suitable to your garden space. It is also possible to make a smaller version of the Victory Garden cold frame. But there is a point of diminishing returns; a cold frame smaller than 2 feet by 3 feet is just too small to be useful. My advice is, get the largest cold frame you can afford; you'll have no trouble putting all the space to use.

Portability We leave our cold frames up all year long because they are in use all year long, and because we have a strip of land along the greenhouse where they are out of sight through the summer. If you would like your cold frame to be out of the way when your garden is at its best, portability is an issue. Most cold frames can be moved, but the ones available commercially must usually be stored intact. We have included in our design loose-pin hinges for the corners and cover so the frame can be collapsed and stored flat.

Ventilation During midwinter, our cold frames are shut tight; in summer, they are wide open. But during the spring and fall, when their function is to protect young plants from the full effects of the weather changes, they must be ventilated daily according to the temperature and sunlight conditions. When the daytime temperatures are 60 degrees or higher, I open the cover completely. On a sunny day when temperatures are in the 40- to 60-degree range, I use the ventilator stakes to keep the cover open a few inches; on a cloudy day in this temperature range, I just slip a stick under the cover to open it a crack. Every night, between late afternoon and early morning, and on any day when the temperatures are below 40 degrees, I keep the frame closed. If a hard frost is predicted, I cover the closed frame with a canvas tarp just before sundown and move any frost-sensitive annuals into the greenhouse. Opening and closing the frame is not a time-consuming job, but if you can't be sure that there will always be some-

Watering the plants in the cold frame

one on hand to check the frame twice a day, you might want to buy one of the solar-operated automatic openers on the market. They are heat-sensitive, opening and closing the frame as the internal temperature requires.

The Victory Garden Cold Frame Our cold frame was designed in the months before our first season on television, and although we have modified it some, it is essentially unchanged. It has two qualities that make it especially attractive: the dimensions of the box are designed to make

the most efficient use of a standard sheet of plywood; and the loose-pin hinges securing the corners make it easy to disassemble the frame for flat storage.

The materials are all selected for long life, ease of construction, and cost efficiency. For the cover surface, we use a translucent or clear corrugated fiberglass, which we buy from the local lumber company. This material, if exposed to bright sunlight all summer, will discolor after 5 or 6 years, and actually become opaque. In the Victory Garden, we've been able to prolong the life of our covers by removing them and storing them out of the sunlight for the summer, when they're not needed anyway. If your frame cover will be ex-

posed to year-round sunlight, you might want to consider substituting the more costly greenhouse-grade corrugated fiberglass sold by greenhouse supply companies. It is designed to resist discoloration for 15 to 20 years, even in direct summer sunlight.

The wood in our frame is a combination of exterior-grade plywood, redwood, and common pine. Both the pine and the plywood must be treated with a wood preservative to prevent rotting. The best wood preservatives for this use are either copper or zinc naphthanate; the copper is green, and the zinc clear. They have two advantages over other commonly available preservatives: they can be painted over; and, more importantly, once dry they do not release toxic fumes, as do many other preservatives. We put on three or four coats, giving each a few hours to dry before the next is added. The best time to treat the wood is after the pieces are cut, before they are assembled.

All metal hardware, including screws and bolts, is either brass or rustproofed steel.

In the following specifications, the box of the cold frame is built first, then the cover. In the last step, the frame is assembled.

INSTRUCTIONS AND MATERIALS FOR MAKING THE COLD FRAME

Lumber and Sheet Goods

One half-sheet (4×4-foot) of stock ½-inch exterior-grade plywood (for the walls of the box)

One 16-foot length of 1×3-inch pine, or two 8-foot lengths (for the cover frame)

Three 6-foot lengths of stock corrugated* wood molding (for the cover)

10 feet of 1×1-inch pine or redwood (for the ventilator stakes, and the lath cover braces)

Two 4-foot lengths of 26-inch-wide translucent or clear stock corrugated* fiberglass (for the cover)

Two 6-foot lengths of corrugated* wood stops (for the cover)

23 lengths of 1-inch lath, each 48 inches long (for the lath cover)

Hardware

Eight 2-inch loose-pin backflap hinges (for the corners of the box)

Forty-eight ³/₁₆-inch flathead stove bolts, ¾ inch long, with nuts and washers (for the corners of the box)

Thirteen 1¼-inch #8 roundhead screws with washers (for the ventilator stakes, and the sides and front of the cover)

Four ¾×4-inch angle irons, with sixteen ¾-inch #8 flathead screws if no screws are included with the irons (for the corners of the cover frame)

Seven 1½-inch #8 roundhead screws (for the back of the cover)

Two 2½-inch loose-pin butt hinges, with twelve ½-inch #8 flathead screws if no screws are included with the hinges (to attach the cover to the box)

A small box of 2-penny resin box nails (for the lath cover)

Two 2½-inch hook eyes (so the cover can be locked shut)

* Make sure that the corrugated pieces you buy are gauged to fit together. There is slight variation from manufacturer to manufacturer.

Assembling the Box

1. Cut the half-sheet of plywood into 4 sections as shown. In order to guarantee that the sections are properly sized, measure and cut piece A, then measure and cut piece B, then C and D. Don't mark all the pieces at once, then cut them all at once, as this will not result in true dimensions. (Be sure that you make your sawcuts on the outside of your marking line, rather than inside it or through it.) As a final step, trim the ½ inch or so of waste from the shop edge of the plywood — where the 4×8-foot sheet was halved. (See Figure 1.)

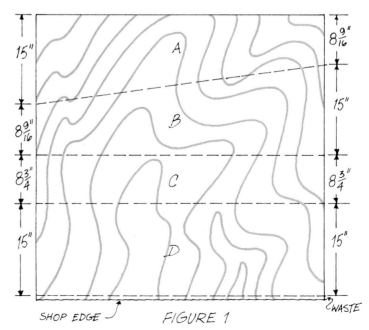

FIGURE 1

2. Trim pieces A and B to measure 46½ inches wide. (See Figure 2.)

3. Treat pieces A, B, C, and D with wood preservative.

4. On the interior surface of pieces A and B, mark the locations for the ventilator stakes, 12 inches back from the short edge, and 8½ inches from the bottom. (See Figure 3.)

5. Assemble pieces A, B, C, and D to form the box, using 2-inch loose-pin backflap hinges and ³/₁₆-inch flathead stove bolts, with nuts and washers.

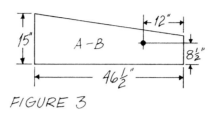

FIGURE 2

FIGURE 3

Predrill the bolt holes with a ³/₁₆-inch bit. Note that the sides, A and B, fit inside the front and back pieces, D and C. (See Figure 4.)

Assembling the Cover

1. Cut two 48-inch lengths of 1×3, and two 43-inch lengths of 1×3. (See Figure 5.) Treat them with wood preservative.

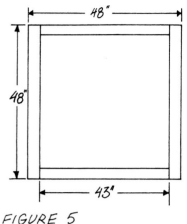

FIGURE 5

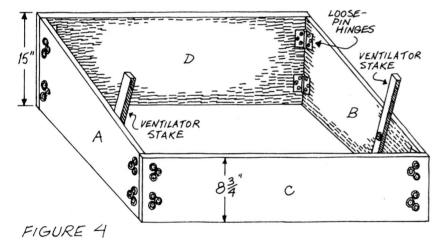

FIGURE 4

6. Drill the 1×1* ventilator stakes 4 inches in from one

* Stock lumber, such as 1×1, 1×3, or 1×6, is always smaller in both dimensions than its name indicates. For instance, 1×1 is actually ¾×¾.

end. Then attach them to the inside surface of the sides where marked. (See Figure 4.) Use 1¼-inch #8 roundhead screws; these stakes are intended to swivel, so don't tighten them completely.

2. Assemble the cover frame as shown, securing the corners with four ¾×4-inch angle irons. If screws are not included with the angle irons, use ¾-inch #8s. (See Figure 6.)

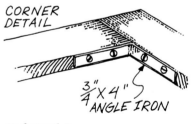

FIGURE 6

3. Cut two lengths of corrugated molding to measure 48 inches from valley to valley. (See Figure 7.) The corrugations in these two lengths should match. If the molding is not redwood, treat with wood preservative.

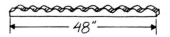

FIGURE 7

4. Lay the two pieces of molding on the top and bottom of the cover frame, flush to the exterior edges. Now measure and cut two lengths of corrugated wood stops to fit along the sides, between the lengths of corrugated molding. (See Figure 8.) Do not fasten the pieces together yet. Treat the wood stops with preservative.

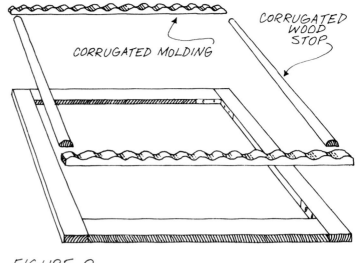

FIGURE 8

5. Lay all the sections of the cover together. First the cover frame, then the lengths of corrugated molding and wood stops, then the two sheets of corrugated fiberglass, overlapping in the center. You will have to position the wood stops on the cover frame to fit properly under the corrugated fiberglass. (See Figure 9.) If necessary while you're working, you can tack any wooden pieces together with 2-penny resin box nails.

6. Cut the third length of corrugated molding to fit across the top of the cover at the back edge. The easiest way to do this is to set the molding on the fiberglass so the corrugations line up, and then trim the molding to fit the 48-inch dimension.

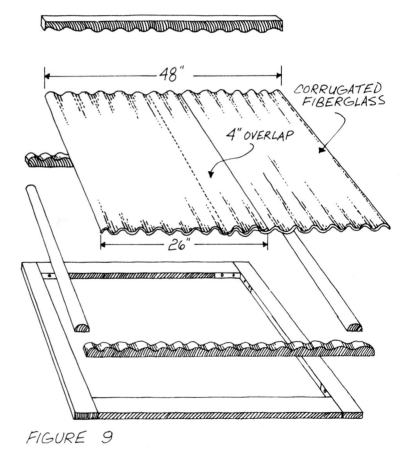

FIGURE 9

7. Fasten the sections of the cover together. First, at every third peak in the corrugation, drill and screw the back of the cover with 1½-inch #8 round-head screws. Then, at every third peak in the corrugation, drill and screw the front of the cover with 1¼-inch #8 round-head screws with washers. Finally, drill and screw the sides of the cover with 1¼-inch #8 roundhead screws with washers, 2 screws to a side. (See Figure 10.)

Assembling the Lath Cover

1. Cut two 46½-inch lengths of 1×3. These are the braces for the lath cover.

2. Secure one length of lath to the two braces as shown, using 2-penny resin box nails. This length of lath should be ¾ inch from the edge of the braces, and the braces should be positioned 12 inches in from the edge of the lath.

3. Separating the lengths of lath by 1 inch, secure the remaining lath to the braces as shown. (See Figure 12.)

4. No hinging is necessary for the lath cover. It will fit over the opening of the frame when the fiberglass cover is removed.

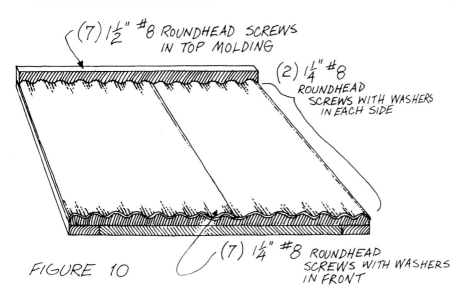

(7) 1½" #8 ROUNDHEAD SCREWS IN TOP MOLDING

(2) 1¼" #8 ROUNDHEAD SCREWS WITH WASHERS IN EACH SIDE

(7) 1¼" #8 ROUNDHEAD SCREWS WITH WASHERS IN FRONT

FIGURE 10

8. Attach the cover to the box with two 2½-inch loose-pin butt hinges, centered 10 inches in from the edge of the box. (See Figure 11.)

FIGURE 11

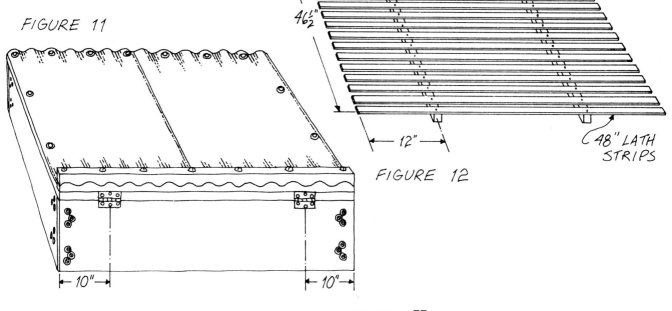

¾"

1"X1" BRACE

1" SPACE BETWEEN LATHS

46½"

12"

48" LATH STRIPS

10"   10"

FIGURE 12

Monthly Checklist

Alyssum
Artemisia
Baby's Breath
Balloonflower
Bee Balm
Canterbury Bell
Carpathian Harebell
Chrysanthemum (Perennial)
Clematis
Cleome
Columbine
Coreopsis
Dahlia
Daylily
Delphinium
English Daisy
Flax
Forget-Me-Not
Foxglove
Gaillardia
Gladiolus
Hollyhock (Perennial)
Iris
Lupine
Maltese Cross
Morning Glory
New England Aster
Painted Daisy
Pansy
Peach-Leafed Bellflower
Phlox (Perennial)
Plumed Bleeding Heart
Purple Loose-Strife
Rose
Shasta Daisy
Sweet Pea
Sweet William

Yellow daylily (see page 96)

APRIL

In the Victory Garden, our last-expected-frost date is April 20, so we can still count on frosty weather this month. But the soil is usually dry enough to work now, and our spring indoor seed-sowing is largely complete, so this is the month when the focus of our attention shifts outdoors for the first time, to the garden itself.

The first task is to finish removing the blanket of mulch that has provided winter protection to the perennials, biennials, and spring-flowering bulbs. I like to have all the mulch removed by the first of April, 3 weeks before the last-expected-frost date, so the shoots aren't kept in the darkness when they're trying to grow. Cold weather isn't much of a threat to these wintered-over plants, but they do tend to be a little tender for the first few days after the mulch is removed, so I keep the mulching material on hand and toss it back over the plants if temperatures in the 20s are predicted. This is the month to keep an eye on the emerging perennials; when they get to be 3 or 4 inches tall, I like to feed them with 5-10-5 (see the September feature).

Another important April job is to transplant the young perennials and biennials that have spent the winter in a nursery row following a July sowing. The plants should be moved as soon as there is 1 or 2 inches of growth to indicate which plant is which. (Remember that balloonflowers are slow to emerge in the spring — we rarely have a glimpse of ours this early in the season — and they can be damaged by indiscriminate digging.) If you haven't sown perennials yourself, you will probably be shopping the garden centers for young plants this time of year. If so, look for the ones that have the fullest, sturdiest growth and the best foliage color. You may find either divisions or spring-sown seedlings; the divisions may be more expensive, but they do produce larger plants the first year.

For most of the spring-flowering bulbs, this is the season of glory, when they occupy the flower garden's center stage all by themselves. When the flowers fade, I cut them off at the base of the stem and scatter the soil with 5-10-5 fertilizer to nourish the bulbs through their ripening period.

Most of the annual seedlings that were sown earlier in the spring need only to be transplanted to six-packs and then set into the cold frame for conditioning in preparation for their move to the garden next month.

Alyssum In April, young alyssum plants, whether sown from seed the previous July and wintered-over in a nursery bed or purchased from a garden center, are ready for transplant to their permanent spots in the perennial border. These are low-growing plants, ranging in height from 6 to 12 inches; they are more horizontal of growth than vertical, spreading 12 to 18 inches across as they grow. With these dimensions, they make excellent edging or rock garden plants. Full sun is best for them, but half-day sunlight is an acceptable alternative.

Following its winter in the nursery bed (see the September feature), an alyssum plant will have a root mass about 4 inches across. In the Victory Garden, where we use these plants primarily as edgers along the front of the perennial border, we use 3 plants together, lined up at minimum spacing about 12 inches apart. However, in the small bed or rock garden, a single plant will make a good show of color. In order to allow the growth to cascade over the front of the border, I set the plants only 2 to 3 inches back from the

Basket of Gold, a variety of alyssum

edge. (For complete transplant instructions, see the August feature.) After they have flowered, I shear off the blossom canopy to prevent the production of seed and help the plant regain its strength.

Alyssum need regular division if they're to be kept in bounds. How frequently this needs to be done depends on the original planting interval. If they are planted in spacious quarters 18 inches apart, they will probably need division only every 2 or 3 years.

Alyssum are tap-rooted perennials; they send down one large, deep root. Then they propagate by natural soil layering: new plants grow where the stems meet the soil. They're like June-bearing strawberries in this regard. If you want to increase your collection, you can simply dig up one of these self-rooted youngsters in the early spring and move it to a new location.

Ⓟ **Artemisia** Close to the front-and-center position of the Victory Garden perennial border there is a soft pillow of gray-green foliage known as the Silver Mound artemisia. This plant is one of my favorites, mostly because it's such a

A full-grown Silver Mound artemisia

treat for the senses. To the eyes, it is soft, cooling, and rest-ful. It has a light fragrance. And, unlike most plants, it in-vites touch. I can't walk by it without reaching down and running my hands along the top of the foliage. Though it does occasionally send up a few forgettable flowers toward the end of the summer, it is grown for its remarkable foliage alone, which softens and gentles the brighter colors and crisper outlines of the plants around it.

For all practical purposes, Silver Mound is the only variety of artemisia available for garden culture, favored pri-marily because it forms a compact plant, about 12 inches in each direction. It does benefit from a summer pruning (see the August entry), but it doesn't require regular division to keep it in bounds. Silver Mound is a variety of *Artemisia Schmidtiana*. Young plants are sold in the spring — April and May in my area — both by garden centers and some mail-order houses. It doesn't come easily from seed; in fact, I've never seen seeds sold commercially. (If you have diffi-culty finding a plant, you can easily take cuttings from a friend's. We do this in August, but the same technique would apply in the spring.)

The procedure for setting in artemisia plants, whether newly purchased or your own wintered-over cut-tings (see the August entry) is the standard one, described in the August feature. We plant them either 1 to a 12-inch site, or 3 together along a row, at 12-inch intervals. Artemi-sias need full sun to do their best, but they will be perfectly acceptable if grown in half-day or even filtered sunlight. They also need a rather dry soil because they can't survive the winter if the soil is too wet. Our soil isn't dry, but the perennial border has a raised bed with good drainage, and our plant has survived several winters without suffering. (If your soil is wet and heavy, and the beds are at ground level, dig out an excavation about 12 inches across and 10 or 12 inches deep. Add 1 part sand to 3 parts soil, refill the hole, and plant.)

The Victory Garden is at the northern limits of the Silver Mound's winter hardiness. At our suburban site, about 10 miles to the northwest, we give the plant a good deal more attention in the fall and a much thicker layer of winter mulch. Even with this extra effort, the specimens there are not up to the ones in the slightly warmer garden only minutes away.

P **Baby's Breath** Baby's breath is an excellent pe-rennial for the border, or for a spot all its own. The standard variety (*Gypsophila paniculata*) is 3 or 4 feet tall at matu-rity, but the overall effect is wispy. The flowers are very

Double-flowered baby's breath

small and white; there's a subtle pink variety as well but it is somewhat less popular. I often plant baby's breath at the end of the perennial border, as an accent. A few stems together will make a beautiful airy bouquet, either fresh or dried. (For drying directions, see the strawflower entry in July.) If all the flower heads are cut back after the June blossom period, the plant will flower again in late August.

Seeds of baby's breath are readily available and easily grown. The problem is that the doubles are far more appealing than the singles, and no variety will produce all double plants from seed. Even varieties labeled as doubles may produce as many single-flowered plants as doubles. There is no way to know until the plants flower, at which point you can spot the doubles easily. In the meantime, several plants must be sown from seed, carried along as seedlings, planted in a nursery bed, and waited for. It's not worth the effort.

My advice instead is simply to buy a small plant from a garden center or catalogue in the spring. These will have been propagated vegetatively from a double-flowered plant, so you can be sure of what you're getting. These young plants come on the market in April, and can be set out immediately.

Baby's breath needs a spot with full or half-day sunlight. They're large plants, so I give them a site 3 or 4 feet across. They're hardy in Zones 4 through 8 (see the Appendix), and come back year after year with little trouble. They stay in bounds and never need division, though they can be divided in the spring. The top growth can be controlled with pinching and pruning, if you wish. Despite their height, they never need staking.

P **Balloonflower** Balloonflowers are very cold-tolerant, and are hardy throughout the country. Gardeners would do well to keep this fact in mind as they wait for their wintered-over plants to poke their heads up through the soil. This species is extremely slow in this regard, but they are rarely killed by cold weather, as gardeners often fear; they're hardy in Zones 3 through 8. When at last there are signs of green, late in April or early in May, these plants should be dug and moved from the nursery bed to their permanent location in the perennial border. I like to put balloonflowers in the center row of the border so the tall flowers are visible throughout their long season, while the foliage, which doesn't have much personality, is kept out of the limelight.

We've concentrated on a variety of balloonflower in the Victory Garden that is shorter than most varieties. Marie's balloonflower sends up blue-violet flowers about 12 inches tall over foliage no taller than 6 to 9 inches. I usually plant these in clusters of 3 or 5, 12 to 15 inches apart to allow for the plants' horizontal spread. Marie's balloonflower cannot be seed-sown, as can the standard varieties. But cutting-grown plants are available from garden centers in the spring. This variety can be propagated by stem cuttings (see the August feature). For more about balloonflowers, see the July entry.

Marie's balloonflower

P **Bee Balm** This plant, named because of the bees' affection for it, is a perennial that increases in size very quickly, sending out underground runners as it ages. The speed with which it grows is a surprise to the unsuspecting gardener: a division only 4 or 5 inches across one spring might be more than 2 feet across a year later; after 3 or 4 years, it could be some 4 feet across. If left alone, it will continue to grow, and eventually it will take over the whole garden. Obviously, the gardener must intervene and divide the plant before this happens.

Bee balms grow from the center outward, reaching their peak in the third year. At that point, the center of the plant begins to lose vigor, while the strongest growth is around the outer edges; it's a pattern I call the doughnut effect. So in the Victory Garden, I divide bee balms in the spring of every fourth year, which allows them time to produce their best show, but stops them before they strangle their neighbors.

The division can be done either in the spring or fall. Spring is by far the better time in the north, so in the Victory Garden, I do this job in April, when the new season's stems are about 2 inches tall. This short growth makes the

Adam, a variety of bee balm

outline of the plant quite clear, both the strong outer section and the exhausted inner section. A plant of this size is difficult to lift whole, so what I do first is perforate the struggling center of the plant, and then "bite" into the doughnut by cutting down through the strong outer circle of growth with a sharp spade. Each division should be 4 to 8 inches across. When all the strong growth has been removed in manageable divisions, I dig out the center and throw it away. Then I excavate the site, working in organic matter, bone meal, and, if a soil test indicates the need, lime, and refill the hole. After setting one division into the spot (see the August feature), I either give the others away or move them to other sites in the garden.

New plants are often available for purchase at this time of the year, but bee balms are easily started from seed, which we do in July, transplanting the seedlings to nursery beds in September. Now, in April, these wintered-over plants are ready for permanent spots in the garden; they will have developed a root mass some 4 or 5 inches across, and new spring growth will just be starting. Bee balms need a spot with full sun (half-day sunlight is all right) and excellent air circulation. We put one plant to a site, and give it a space 2 to 4 feet around to grow into. Before setting the plant in, we give the soil standard springtime soil preparation (see the September feature), having already amply worked the soil in the fall (see After Frost). This planting information also applies to plants purchased in the spring.

In the Victory Garden, we put these large plants in the back of the perennial border. From the design perspective, this is the best spot for them, but it does put them in an area where the air circulation is poor, and they frequently develop mildew. We can usually make it through June, the first month of the flowering period, without a problem, but there is often mildew on the leaves early in July. Mildew, which turns the foliage white, is not a fatal problem but it is quite unsightly, so we respond as soon as we see it. Our first line of defense is a dusting of sulfur. If this doesn't do the trick, we cut the plants back to 3 or 4 inches from the ground early in July; they usually have a chance to recuperate and flower again in late summer.

Ⓑ **Canterbury Bell** In the Victory Garden, we treat all our biennials alike. We sow them in pots in midsummer (see the July entry), transplant them into nursery rows in September, and winter them over with the perennials once frost is in the ground (see After Frost). This month, as the warm weather comes again, they are ready to take their permanent places in the garden. To do their best, they need

Opposite: Canterbury bells, grown from a mix

a spot with full sunlight, but they will do quite well in half-day sunlight, too.

The first step is to remove the mulch, which we do in two stages in order to avoid suddenly exposing the plants to the full effects of the sun (see After Frost for additional information). Then we lift the individual Canterbury bell plants out and set them into the perennial border for some June color. They can be added to the annual bed, but their subtle colors and short blossom period — only 2 or 3 weeks — make them better suited to the perennial border.

In terms of spring soil preparation, Canterbury bells are treated as annuals, even though they're put into the perennial border (see the May feature). At maturity, Canterbury bells stand 2 to 2½ feet tall, with a spread of about 12 to 18 inches, so we space them at 18-inch intervals. After transplant, we water them with transplant solution (see the July feature), and off they go. They usually need the help of a single stake later in the summer to help them stand up straight. (For staking directions, see the July feature.)

P **Carpathian Harebell** Like so many of the July-sown perennials, Carpathian harebells have root masses some 4 inches across by spring, when they are ready to be moved from their nursery bed to permanent spacing in the

Blue Clips, a variety of Carpathian harebell

garden. At 6 to 8 inches tall, they are candidates for the rock garden, the edge of the path, or the front of the perennial border. Anyplace, in fact, where their short stature is well used and they have either full, half-day, or filtered sunlight. I like them as edging plants, so after routine soil preparation, I line 3 plants up in a row 9 to 15 inches apart. They can be planted singly, but they are so small that the larger planting gives them a better effect.

Carpathian harebells are very slow growing, so they don't tend to outgrow their space quickly. But they do exhaust the nutrients in the soil, so every 3 to 5 years, in April, I divide the plants into 4- or 5-inch sections, and set them back into reworked soil. (Garden centers also sell young divisions at this time of year; the planting routine is the same.)

P **Chrysanthemum (Perennial)** In the case of hardy chrysanthemums, the word perennial must be used advisedly, as their ability to survive winter is not their best quality. They can be brought through, if nature cooperates, with a careful winter mulching. Our loss to winterkill is fairly minimal with this treatment. Now, in the spring, the mulch can be removed in the standard two-step operation and, cross your fingers, dozens of new little shoots will be exposed to the world. (For more about winter mulching, see After Frost.) A plant going into its second season can be left as is if you want, but an older plant needs to be divided to produce the best plants.

In the Victory Garden we divide chrysanthemum plants when they reach 4 or 5 inches in height. What I do is just dig up the whole plant and go to work. In some varieties, single-stemmed divisions will come easily from the root mass, almost peeling off in well-rooted, discrete units. Other varieties are not so cooperative; these I either divide into quarters or separate the small offshoots that develop along the outer edge of the wintered-over plant. Whether you wind up with single-stemmed or clump divisions, with a regular program of pinching back you will have fine, large, densely flowered plants in the fall.

In the Victory Garden we move young single-stemmed plants into six-packs and larger clumps into suitably sized pots, and keep them in the greenhouse until they're in bud. This is a space-economy move for us, as we just can't afford to turn over a good amount of garden space to plants that won't flower until the fall. For the home gardener, a nursery bed is probably a better alternative.

Garden centers sometimes sell young plants in 2½-inch pots in the spring; these have been propagated by stem

One of the many hardy chrysanthemums on the market

cutting. They're good buys and a good idea if you can give them a place to develop. You can put them in their flowering spot if you don't mind looking at flowerless plants all summer. Or you can put them elsewhere, in prepared soil and full or half-day sunshine, until they're in bud. These youngsters should be pinched back too. (See the May entry.)

🅿 **Clematis** The main selling point of this perennial vine is the astonishing density of the flowers on the mature plant — it seems to be nothing less than a great wall of color. It's not a good plant for the impatient, as it spends approximately 7 sparse-flowering years reaching maturity, but for those among you who are willing to wait, it's a marvelous plant. It's easy to care for and extremely long-lived. And it blossoms for most of the summer.

In the past, northern gardeners had to choose clematis carefully because some varieties were on a 2-year cycle, flowering the second year from canes produced the first. These had to be avoided in cold-winter areas because the first-year canes were too tender to make it through. Now there are very few of these 2-season clematis on the market; catalogues no longer even mention the problem. The new varieties are widely available from seed houses and garden centers in the spring. In the Victory Garden, we've grown a purple-flowered variety, *Clematis jackmanii*, which is one of the best in my opinion; Ramona, which has large, light-blue flowers; and the white-flowered Candidissima.

If you ask an old-timer about planting clematis, you will hear one of gardening's most venerable sayings: clematis like their heads in the sun and their feet in the shade. In other words, they like their roots cool and shady and their foliage sunlit. If you don't have a spot that offers this condition, plant them in full or half-day sun, and mulch the soil around the plant. In the Victory Garden, we put a 12-inch circle of pine bark or wood chips, about 2 inches deep, around the base of the plants, making sure that there is a 2-inch unmulched circle around the stems. Then in a circle 18 inches out from the plant, we set in low-growing annuals, such as impatiens or begonias. This combination of mulch and annuals minimizes root disturbance while dressing up the area around the plants. (At the end of the season, I pull out the annuals and remove the summer mulch so I can provide a winter mulch to help them through the cold weather. For more, see After Frost.)

The procedure for setting in the plants is the standard one (see the August feature). The important aspect of this job is to provide a support so the plants can begin climbing immediately; if they can't climb, their growth is poor. I usually use a sturdy nylon netting. In the Victory Garden the clematis are growing up along a stockade fence, so we've just stapled the netting to the top of the fence, and staked the bottom of the netting out about 10 inches from the fence, giving the netting an angle and creating space for air to circulate between the plant and the fence. It is possible to grow clematis along an open area — like a porch, for instance — so long as the support is sturdy enough. The natural growth inclination of clematis is tall and narrow. During their first year, the plants grow about 8 or 10 feet straight up, with almost no side growth. If they're pinched at the beginning of the second year, they will begin to spread outward. But by the placement of the netting, you can train them to go where you want — even, once they're 2 feet tall or so, horizontally.

For established plants, regular spring care is fairly simple. The stems break easily, so in April, when new growth starts, I prune away any damaged stems that haven't made it through the winter. Before mulching and planting the annuals to provide shade for the roots, I scatter

Clematis jackmanii *growing in the Victory Garden*

5-10-5 fertilizer around the soil, no closer to the stem than 2 or 3 inches, to avoid burning. The fertilizer can go right on top of the mulch and be watered in. (For more about fertilizers, see the July feature.)

A **Cleome** At 6 to 8 inches across, the flower clusters of these annuals are among the largest blooms in the garden, but for all their size, they are light and airy and graceful. The flower colors are white and shades of pink. The foliage is very handsome and unusual in texture, always a good quality in a flowering plant; it's also thorny and sticky. At maturity, the plants are 3 to 4 feet tall and 2 to 3 feet across; there are no dwarf varieties on the market. Their size makes them a good choice for a large informal area that needs filling quickly.

Most of the seed catalogues sell a white-flowered cleome named Helen Campbell, as well as several varieties of the strain Queen, whose flowers are various shades of pink and lilac. We've grown nearly all of these in the Victory Garden. Their botanical name is *Cleome Hasslerana*. They are sometimes called spider flowers, a reference to their long and noticeable stamens.

Cleome grows so big so quickly that the plants need only 3 weeks after sowing to reach set-out size. If they're allowed more time to grow indoors, they outgrow their six-packs before the outdoor weather is warm enough for them, necessitating an extra transplant to larger containers. In the Victory Garden, we sow the seeds the second week of April; the procedure is the standard one, except that these are plants that should *not* be pinched back (see the August feature). After a few days in the cold frame toward the end of

A Rose Queen cleome, not quite at its peak

the month, they're ready for the garden the first of May. Given full or half-day sun, they'll bloom full time from summer to frost.

P **Columbine** Columbine plants bloom in the early summer, along with lupines, iris, daylilies, Oriental poppies, and alyssum. The taller varieties, especially the long-spurred hybrids, are beautifully graceful; they mature at 3 to 4 feet tall, with a spread of 18 to 24 inches. They're a spectacular plant for the back of the border. In the Victory Garden, we've made more use of a dwarf variety called Nana, which at 12 to 18 inches tall and 10 to 15 inches across is more appropriate to the scale of our border. When Nana is in blos-

som, the flowers extend another 6 inches above the foliage, making this a good choice for the intermediate row of the border.

Our perennial border is in full sunshine all day, and our columbines have done well there. But one of the attributes of this plant is that it grows well in, and actually prefers, half-day sunlight. All the varieties will grow in a spot where the summer sun is fairly weak as long as they have the advantage of half-day sunlight through the spring. (For seed-sowing, see the July entry.)

McKana's Giant Hybrid, a long-spurred variety of columbine

P **Coreopsis** There are several species of coreopsis grown in the flower garden. Our favorite is a species called the threadleaf coreopsis (*Coreopsis verticillata*), named for its threadlike, ferny foliage. I like this plant for several reasons: it has a clear lemon-yellow flower through the summer, when this color is hard to come by in the perennial border; it's virtually pest-free; and it has a very long flowering period for a perennial, from June through September. It's an extremely hardy plant, native to the northeastern regions of the United States. In fact, *C. verticillata* is the original species plant; it hasn't been hybridized at all. It lives a long life, spreads rapidly, and demands little.

For some reason, though, it is not an easy plant to find. The seeds aren't sold by seed houses, though seeds of other species are. We have been able to find divisions in the spring, however. We plant them in the intermediate row of our perennial border (they're beautiful next to perennial flax). At maturity, the plants are 18 to 24 inches tall. We give each plant a spot 12 to 18 inches across, which it fills in quickly.

In the Victory Garden we divide coreopsis every 3 or 4 years, but they could be planted in a less-formal site and allowed to naturalize. They spread quickly, sending up offshoots from the roots.

A **Dahlia** I'm a thrifty Yankee by nature. If I see a way to increase the return on an investment, I take it. Most tuberous dahlias, for instance, are inexpensive, but there are rare and wondrous varieties available from the specialty houses that are very costly. I buy them anyway, because I know that propagation is so easy and so productive.

I begin with plants started into growth last month (see the March entry). By April, they have produced foliage 8 to 10 inches tall. With no damage to the parent plant whatsoever, several 3- or 4-inch stem cuttings can be taken and rooted in perlite. When they've rooted, I move them to six-packs filled with potting soil (see the August feature). The

Opposite: Threadleaf coreopsis, an excellent source of cut flowers

result is many plants from one; they will all, parent and off-spring, flower the first year and produce full-size tubers by the end of the season.

Toward the end of April, I set all the plants into the cold frame for 5 to 7 days. (These are very frost-sensitive plants, so don't put them into the cold frame too early.) The parent plant may be too tall to fit into the frame, in which case it is a good idea to set the plant outside for several days before planting, bringing the plant inside in the late afternoon to protect it from the cool night temperatures. All the plants are then ready for open garden next month.

P   **Daylily**   Daylilies have a very fast grip on life. They're one of the hardest perennials to kill, which explains why they are so often the only survivors in an abandoned garden. Their long lease on life is not their only selling point. Though they're best in half-day sunlight, they'll also tolerate full or filtered sun. They grow quickly, are rarely bothered by insects or diseases, and all in all require very little attention. They're called daylilies because each single flower lasts only one day; even so, they make nice cut flowers for a single event.

As a group, daylilies are tall, wide, and handsome. Depending on the variety, the flowers range from 2 to 4 feet tall, and the foliage from 18 to 24 inches tall. Tetraploid daylilies are a little harder to find, and significantly more expensive, but they are more vigorous, and have the added advantage of larger flowers on shorter plants; tetraploids are all under 2 feet tall. A single daylily plant blooms for about 4 weeks, but there are early-, mid-, and late-season daylily varieties, so by selecting carefully, it's possible to have plants in bloom from May through early August. When buying, the important qualities are time of bloom, height, and color. All varieties on the market today are hybrids of the genus *Hemerocallis*. Hardiness varies with the variety but there's a choice for every area.

Young daylily plants come onto the market in the spring, and they are available through many of the seed houses. (If you would like to see a staggering range of daylily varieties, look at one of the specialty house catalogues.) The catalogues may use varietal names, or they may identify the plants by color only. The mail-order houses will probably ship the plants bare-root; local garden centers will most likely pot them before selling them. (For more, see the August feature.)

The setting-in procedure for daylilies is the standard one (see the August feature). At maturity, a single daylily plant can be as large as 2 feet across, so they can be planted, one to a site, in the center of a 2-foot space. But because daylilies do not produce much of a flower show their first year, we sometimes set them in a cluster of 3 plants in a triangle formation. In this case, they need a much larger planting site, some 4 feet across, to give them room enough to develop; they will also need dividing more frequently.

▣ **Delphinium** In the Victory Garden, we plant both the tall and the dwarf varieties of delphinium, sowing the seeds in July and wintering the plants in nursery beds (see the September feature). Now in April it's time to move them to their flowering spots, in either full or half-day sunlight. We plant both the tall and dwarf varieties in 3-plant clusters, spacing the taller ones 18 to 24 inches apart and the dwarf at intervals of 12 to 15 inches. The taller delphiniums will need the support of single stakes as they mature.

Giant Pacific, a mixed variety of bee delphinium

Locating delphiniums requires thinking ahead. The tall-growing varieties reach heights of 4 to 6 feet when they're in bloom, but up to half of that height is in the flower spikes. After their June to July flowering, they should be cut back for a second, less-dramatic late-summer blossom period. This will leave foliage only 2 or 3 feet tall for a good part of the summer. The dwarf varieties of delphinium, though shorter at 1½ to 3 feet flowering height, follow the same foliage-to-flowering proportions. So in planting, delphiniums must be located where their foliage won't be shaded by taller-growing plants, and where their tall flowers won't obscure the sightline to other blossoms.

Ⓑ **English Daisy** Along with the other biennials in the Victory Garden, we move our young English daisy plants to their flowering location in mid-April, after removing the protective winter mulch in the standard two-stage operation (see After Frost).

These are short plants (6 to 9 inches tall), so they're good at the front of the perennial border, as short-lived members of the annual border, or as edging plants; they're appealing next to sweet Williams, or around a tall plant, like perennial phlox. They're best in full sun but will also tolerate half-day sunlight.

Before setting the plants in, we do standard springtime soil preparation, treating English daisies as annuals in this regard (see the May feature). Then we lift the plants out of the nursery bed, set them into the garden at 6- to 9-inch intervals to account for the spread of the foliage, and water them with transplant solution (see the July feature).

English daisies are at their best in the cool spring. They flower 4 to 6 weeks in June and early July, but their

Rose Buttons, a variety of English daisy

blossom show lets up from that point on. They seem to attract aphids once the weather warms up, so although they may throw occasional flowers till frost, the reward isn't worth the wait. We pull the plants in July and give the space over to another plant, such as chrysanthemums.

P **Flax** In the Victory Garden we start flax from seed in July and winter-over the plants in a nursery bed until spring. Now they're ready to be moved to their flowering spot. (If you haven't sown seeds yourself, you may be out of luck, as these are not the most easily available of perennials in the spring.) Depending on the variety and growing conditions, flax reach a height of 12 to 18 inches, with a spread of 9 to 12 inches, so I set them in 9 to 12 inches apart. They're best in full sunlight, but they will grow in half-day or filtered light as well.

Young flax plants do not branch well on their own; they have a tendency to send up long stems topped with single flowers. So after I move them to their permanent spots I pinch the tips back once to encourage branching. Even with this treatment, they will come into flower in late June and continue into July.

After a few years, flax will exhaust the soil they're growing in, and show a loss of vigor. They are not good candidates for division, so at this point I suggest starting new plants from seed (see the July entry).

Ⓑ **Forget-Me-Not** Young plants of these biennials are very commonplace in garden centers in the spring, but in the Victory Garden we sow our own seeds in midsummer (see the July entry), winter the plants over in a nursery bed, and are now ready to move them to their flowering spots. They're adaptable to a range of sites, but I particularly like their small, airy, blue flowers interplanted among stiff, dramatic, boldly colored tulips. This is an old-fashioned combination that still retains its appeal. I've also used them in rock gardens, and as edging plants along the front of either the annual or perennial bed.

Forget-me-nots have a roundish look, standing 6 to 9 inches in all directions. They do their best in half-day and filtered light. So when I set them in, I give them a spot out of the direct sun, and set them in at 6- to 9-inch intervals. Then I wait for their 6-week flower show through May and June.

Ⓑ **Foxglove** We use foxglove exclusively in the perennial border in the Victory Garden, where their height and softly colored flowers are at home. The standard varieties can grow to heights of 4 to 5 feet; even Foxy, the shorter variety we've grown and liked in the Victory Garden, will be some 3 feet tall at maturity. I particularly like the combination of the tall, spiked foxglove next to the shorter, rounder mass of peonies.

We start our own plants from seeds in the summer (see the July entry), but plants are easy to find in garden centers in the spring, usually as mixes. Both the standard and dwarf varieties spread 12 to 18 inches, so we give each plant a site of this size to grow into. We generally cluster Foxy in groups of 3 or 5.

Standard varieties of foxglove tend to become perennial because they both self-sow and send up basal offshoots. Because these are hybrids, the self-sown seedlings will not breed true, so we pull these out. The offshoots can be left, however, for another crop of lovely flowers the following year. (Foxy is not quite so eager to propagate itself. It doesn't self-sow and rarely sends up offshoots, so I just start new plants from seed every summer.)

One of the commonly available blue-flowered forget-me-nots

Standard-size foxgloves of the Excelsior strain

Foxglove's Latin name is *Digitalis purpurea*; it is the source of digitalis, a medicine used in the treatment of heart disease. However, the flowers themselves are toxic; don't let children nibble on them.

P **Gaillardia** Gaillardias, or blanketflowers, are very commonplace in the garden centers in the spring, but we usually start our own plants in midsummer (see the July entry), either by seed or by cutting. In September we move these young plants to the nursery bed where they stay, protected by mulch, for the winter. Now, as April brings warm weather, they can be dug up and moved to a spot with full or half-day sun. The standard varieties, such as Dazzler, grow to be over 3 feet tall, so we put these toward the middle or back of the border. They will need peripheral staking as the season advances. The dwarf varieties, standing about 12 inches tall, are better toward the front edge. For the standard varieties, I set one plant into a prepared site 18 to 24 inches across. I think the dwarf varieties are better clustered, so I put 3 together, 10 to 12 inches apart.

Gaillardias need division after 3 to 5 years in the garden. We do this job in April, discarding the poor growth in the center of the plant and cutting the remaining vigorous growth into sections 4 to 6 inches across. We follow the above planting routine for resetting these divisions, or for planting ones bought from a garden center. If you would like to propagate your gaillardia without dividing a plant that is still doing well, you can dig up one of the offshoots that will develop along the outer circle of the plant.

A Dazzler gaillardia, with the petal damage common to gaillardias

Ⓐ **Gladiolus** Gladioluses are known mostly for the spectacular cut flowers they produce — for cutting tips, see the June entry — but they're also wonderful garden plants, even if you don't intend to bring the flowers indoors. Either way, the blossoms are very dramatic, and come in every imaginable color, including some of the best greens around. Depending on the variety, the plants will stand 3 to 5 feet tall; there are some dwarf varieties that are less than 3 feet tall. And there's a hardy dwarf, too, which can be planted in the fall with other spring-flowering bulbs. The gardener has enormous choice when selecting glads for the garden.

Gladiolus corms, sometimes mistakenly called bulbs (see the October feature), are easy to find in garden centers and catalogues. The most expensive are the largest, known as "top size." These are the ones I buy, but there is something to be said for buying smaller corms, though they produce somewhat shorter flower stems. The economy comes from the fact that all corms produce a number of new corms at the end of every growing season. Of the new corms, several are young, pea-sized corms, called cormels, that are not yet large enough to flower. But there are always 2 or 3 flowering-size corms among the new generation, and one is usually large enough to qualify as top size. One corm sends up 1 or 2 flower spikes. Cormels need a year or two to grow to full size. Because they are so small, I advise planting them in a separate nursery row, about 2 inches deep and 4 to 6 inches apart, in the spring. (See the October entry.)

The gladiolus blossom period lasts about a week. In the Victory Garden, we keep glads coming all summer with successive plantings, every week or so, from mid-April through early August. (The shoots are frost-sensitive, so don't plant too early.) The early plantings take 8 or 10 weeks to flower because the weather is cool; in the warmer weather, glads flower in about 6 to 8 weeks. So our planting schedule keeps us chest-high in gladioluses from June through frost.

In the Victory Garden, we grow glads in the perennial border because they're too tall for other sites. They

A miniature bicolor gladiolus

need full sun; unlike many plants, they have no tolerance for less-than-ideal light conditions. After adding some organic matter and bone meal to the soil, we're ready to plant. We cluster an uneven number of same-variety corms, usually 3 or 5, 6 to 9 inches apart. To avoid the appearance of a line-up, we arrange them randomly. Then we plant the corms, rounded side down; they should be 3 times as deep as the height of the corm, so the planting depth varies depending on the size of the individual corm.

A single-flowered perennial hollyhock

P **Hollyhock (Perennial)** Hollyhocks are tall plants, reaching heights of 4 to 6 feet, so they belong at the back of the perennial border. Now that spring weather is here, I dig up the young plants that have spent the winter in nursery rows (see the September feature), and set them into prepared soil, one plant to a space 2 to 3 feet wide. (See the August feature for more.) They need no further attention until next month, when the growth will be tall enough to need staking; we give each flowering stem a single stake (see the July feature).

Hollyhocks need a large, carefully chosen planting site; they'll take half-day sunlight, but the more the better. They're broad in addition to being tall, spreading 2 to 3 feet across after a season or two in the ground. They're also very prone to rust fungus, which appears as small bumps, usually red, on the foliage. This is a particular problem in humid areas. We've had a couple of unusually dry summers when the rust problems haven't been too bad, but more often than not it's been a problem for us in the Victory Garden. One of the best remedies for rust is in fact a preventive — good air circulation. Given the size of the mature plants, providing good air circulation means giving them a very large section, 2 to 3 feet across. In the Victory Garden we had no spot for hollyhocks except against the fence, and while we have had rust, most years we've been able to get a fairly long season of flowers before the problem becomes serious.

We no longer spray hollyhocks regularly with a fungicide to prevent rust. Even if rust is a problem, the plants usually continue to flower — the disease affects the foliage, not the blossoms. Throughout the flowering season, I keep an eye on the plants, checking the undersides of the leaves especially, looking for the little brownish bumps that come with rust. If the plants are hit, I wait until late in the flowering period and cut them back to healthy foliage, leaving behind stems and leaves that can grow for another few weeks and help the plants build strength for another year. If I make it through the whole summer without problems, I consider myself lucky, but I take precautions against unseen rust wintering-over in the foliage by cutting the plants back to soil level just before the winter mulch goes on. All this cut foliage must be removed from the garden and burned or discarded with the trash.

P **Iris** There are least 200 species of iris known to botanists. In most, the leaves grow from the crown of the plant, right at the soil line, while exquisite flowers sit above the foliage on strong, straight stems. From species to species, irises vary in size and color, but they share a unique configuration. Half of the petals, usually 3, stand upright, and are called standards. And half (again, usually 3), hang down from the flower's crown; these are called falls. The size of the petals, their number, and exact position are a little different from species to species.

Bearded iris flowers

Although there are some bulbous irises, the most common irises available from the garden come from rhizomes, which are thick storage roots that grow horizontally at or just below the surface of the soil (see the October feature). Among the rhizomatous irises, there are two types, bearded and beardless, a reference to whether or not the flowers have a fuzzy strip, often in a contrasting color, along the inside center of the falls. Bearded irises dominate the market, but the beardless have their uses as well. (Crested irises are a third type; they are handled like beardless irises.)

Bearded irises, also known as pogon or German irises, bloom for 2 or 3 weeks through June and July. They

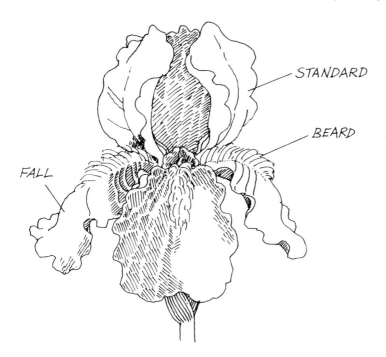

New growth from a bearded iris plant

come on the market in April and are widely sold both by garden centers and mail-order houses. There are many varieties available, offering by far the best color range among irises; with the exception of clear red, nearly every flower color is represented. Depending on the variety, the heights range from under 10 inches tall to 3 feet or more. When bearded irises are sold, they are usually identified both by color and by height.

At this time of the year, bearded irises are available from garden centers as growing, potted divisions. These can simply be planted in a site 12 inches across at the same depth they grew in the pot. (For more, see the August feature.) You'll save some money buying bearded irises if you wait until June, and buy the newly divided rhizomes (see the June entry). Whichever way you decide to begin your collection, you should treat established plants — those more than a year old — to some 5-10-5 fertilizer every April. Beyond this minimal effort, bearded irises present no maintenance problems until they have been in the ground for 3 to 5 years, when they need division (see the June entry).

Beardless, or apogon, irises differ from their bearded relatives in more than the beard. They offer much less variety of height and color, but they have the advantage of doing well in moist, shady places, requiring only half-day or filtered sunlight.

Of all the beardless irises, the Siberian irises are the most forgiving and easiest to grow. They're one of the few plants that actually thrive in the moist sites that often present garden problems. (In the Victory Garden, they are exposed to more sun and drier conditions than they would like, but we've been able to keep them fairly happy with a careful watering schedule, especially through a dry spring, as they send up a great deal of growth early in the season.) The individual flowers are very long-lasting; they come in white and shades of blue and purple. The plants themselves are usually about 2½ feet tall.

Japanese iris, another of the beardless varieties, is a more specialized plant. It needs a soil even moister than Siberian iris, and soil on the acid side (pH 5.5 to 6.5). It's done all right in the Victory Garden because we've tended it so carefully, but it's really meant for a spot where there's more moisture in the soil, and less sunlight. The flower colors are limited to white and shades of blue and purple. The breeding of Japanese irises has produced some varieties with enormous flowers. In my opinion, the large ones have lost all their grace. The single-flowered varieties are the nicest.

Beardless irises also need regular division every 3 to 5 years. As they grow, the centers of the plants lose vigor,

Opposite: A planting of Siberian beardless irises

and the strongest parts are concentrated around the outer edges. Beardless irises can be divided according to the timetable for the bearded (right after flowering in early summer), but they respond better if they're divided in the early spring, just as they begin growth. Though they're called rhizomatous, the roots of beardless irises are different from those of the bearded; rather than one large rhizome with 1 or 2 smaller ones attached, these clumps have a very tough network of smaller, fleshy roots. The only way to divide them is with an axe, a hatchet, or a sharp spade. In dividing, I cut the vigorous growth into individual clumps 4 to 6 inches across and discard the weak inner section. After working bone meal and organic matter into the soil, and lime if needed to correct the pH, I plant them, one division to a site, at intervals of 15 to 18 inches. The clumps should be planted at the same level at which they were growing before. After they're planted, I fertilize new plants with transplant solution. (This information also governs the setting-in of a newly purchased, potted division.)

For more information about division and planting, see the August feature.

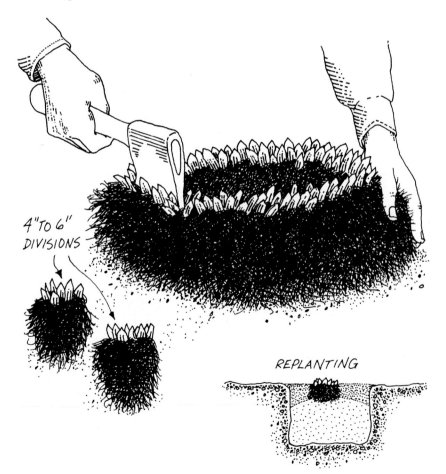

4" TO 6" DIVISIONS

REPLANTING

P **Lupine** Although the flowers reach an impressive 3 to 5 feet in height, lupines must be considered intermediate-height plants because the foliage itself is rarely taller than 18 inches. This means that for most of the season, with the exception of the June blossoming period, there is only foliage to look at in the garden; it's very good-looking foliage, so I like to locate the plant where the foliage can be seen and where it will receive its share of sunlight.

So in April, when we move our young plants from their nursery bed (see the September feature), we give them a spot in the center row of the perennial border. We like to put 3 plants together in a cluster, each about 18 inches apart in a spot 3 feet across. I particularly like the plant next to iris, which blooms at the same time. Lupines are best in full sunlight, but half-day sun will suit them, too.

Standard-size Russell lupines, with the characteristic bicolored flower

Occasionally the tall-growing flower stems will need the support of a single stake (see the July feature). Other than that, they need no further attention. After 3 or 4 years in the ground, the plants peter out and should be replaced with new plants.

For more about lupines, see the July entry.

P **Maltese Cross** By spring, young Maltese cross plants sown in July and wintered-over in a nursery bed have developed a root mass some 4 or 5 inches across. This month, they're ready to be dug and moved to a permanent site in the perennial border, each plant to a site 2 or 3 feet across. If you haven't started plants of your own, you should be able to find seed-grown plants and divisions at garden centers this month.

The red-flowered varieties of Maltese cross plants produce vividly colored flowers on large plants. It's a good hot spot in the garden, one I usually surround with paler colors — blues and soft yellows. If other bright reds or oranges were planted nearby, the color balance of the border could be disturbed. They need full or half-day sunlight.

After 3 or 4 years in the garden, Maltese cross plants will need division. These are among the many perennials that lose vigor in the center of the plant as they age while the strong growth moves outward. So in dividing, I cut the vigorous growth into 4- to 6-inch divisions. A single division should occupy a space 2 to 3 feet across. (For complete division information, see the August feature.)

In May, we provide these plants with stakes around their foliage to help keep the heavy growth upright. And in July, we cut the plants back to stimulate a second flowering later in the season.

A **Morning Glory** Most annuals, set into the ground after the danger of spring frost, will begin growing right away. Morning glories require warmth to grow well. They aren't damaged if they're set out with the other annuals the first of May, but they don't progress. So we time our morning glories to go into the ground around Memorial Day, sowing the seeds around the middle of April.

Morning glories are annual vines that climb eagerly if given a support. There is a great deal of height difference depending on the variety. At 10 to 15 feet, Heavenly Blue is among the taller. The Early Call series offers some of the shortest plants, at 6 or 8 feet. All varieties grow quickly; we've had plants 6 or 8 feet tall by the fourth of July.

No variety of morning glory has much of a spread, so for a good show of color several plants must be grown. In

Opposite: The red-flowered Maltese cross, a good addition to the cut-flower bouquet

Morning glories, the variety Heavenly Blue

quantity, they're an excellent choice for an immediate show of substantial foliage and color. The flowers themselves are fairly large, at 3 to 5 inches across, and numerous; the plants flower all season long. The traditional color of morning glory flowers is sky blue, but there are now several shades of blue available, as well as white and rose. In the Victory Garden, we've grown both blue and white varieties. The plants are called morning glories because, originally, the flowers opened only in the morning, closing as the midday sun became hot. The new hybrids are more tolerant of bright light and heat. The Early Call series is quite good on this score; these are also the first varieties to bloom. All varieties, while best in full sunlight, benefit from protection from the noonday sun. In fact they'll tolerate anything more than half-day sunlight.

Morning glory seeds are widely available through mail-order catalogues. Their botanical name is *Ipomoea purpurea*. The seeds are tough-coated, so I put them in hot tap water and let them cool in the water overnight. Because the seedlings do not transplant well, I sow the seeds directly in individual peat pots or six-packs, putting 2 or 3 seeds together. When the seedlings are about 2 inches tall, I thin all but the strongest seedling in a compartment. The seedlings will grow very quickly, and need a small stake to keep them upright, even before they're moved outdoors. Before setting the plants into the garden, I put them into the cold frame for 5 to 7 days to become conditioned.

P **New England Aster** Like most true asters, this is a perennial, *Aster novae-angliae*. (For the most common of the annual asters, see the March entry.) New England asters, sometimes known as Michaelmas daisies, are recommended both by their blossom time and their bulk. They flower in the fall, when most perennials have gone by. And they're heavy with flowers on great large plants that are not only tall but full and bushy. We've grown two varieties in the Victory Garden: Eventide, which has purple flowers, and Harrington's Pink, which bears pink blossoms. They are both, like all New England asters, daisy-flowered. In our garden, they reach a height of 4 to 5 feet. However, their height can be controlled somewhat, and more flowers produced, by pinching the tips once in May or June.

New England aster seeds are never sold — they don't breed true — but plants are sold by garden centers in the spring. Usually these are potted divisions in 6-inch containers. They grow to be so large — they'll double in size over a year — that only one plant is put in an area 18 to 24 inches across.

New England asters are among the fastest-growing perennials around; if they're grown in an open setting, where they are not in conflict with other plants, this isn't a

Harrington's Pink, a variety of New England aster

problem, but if they're sharing a limited space with other plants they will need division every other year or they'll take over. In the Victory Garden, this job can be done either in the spring or in the fall after they flower. (If your fall frost date is earlier than ours, spring division is a better bet.) A spring division will send up flowers the same year.

In the Victory Garden, we plant these beauties in a spot that is 18 to 24 inches across, which our 4- to 6-inch divisions fill in in 2 or 3 years. If the ground around them looks a little bare the first season, annuals can be used to provide color. New England asters like a spot where they're in full sun, but half-day sunlight will do.

For a discussion about dividing plants, see the August feature.

Ⓟ **Painted Daisy** Young painted daisies, started from seed in July and wintered-over in a nursery bed, are ready this month to join the other plants in the perennial border. Though the flowers rise to a height of 2 or more feet, the foliage is only 15 to 20 inches tall, so we treat painted daisies as intermediate-height plants.

We cluster 3 young plants together, 12 to 15 inches apart, either in the middle row of the perennial border, or in the rock garden. Painted daisies bloom in June, with lupine and columbine. In our garden, they grow in full sunlight; this is their preference, but they also do well in half-day or filtered sun. In May, we provide the major stem of each plant with the support of a single stake. And in June, after they've flowered, we cut back the flower stems to encourage a second bloom later in the summer.

Painted daisies can be divided, either in the spring or fall. However, old plants stay well in bounds, and new specimens grow easily from seed. So in the Victory Garden, we start new plants rather than divide the old.

A painted daisy in early spring

Ⓑ **Pansy** This is the month we move our young pansies from their nursery bed (see the September feature) into flowering spots in the garden.

Pansies have the color profusion and long season of annuals, but being hardy they come into flower much earlier in the season. However, in the Victory Garden, where immediacy of color is more important than a long season, we plant the pansies at very close intervals (4 to 6 inches apart) between the tulip bulbs, which are just beginning to show signs of growth in April. The two crops blossom together in May, and because the pansies are so close together, the bed is a solid mass of color quite early in the spring. After the tulips have gone by, we pull the bulbs and the pansy plants out, and give the spot over to annuals. (See the tulip entry in October for more.)

The home gardener probably views this as an extravagant use of pansies; in my own garden at home, so do I. After all, if the plants are given room enough to grow, and if the faded flowers are regularly removed, the new, heat-tolerant varieties blossom until frost; but because of the tight spacing in the Victory Garden, the plants must be treated as short-term flowers since they become overcrowded so quickly. The alternative to our treatment is to handle the pansies as long-term annuals, and plant them in masses, 6 to 9 inches apart, either in the annual bed or along the garden walk. They're best in a spot with half-day sunlight, but they will tolerate full or filtered sun, too. (They deteriorate faster in full sun.) Depending on the growing conditions, they will reach heights of 6 to 12 inches.

Pansies are very eager to set seed; if you allow the flowers to fade on the plants, and the seeds to ripen, you'll lose the crop. The solution is to check the plants regularly,

Butterfly Hybrids, one of the larger-flowered pansy varieties on the market

and snip off faded blossoms and the seed pod directly behind the flowers. Even with this effort, the plants are apt to look exhausted by midsummer, so I usually sheer the plants back to about half their height when they begin to suffer. In a few weeks, they come back into flower with a new lease on life.

P **Peach-Leafed Bellflower** These are fairly tall-growing plants, reaching heights of 2 or 3 feet, but at only 12 to 18 inches across, they have a mostly vertical look. In the Victory Garden, we plant them across the back or middle of the perennial border. Their tall, narrow flower spikes are particularly handsome next to rounder, fuller plants, such as phlox.

There are two April chores for peach-leafed bellflowers, one for young plants and one for old. Young plants — those started from seed in July and wintered-over in a nursery bed — are ready now to take their place in the perennial border. To add width, we cluster 3 plants tightly together at 12- to 18-inch intervals. These plants do well in full- or half-day sunlight.

Older plants — those that have been in the ground 4 or 5 years — need division in April to remove the weakening center of the plant and give the stronger outer growth a chance to develop. I cut divisions 4 to 6 inches across, and plant them in prepared soil as above. (For more about division, see the August feature.)

P **Phlox (Perennial)** There are several species of perennial phlox for garden culture. We've grown two of the most common: Carolina phlox (*Phlox carolina*) and garden phlox (*P. paniculata*). Both are best in full sun but they will also tolerate half-day sunlight. Both produce large, rounded flower clusters.

Of the two, my preference is for the Carolinas, especially the variety Miss Lingard, the star of the Victory Garden perennial border. I would rather sacrifice many of the other flowers in the garden than lose Miss Lingard's abundant clear-white flowers. There are also handsome pink-flowered varieties. All Carolina phlox are sterile. Because they do not set viable seed, they do not self-sow, which saves them from the "reversion" problem that garden phlox face. Carolina phlox bloom for about 6 weeks in June and July, and if the seed heads and flowers are cut off after the first flowering (see the July feature), they blossom again in the fall. That's an unusual trait for a perennial, and an added bonus from an already excellent plant.

Garden phlox, at 2½ to 3 feet tall, are about the same height as the Carolina, and the flower clusters are nearly the

Miss Lingard phlox in the Victory Garden perennial border

same size. The color range is better than the Carolina, adding various shades of purple and red to the Carolina's white and pink. (We've grown the white-flowered White Admiral; American Legion, which is red-flowered; and Prince George, a fragrant variety with orange-red flowers.) Garden phlox flower in late summer for a month or more, a shorter period than the Carolinas; garden phlox also do not have the second flowering ability of Carolina phlox.

Unlike the Carolinas, garden phlox set seeds, which will self-sow in late summer if the seed pods are allowed to ripen. Because the varieties grown today are hybrids, the seedlings that result are not always the same as the parents.

Usually they are poor-looking, producing muddy-purple flowers. These nearly wild seedlings are also tougher than the cultivated plants, with the result that the self-sown seedlings survive and crowd out the original variety. This process is usually called reverting, but it's not really an accurate term; it's actually self-sowing. To prevent it, the gardener must diligently remove faded blossoms before the seeds ripen. This is good housekeeping anyway, and it helps the plant stay in bloom for the longest possible period of time.

We started our perennial phlox collection from young plants bought in the spring. They are more available from garden centers than from catalogues. After digging the hole and preparing the soil (see the August feature), I set the plants in, one to a site, at intervals of 2 to 3 feet. They send up a few flowers their first summer, and reach their stride in the years following.

If they're grown in an isolated spot, where they're not in conflict for space, they can be allowed to continue growing; if they're grown in a garden setting, both Carolina and garden phlox need dividing every 3 to 5 years. The division can be done either in the spring (April in the Victory Garden) or in the fall after flowering. Each division should have 3 to 6 green shoots, and be set into prepared soil at 2- to 3-foot intervals.

The long-flowering plumed bleeding heart

P **Plumed Bleeding Heart** Ordinarily, we start our perennials from seed, but plumed bleeding heart seeds are not readily available, so we buy plants in the spring. (You may find seeds from a nursery or catalogue that specializes in wildflowers.) The divisions and seedlings sold by garden centers in the spring are a little more expensive than those of some other plants, but single plants are a fairly good size, so only a plant or two are needed.

For reasons that escape me, the plumed, or fringed, bleeding heart (*Dicentra eximia*) is not as well known as the common bleeding heart (*D. spectabilis*), though it is in many ways the better plant. It's bushier and more compact at 12 to 15 inches tall; by contrast, the common bleeding heart, which is often sold by mail-order seed houses, is 3 feet tall, and rank of growth. The plumed bleeding heart has attractive, fernlike foliage. And it blossoms all summer, while the common bleeding heart has finished its flowering season by early summer. Both types produce pink and white flowers.

After digging a hole and enriching the soil with organic matter, I give each plant a spot 1 foot across. A division 4 to 6 inches across will fill this space in 2 to 4 years; a seedling will take a little longer. These plants are best in half-day sunlight, but they'll tolerate full and filtered sun,

The beautifully flowered but short-lived common bleeding heart

too. They're good plants for woodlands and fairly deep shade. After 3 to 5 growing seasons, the plants will have grown so large that they need division, exhibiting the dough-nut effect common to established clump-rooted perennials (see the August feature). We do this job in the spring, before the tight leaves unfold. The roots are fragile and pull apart quite easily. Once the entire clump is dug up and divided into clumps about 6 inches across, divisions can be set into the ground just like newly purchased plants.

Once you have the plant, you can propagate it by seed you harvest yourself. Make sure you plant the seeds right away while they're fresh. They may germinate immediately, or they may wait and sprout in the spring.

Purple Loose-Strife In the Victory Garden, we sow most of our perennials in July, move them to nursery beds in September, and let them winter there under a protective layer of mulch. Now, in April, they are ready to be moved to their permanent location in the perennial border.

One of the commonly available varieties of purple loose-strife

After routine soil improvement (see the August feature), I lift the young purple loose-strife plants (with their soil mass 4 to 6 inches across), and relocate them, one plant to a site 2 or 3 feet across. With a mature height of 3 or 4 feet, these plants belong at the back of the perennial border. They're best in half-day sun, but grow well in full or filtered sunlight, too. After transplant I pinch the tips back once to encourage branching.

After 3 to 5 years in the garden, this perennial will develop vigor problems at the center of the plant and need division. At this point, a plant begun as a seedling could easily be 3 feet across, so several divisions, 4 to 6 inches each, can be taken from one plant. After the soil is excavated and improved, each division is reset in a 2- to 3-foot site.

P **Rose** Roses are the world's favorite flower. For shape, color, and fragrance, they are without equal. Despite a somewhat short vase life, they are the unquestioned monarch of cut flowers. But for all their beauty, today's roses are among the most difficult plants to grow. All plants are subject to damage from pests, disease, cold weather, and poor drainage, but roses are more sensitive on all counts, cold in particular.

In the old days, roses were not a worry. The ones most commonly grown were species roses — meaning they grow naturally in the wild — native to temperate-climate sections of Asia. These can be grown easily almost anywhere in this country, because when cool weather comes in the fall, they follow their natural inclination and enter dormancy. They resume growth in the spring, and flower for about a month in early summer. The flowers themselves are generally small but fairly numerous, and often fragrant.

In the years since World War II, these roses have become less and less common commercially. Even their names — china, alba, damask — have an old-fashioned sound now. In fact, they are commonly referred to as old roses to distinguish them from the very different hybrids that dominate today's market. These new hybrids are genetically complicated offspring of roses native to warm climates, where they are able to put their energies into flowers with spectacular results. The problem with these warm-weather natives, and their hybrid offspring, is that they do not have a dormancy mechanism; in their native environment, they just keep growing year-round. If subjected to a season of frozen earth, they could die back completely.

The solution to this problem has been the grafting process, the joining of the roots of a hardy plant to the top-growth of a fragile hybrid. This is an actual mechanical process, done in rose nurseries plant by plant. With the hardy roots as understock, the beautiful hybrid roses are much better able to survive winter. But the bud union, the point where the two plants are joined, is, literally, the weak link. And the grafted rose's ability to withstand winter depends on good drainage, on the careful positioning of the bud union during planting, on the particulars of the winter (very cold, snowless winters are the worst), and on the amount of protection provided by the gardener every fall (see After Frost).

Buying Roses The most commonly available roses are, in order of popularity, hybrid teas, floribundas, grandifloras, and miniatures. All but the miniatures are grafted.

Hybrid teas are among the oldest of the current hybrids, dating back to the mid-nineteenth century. The parents were a fragile but long-blooming tea rose and a vigorous hybrid perpetual. Hybrid teas are probably the best of the cut-flower roses. They send up large flowers — as big as 6 or 7 inches across — on straight stems. Peace, a variety of hybrid tea, is one of the most popular roses grown; it was introduced just after World War II, and named in honor of the war's end. Double Delight is an All-America Winner, and one of the most fragrant introductions of recent years.

Floribunda roses are crosses between hybrid teas and free-flowering polyantha roses. They produce a very full, well-flowered plant, a claim most roses can't make. Each stem bears several flowers, so many, in fact, that one stem makes a bouquet. The flowers themselves are generally smaller than those of the hybrid teas, but they're still 3 or 4 inches across. We've grown Redgold, Europeana, Gene Boerner, and Pinocchio.

The grandiflora roses are the offspring of hybrid teas and floribundas, a combination that produces plants with larger flowers than the floribundas in greater number than the hybrid teas. Queen Elizabeth is one of the most popular varieties.

Miniature roses are genetically hardy, so they are not grafted. They are small versions of full-size plants, and perfectly scaled. At no more than 15 inches tall, they are small enough to be grown in pots (see the June feature), but they make a nice addition to the garden bed, too. Of all the popular roses, they are the most hardy.

Varieties of all types of roses are widely available from garden centers, catalogues, even supermarkets. The bush roses — so named because of their shape — dominate the market. As mature plants, they produce several canes, and, in this climate, reach heights of 3 to 4 feet. In addition

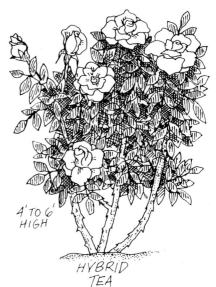

4' TO 6' HIGH

HYBRID TEA

2' TO 3' HIGH

FLORIBUNDA

4' TO 6' HIGH

GRANDIFLORA

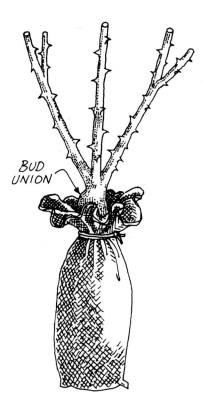

BUD UNION

BARE-ROOT ROSE

Opposite: Redgold, a floribunda rose

to the bush roses, some sellers, especially the mail-order houses and larger garden centers, will carry climbing roses and tree roses. Climbing roses are actually misnamed, as they have no mechanism with which to climb; in fact, they are long-caned selections of bush roses, and will stand upright only if they are woven through or tied to some sort of support. Tree roses are double grafts. First the hardy understock is grafted to a single, long cane from which the buds are removed; then the desired flowering variety is grafted on top. Tree roses are expensive and too formal for most gardens; in addition, they do not stand without support, and they require elaborate winter protection. For my money, the bush roses are the best choice. (Some roses in each category are fragrant, while others are not. If fragrance matters to you, read the descriptive copy carefully.)

If you buy a plant locally, it will probably be potted and growing; it may even be in bud or flowering. Potted roses can be planted outdoors anytime between the last spring frost and 2 months shy of the first fall frost.

Most mail-order houses ship roses only in the spring, and they ship only bare-root plants, which have been held in dormancy by refrigeration. They arrive, often betraying no sign of life, with their roots wrapped in moistened medium. If possible, bare-root plants should be set into the ground right away, before warm temperatures trigger their growth and dry their roots. If you can't plant them immediately, heel them in; that is, remove the plastic wrapped around the roots, set them at an angle in a trench, cover the roots with soil, and water well. Be sure to check them regularly and keep the medium moist.

Planting Roses need a location where the drainage is good and the sun shines for at least 6 hours a day. From a distance, some rose varieties can seem unimpressive, and fragrance is lost, so I always like to put my roses in a spot where I can regularly see and appreciate them. Hybrid roses are extremely susceptible to insect and disease damage. Though the hybridizers are gradually improving them on this score, they still need diligent spraying or dusting to rid them of unwanted visitors (see the May entry). This is easier to provide if the roses are grown in a bed by themselves, with only other roses for company. At our suburban site, for instance, we have over 90 roses growing in their own private garden. With 3 feet separating the plants on all sides, air is allowed to circulate freely, reducing the chances for moisture-related diseases.

I must confess, though, that in the Victory Garden perennial border we have several roses growing happily,

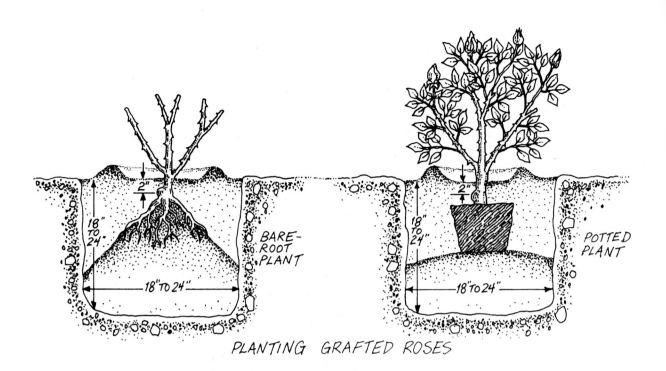

PLANTING GRAFTED ROSES

even though they are closer to other plants than generally advised. I attribute their success to very careful spraying and mulching, to the excellent drainage provided by our raised-bed perennial border, and to the protection from harsh winter winds provided by the fence behind the border. It is also true that the Victory Garden is more protected than the average backyard plot. We are close enough to the city and the ocean to enjoy relatively warm temperatures, and far enough from other gardens — at least half a mile — to be effectively quarantined from neighboring insects and diseases.

Sometimes gardeners are advised to do very elaborate soil preparation for roses. It's true that roses demand more attention than most plants, but for the beginner, two things matter in particular: the size of the hole and the amount of organic material added. Both contribute to good soil drainage.

Ideally, roses need a hole 18 to 24 inches deep, and about as wide. This is larger than may be manageable in some soil, but the hole should be as close to these dimensions as possible. To the excavated soil, I add lime if a soil test indicates the need (roses grow best in a pH of 6.0 to 6.8), as well as bone meal. Then I work in the organic material that will both nourish the plants and assist in drainage. I use compost if I have it, otherwise leaf mold or old cow manure. Peat moss and composted cow manure can be bought from garden centers for this, too. Combinations of several types of organic material are also fine. Ideally, the soil should be about one-third organic matter. If the soil is quite heavy, I recommend working in a 2-inch layer of sand to improve drainage. Poor drainage means ice damage to roots during winter, which can kill the plants. This seems to explain the rather high mortality rate among the roses at our suburban site, which grow in heavy soil on the downhill side of a long grade.

Miniature roses will be sold potted; they should be planted at the same level they were growing in the pot (see the August feature). With grafted roses, the planting depth varies. In areas where the average winter temperatures fall below $-10°F$, the bud union should be 2 inches below the soil surface. In areas where the minimum winter temperatures are in the $-10°$ to $+10°F$ range, the bud union should be 1 inch deep. The bud union can be just at the soil surface if winter temperatures stay above 10°F. When I plant roses I fill in the bottom of the hole with the improved soil so that the plant will be raised to the right position when set in; the bottom portion of soil must be firmed when these measurements are done, or it will settle and pull the plant down so the bud union is out of position.

If you're setting in a potted plant, the bud union will be visible in the pot, above the soil line. The procedure for setting in a potted rose is the standard one (see the August feature), except that the usual rule to set a plant in at the same depth it grew in the pot is not in effect because it's the depth of the bud union that matters with roses. If you've bought a bare-root plant, it will probably arrive already pruned down to 3 or 4 well-placed canes; if your plant has more canes than this, prune it according to the directions below, as too many canes will overtax the plant's strength during the first year. Prune damaged lengths of roots, too, but be conservative about it, and remove only damaged sections. Then soak the roots in water for a couple of hours before planting.

When planting a bare-root plant, the roots should sit on a mounded shape of soil, so they are able to drape downward. This may take some doing, getting both the right height and the mounded shape, but it's important. Once the mound is the proper size to bring the bud union into position, the plant can be set in. If there is a piece of root that doesn't fit, prune it as minimally as you can; at this point, you don't want to overprune. Next, fill in about half the remaining hole with soil, and add water. When it drains, fill in the rest of the hole and water again. Once the plant is in the ground, build up a rim of soil, 8 or 10 inches across, to trap water and aim it down toward the roots.

Springtime Care Once rose plants are established, after a year in the ground, there are three important springtime chores: removing the winter mulch; pruning the canes; and fertilizing. I do these jobs in the Victory Garden in April, when the plants are just coming out of dormancy. Our last-expected-frost date is April 20, but I can take care of these jobs a week or two before this, as the plants will survive freezing temperatures without damage. (I do leave the mulch nearby, on the remote chance that temperatures in the low-20s are expected. I'd rather spend a few minutes mounding some mulch around them for the night than lose the plants to a freak frost.) It is not a good idea to leave these jobs for later in the spring, as actively-growing canes are more apt to suffer damage from all the handling.

When removing the mulch, I use my hands (wearing gloves!) to pull away most of the mulching material, and then aim a stream of water at the plants to clear the stems. It's important not to work roughly, or to use sharp metal tools, because any new shoots will be easily injured. With herbaceous perennials, I advise removing the mulch in 2 stages, but in the case of roses, I remove it all at once.

The next job is to prune away dead canes, and dead sections of canes, so that the plant faces the new season with only live growth. Dead canes are usually easy to spot by their black or brown color; living canes, even this early in the season when they're just coming out of dormancy, have green bark. (If you're not sure which canes are dead, wait a few days until the new growth starts to break; any cane, or section of a cane, that produces new growth is alive.) In the Victory Garden we usually make it through winter in very good shape, with only a few dead cane tips. At our suburban site, though, the winterkill is so severe that every year some plants die back to the bud union; however, if the bud union is well-protected through the winter (see After Frost), it will survive and send up new canes from the hundreds of dormant eyes that lie within the union.

When pruning, only the dead canes, or the dead tips of live canes, need be removed. Pruning must also eliminate any areas where canes rub together, as the abrasion that results will create an entry point for disease. The pruning job cannot be haphazard, because it determines the ultimate shape of the plant.

There are two approaches to rose pruning. A high prune is the conservative one, removing only damaged or inward-facing canes, or those that rub together; this results in more flowers on taller plants. A low prune removes more of the plant's live growth, and produces shorter plants with fewer but larger flowers. In the Victory Garden, we do a high prune because our bushes are in the background, and we need the height. But in the more hostile environment of the suburban site, we must often prune to the bud union in order to remove dead vegetation and save the plant.

In either case the pruning cut should be just above a bud that points outward, even if this means sacrificing several buds facing the wrong direction. If the plant is not pruned correctly, it will send out canes every which way and won't be well shaped as it grows.

Rose diseases are among the most serious of gardening problems. There is more on this subject in subsequent entries, but for springtime care the important task is to clear away old canes and leaves. I never allow old vegetation to stay on the ground where it can infest the current season's young growth. I clear away the refuse completely, and either put it out with the trash or burn it.

Finally, established plants need their first dose of fertilizer this month. I put ¼ cup of 5-10-5 in a ring about 6 inches from the crown, and then water it in. I repeat the feedings in June and midsummer, making sure to give the plants no fertilizer in the last 2 or 3 months before the first expected fall frost.

P **Shasta Daisy** After 3 or 4 years in the ground, these perennials are so large that their centers lose vigor while the outer rim of the plant is strong and healthy. They need division at this point. This job can be done anytime during the growing season, but the best time is spring or fall; if they're divided while they're in bloom, several healthy flowers will fall from the plant.

The roots will come apart easily. After digging out and discarding the weakened center of the plant, I divide the strong growth into sections about 6 inches across. Shasta daisies nearly double in size every year, so I give the full-size plants a spot 18 to 24 inches across, and the dwarf varieties an area 12 to 18 inches across. One full-size plant is substantial enough to occupy a site on its own, but I usually cluster 3 of the dwarf varieties together. In the Victory Garden, all our perennials enjoy full-day sunlight, but these plants would do well on half-day sun. These new divisions will send up a few flowers their first year, and then reach their stride in their second year.

April is also the time to move the young plants that were started as seedlings last July, and wintered over in a nursery row. After several months in the ground, they will have developed a root mass 4 to 6 inches across, so they can be treated as the young divisions, above.

For more about shasta daisies, see the July entry.

A dwarf shasta daisy

A **Sweet Pea** Sweet peas (sown in March) do beautifully in cool weather and miserably in hot, so it's imperative to get them into the garden as early in the spring as possible, as soon as there's no further danger of hard frost. They need a site where they get full, or at least half-day, sun. In the Victory Garden, we set them out in mid-April, after 2 weeks in the cold frame. They're the first show of green in the annual border.

Sweet peas must be provided with a structure to climb. I use a standard black nylon netting, supported by redwood stakes at 3-foot intervals. The netting should go up before the plants go in. The netting does not need to touch the soil, as the seedlings will be able to support a few inches of growth without collapsing; I usually set up the netting so it's 4 to 6 inches from the ground. It is important that the netting be tall enough (about 5 feet) to accommodate the full height of the mature plants. They'll climb on their own. I set the plants in at intervals of 6 to 9 inches, about 1 or 2 inches from the netting. In the garden, where the netting is freestanding and not up against a structure, I put in a second

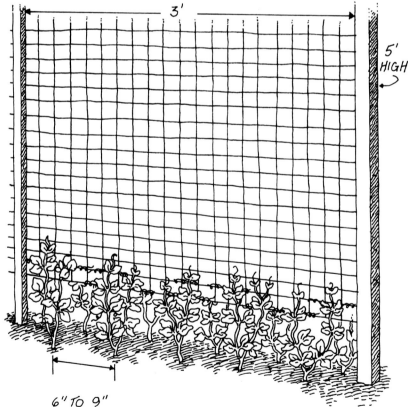

3'

5' HIGH

6" TO 9" APART ON BOTH SIDES OF NETTING

row of seedlings on the other side of the netting, staggering the locations so that 2 plants are not climbing the same section of netting.

As an alternative to the netting, the seedlings can be set in 3 rows, 6 to 9 inches apart, with pea brush worked in throughout the bed. (Pea brush is nothing but the well-branched, fairly strong twigs of deciduous trees. It was the original gardening solution to sweet peas' need for support.)

A warm-weather mulch (see the July feature) helps sweet peas resist the effects of hot weather by keeping the soil temperature down. We use either salt marsh hay or partially decomposed compost. The hay is easily removed after the peas are gone, and the compost can just be worked into the soil. (Wood chips or pine bark are other choices. They're better looking than either of the other two mulches, but sometimes harder to remove.) In any case, the mulch should cover the soil for 8 inches around the plants. In our netting set-up, the best procedure is to set down two strips of mulch, each about 6 inches wide, on either side of and between the seedlings, but no closer to the plants' stems than 2 inches.

Sweet peas will blossom until the weather turns too warm for them. At that point we pull them out and make way for more heat-tolerant plants.

Ⓑ **Sweet William** Along with our other biennials, the Victory Garden sweet William crop is sown from seed in midsummer (see the July entry), moved to nursery beds in September, and protected with a winter mulch till spring. Now it's time to set them into their flowering spots, either in the annual bed or in the perennial border. Sweet Williams are best in full sun, but they'll flower even in filtered sun, if they're to be pulled after flowering. In terms of soil preparation, all biennials are treated as annuals (see the May feature). In the Victory Garden we grow dwarf varieties of sweet William, which are 6 to 9 inches tall at maturity; for a concentrated effect, we usually mass several plants together at 9- to 12-inch intervals.

Sweet Williams bloom for about a month in June. If the seed pods are allowed to mature, the plants will self-sow. These seedlings will survive winter if mulched. We usually pull our plants after they flower, but the home gardener may feel more inclined to save a few volunteers and let them mature.

Pinocchio, a variety of sweet William

SPACE AND SUN

In one way, flowering plants are very much like people. The healthier they are, the better they look. I'm not referring here to slight differences in the vigor of the plants, visible only under scrutiny. What I mean is that in unhealthy plants, flower production can be reduced to a noticeable and disheartening degree, even if the foliage is still presentable. Unhealthy plants are also far more susceptible to pest and disease damage.

Plants owe their good health to many factors: to sturdy, disease-resistant varieties; to good growing conditions; to an attentive gardener who keeps the old blossoms picked, the soil moist, the plants fed. But if there is one factor that matters more than the others, it is making the most of your site's natural conditions, and choosing plants that will do well there. The handsomest gardens are those in which plants have the sunlight they need, where the soil is well prepared (see After Frost), and where the air circulates freely around their foliage.

Sunlight In most gardens, the amount of sunlight is a given unless trees can be taken down and buildings demolished. The important thing for the gardener is not to try to change the patterns of sun and shade in the garden site, but to learn them and work with them. For instance, you may love roses, but if you live in a pine grove, where only an occasional ray of sunlight reaches the ground, roses are simply out of the question.

The amount of sunlight a plant needs depends largely on the environment to which it is native. If in the wild plants grow on the deeply shaded forest floor, they will not be able to tolerate an open field where the sun beats down on them all day. By contrast, plants accustomed to full sunlight need full sunlight, or close to it, to do their best.

This does not mean that the gardener must replicate nature's conditions completely; most growing plants are more flexible than that. They do best if grown in optimum light conditions, but they may also make a respectable show in less-than-perfect light. I certainly wouldn't advise a gardener against growing annuals, for instance, if the available site is sunny for an hour or two less every day than is recommended. In the entries, I have indicated the light conditions that will bring the plant to its best condition, but I have also indicated acceptable alternatives. The following chart clarifies the terminology I've used:

Air Circulation For the novice gardener, good air circulation is one of the hardest elements to plan for. When all you're holding is a seedling with a couple of inches of foliage, it's difficult to envision how large the plant will be after 2 months in the ground. As a result, it's difficult to know how much room to allow the plant in the garden. But space is one of the major determinants of the plant's health. If air cannot move freely around and between plants, moisture rising from the soil stagnates around the lower foliage and roots, and this combination of stillness and moisture often encourages disease. In addition, plants growing too close together are in competition for soil and air space, light, and nutrients.

Both the vertical and horizontal dimensions of the plant are important to spacing. There is no way to anticipate this precisely, because the plant's size is affected both by genetic characteristics and by growing conditions. When catalogues list heights and spreads of plants, they are basing the information on their own test gardens where plants are offered optimum conditions. In each of the entries in this book, I have given the spread range, the plant's horizontal dimension at maturity, that I expect in the Victory Garden.

The variation in heights in the garden creates the possibil-

Sunlight Terminology

Full sunlight: *Unfiltered, uninterrupted sunlight all day. This is the site for roses or vegetables.*

Half-day sunlight: *Five or 6 hours of open sunlight a day, with shade or filtered sun the rest of the day.*

Filtered sunlight: *Dappled sun, either all day long, or interrupted for up to 4 hours by either direct sunlight or shade.*

Shade: *Solid, sunless shade, such as provided by a building or a dense overhang of foliage.*

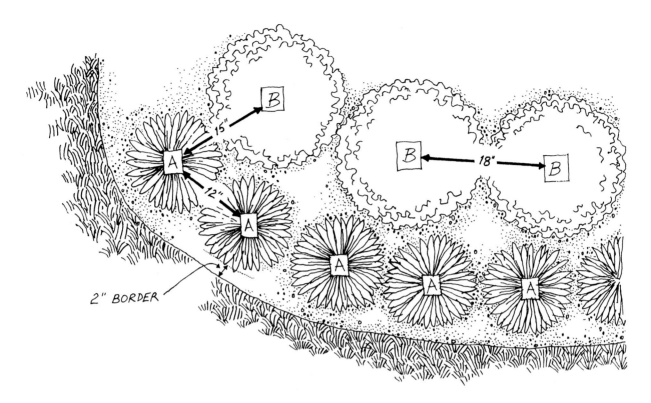

2" BORDER

ity that a tall plant will shade a shorter neighbor. This is usually taken care of by planting the tall plants behind (to the north of) the shorter ones.

Accounting for the horizontal dimension — the spread of the foliage at maturity — requires more planning. Plants should be spaced for best health, best effect, and ease of maintenance. They should be far enough apart for good air circulation and uncrowded growing conditions, yet close enough together so the garden seems unified; if the plants are too far apart, the garden has a here-a-flower-there-a-flower look. When planting, you can use as your interval between the plants any distance covered by the spread range; in other words, if a plant has a spread

of 6 to 9 inches, the plants should be set in 6 to 9 inches apart, all seedlings of one variety at the same interval. The closer together the plants are, the fuller the bed will look earlier in the season; however, close spacing will cut down on air circulation, which makes the plants more prone to disease problems. I think the home gardener is better advised to set plants in at the maximum spacing. It will take a little longer for the bed to fill in, but the plants will be healthier and easier to maintain.

When spacing one species from another with a different horizontal dimension, the rule is to split the difference, the goal being a continuous flow of color without gaps. For instance, if you were planting one variety with a 12-inch spread next to another with an 18-inch spread, the space

between the two varieties should be 15 inches (see the illustration). The same rule holds for large plants. If a plant with a 2-foot spread is next to one with a 4-foot spread, they should be spaced 3 feet apart.

When it comes time to plant, I always mark the sites carefully. Guesswork in determining intervals usually shows in the results. A little bone meal is a good marker. Finally, I set the plants in in staggered rows, which is more informal and graceful than the checkerboard approach.

MAY

Monthly Checklist

Ageratum
Aster (Annual)
Browallia
Caladium
Calendula
Celosia
Chrysanthemum (Annual)
Chrysanthemum (Perennial)
Cleome
Coleus
Cornflower
Cosmos
Dahlia
Dusty Miller
Gazania
Geranium
Globe Amaranth
Gloriosa Daisy
Hollyhock (Annual)
Impatiens
Lobelia
Marigold
Morning Glory
Nasturtium
Nicotiana
Nierembergia
Petunia
Phlox (Annual)
Pinks
Portulaca
Rose
Salvia
Scabiosa
Snapdragon
Statice
Strawflower
Swan River Daisy
Sweet Alyssum
Tulip
Verbena
Vinca
Wax Begonia
Zinnia

Sunshine, a variety of gazania
(see page 145)

MAY

Our May first set-out date for the annuals that we've been nursing along through the spring makes the beginning of this month one of the busiest times in the Victory Garden. But because the planning and preparation have already been done, the chore moves along fairly quickly and in no time at all there are small living plants where before there was only soil. Planting annuals is one of gardening's most satisfying jobs.

Because the bright sun can be too much for these young plants, I like to work on a cloudy day — or late in the afternoon — so they aren't overtaxed as they're getting accustomed to new quarters. After I transplant them I cover them lightly with a little salt marsh hay, just for a day or two, to shade them further from the sun. (For complete information about transplanting, see the August feature.) Once all the plants are in the ground, I water them with transplant solution (see the July feature).

May continues the season of the spring-flowering bulbs, with only the very early minor bulbs completely gone by now. Lilies-of-the-valley often make their first appearance this month. Keep in mind that in grassy areas where bulbs are naturalized, lawn-mowing must be postponed until the foliage has had time to wither and brown completely; if you cut the leaves before this, the bulb is deprived of a crucial ripening period.

In the Victory Garden, most of our favorite tulips come on in May. Like so many bulb flowers, tulips make excellent cut flowers. If you're as partial to this use of tulips as I am, I have a tip for you. The base of the tulip stem, where the growth is hard and white, is too tough to absorb water easily. You can take care of this problem by slicing up into this tough section about 1 inch, exposing the tender interior tissue that is much more efficient at absorbing water.

In both the annual and perennial gardens, this is the month to put stakes in place, so that as the foliage matures it hides the plants' supports. Later in the season, when the plants are in bud, only the twine need be added to help the plants stand straight (see the July feature).

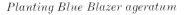

A   **Ageratum** If you're in the market for seedlings in the spring, you should have no trouble at all finding ageratums, as they're one of the most popular of the bedding plants. There are several excellent blue varieties from which to choose; there are pinks and whites, too, but the blues are preferable. Our favorite in the Victory Garden is a variety called Blue Blazer. We sow the seeds in March, and have garden-size seedlings by our annual set-out date of May 1. (See the March entry.)

    I've always been partial to the combination of blue and yellow flowers, so I often grow ageratum as a counterpart to marigolds, either in a window box, a pot, or in the annual bed. They're also handsome with pink petunias or white lobelias. We planted a beautiful window box one year by combining blue ageratum, dusty miller, and verbena Blaze. Ageratums are adaptable to any site so long as they have full or half-day sunlight. When I put them into the garden, I cluster 3 or 5 plants together, 6 to 12 inches apart; even-numbered plantings tend to make the cluster look

Planting Blue Blazer ageratum

boxy. (For more about container gardening, see the June feature.)

When they're at their peak, ageratums are covered with flowers, but they don't have as long a life as some other annuals. They have a tendency to lose vigor in midsummer, after they've been in flower several weeks. They can be pruned back a couple of inches at this point, to allow the new growth to come in for another show of flowers for the fall. Some years we just start new seedlings in June, and have fresh plants to replace the March sowing when they begin to show signs of wear and tear. The advantage to this approach is that we have ageratums all summer long, without the recovery period that shearing-back necessitates.

A **Aster (Annual)** Asters have always had their problems with plant diseases — wilt, mildew, and yellows in particular — but plant breeders have developed varieties that are better able to stand up to these long-time enemies. Wilt is dangerous because it lives over in the soil from year to

The flowers of Red Mound, a variety of annual aster, have yellow centers when fully open

year, but by planting asters in a different location every spring, and by selecting wilt-resistant varieties (such as Red Mound), wilt problems can be held to a minimum. Mildew is still a worry — it's been a frequent visitor in the Victory Garden — but it's fairly easy to control with a fungicide such as benomyl.

The real threat to asters comes from yellows, a viral disease carried by an insect, the six-spotted leaf hopper. The symptoms of this very destructive disease include stunted growth, yellow foliage, distorted flowers, and buds that fail to open. We've never had a case of yellows in the Victory Garden. I attribute our good fortune to luck, to the Victory Garden's isolation from neighboring gardens, and to the fact that we've grown mostly Red Mound, which is one of the varieties that has been bred for yellows tolerance. It is not resistant to yellows — no variety is — but it is somewhat less susceptible than some of the other varieties. Yellows is a more common problem, even for tolerant varieties, in sub-urban gardens, where the insects can easily move from garden to garden through the neighborhood. The only way to control it is by controlling the carrier insects, and the only way to do this is with heavy use of insecticide, or netting protection for each plant. Neither choice is appealing. I'd advise the gardener with yellows problems to pull the plants out and fill the spots with a less-demanding flower.

It might appear that asters have nothing to recommend them, but this is not the case if they're healthy. They're an excellent plant for very hot locations, as they stand up beautifully to blistering weather, blooming right through the months of July and August when many annuals are struggling. They have a profusion of flowers with an excellent color range and are good for cutting. If they're well planted and well cared for, many of their disease problems can be kept in control. They need the best cultural conditions possible, all designed to keep moisture at a minimum, as moisture creates an environment hospitable to disease. We do this by giving the plants enough air space, setting them in a spot 2 inches or so bigger all around than the mature spread of the plant: that is, we put Red Mound, with a mature spread of 12 inches, in a 14-inch site. Then we give the plants a spot with full sunlight; half-day sun will do, but the more sunlight they receive, the drier they stay. Finally, we use a drip irrigation system (see the July feature) so the foliage isn't wet any more than necessary.

[A] **Browallia** By May 1, the date our annuals are transplanted into the open garden, the browallias started from seed (see the February entry) are still quite small, but

A blue-flowered browallia in a hanging basket

they're ready for the open air. If you don t have seedlings you've been nursing along, you should be able to find some easily in a garden center, as these are popular plants and widely available. In the Victory Garden, we've grown mostly the trailing varieties, using them in window boxes and hanging baskets.

If we grow browallias in a window box, we space them about 6 inches apart; they have a graceful curving habit that will attractively cover the edge of the box. For a hanging basket arrangement, I'd put 3 plants together in an 8-inch pot. These are excellent shade-tolerant plants, at their best in half-day sunlight; they'll grow perfectly well in full or filtered sun, too. The blossom colors are apt to fade some in full sunlight. At 12 inches in height, browallias are tall enough to be used alone, either one color or both together. But they also combine nicely with small marigolds or with white alyssum. Any of these combinations will make a beautiful window-box display. (For more about window boxes, see the June feature.)

In my area, browallia plants bloom well in the early summer, but they begin to lose their looks in hot weather, when the growth tends to harden. They can be cut back at that point, but the new growth is often disappointing, so I prefer to start new plants in April or May to have a replacement crop at the ready when the first sowing peters out. Browallias are grown as annuals but they are in fact tender perennials. Most other such plants — like fuchsia and geranium — can be propagated by cutting and grown indoors over winter; while browallias can be treated in this way, they tend to lose steam when they're about a year and a half old, so I just let each season's crop die with the frost and start new seedlings every year.

Caladium Caladiums survive deep shade better than almost any decorative plant. In fact, they will scorch in anything brighter than filtered sunlight. They are not an important part of the Victory Garden itself, where we can offer them neither shade nor the natural setting where they look their best. But they've done very handsomely for us in the shady areas of the suburban site. We start the tubers into growth in March, and set them into the garden around mid- to late May, when the outside nighttime air temperature is reliably in the 45- to 50-degree range. You may find caladium tubers on the market in May and be tempted to plant them outside now; this will work, but you won't have showy plants until August. It's hardly worth the effort.

If the number of tubers to be planted is small — say, 4 or 5 — I often plant them pots and all, which saves the

Opposite: Freshly planted caladiums in a shady spot in the suburban garden

tubers the disturbance of transplant, and makes it easier to dig them up in the fall. The problem with this technique is that the plants require more individual care, isolated as they are from the soil around them. They're more apt to dry out in the pots, so they have to be watched carefully and kept watered. They're also cut off from food supplies if they're planted in their pots, so before setting them out I put a light ring of slow-release fertilizer on the surface of the potted soil, and feed them again in midsummer with a water-soluble fertilizer. For a number of plants, it is less effort to unpot the tubers and set them into prepared garden soil, fertilizing them as we would any annual. In either case, the dwarf variety that we grow in the Victory Garden has a 12- to 18-inch spread at maturity, so I set the plants out at 12- to 18-inch intervals. They look best if they're arranged somewhat irregularly, rather than in straight rows. (See the October entry for instructions on digging and storing the tubers so they can be grown year after year.)

Orange Coronet calendulas

A   **Calendula**   This lovely annual may not be easy to find as a seedling crop in garden centers. In the Victory Garden, we start the seeds ourselves (see the March entry), and have plants ready for the open garden on the first day of May. They need full sun to do their best, but they also grow well in half-day or filtered sunlight.

Calendulas are old favorites of mine, but I can't call them free-flowering. They're cool-weather plants that in even the best of spring and fall weather conditions are fairly sparse-flowered; in hot summer, they're able to manage only an occasional blossom. They aren't really a good choice for the annual bed for this reason, but the yellow varieties are a nice addition to the herb garden, where their now-and-then flowers are a bonus instead of a drawback. (The orange-flowered varieties are too bright for the soft colors of an herb garden.) There's a rightness in this, too, as calendula flower petals are an old-time herb. The flowers are held on long, sturdy stems, so they're good for cutting. And when the weather is too hot for flowers, the foliage is still an attractive addition to the herb garden.

Tall varieties of calendula, in the 18- to 24-inch range, spread 12 to 15 inches at maturity. The dwarf varieties are about 12 inches tall when full grown, spreading 6 to 9 inches. I usually put 2 or 3 plants in the herb garden, one plant to a site, giving each a space large enough to accommodate its spread; the clustering approach that we use to keep the annual and perennial beds looking full would upset the balance of the herb garden, in which it is more the custom to plant single specimens of many kinds of plants.

A **Celosia** The red-plumed celosia we've been growing for several seasons in the Victory Garden is an unusual combination of breezy grace and vivid color. It adds an interesting touch to the annual border, where the dwarf varieties will stand about 12 inches tall and spread 9 to 12 inches. We sow the seeds indoors in early spring (see the March entry) — seedlings should be available at garden centers, too — and set them into the garden along with the other annuals on our set-out date of May 1. To give the planting a little width, I usually set 3 plants together to a site, 12 to 15 inches apart. Half-day sunlight will suit their needs, but they're better if grown in full sun.

The plumes will begin to appear in June and continue through frost. Each one is very long-lasting, whether on the plants or dried for indoor arrangements (see the strawflower entry in July for directions). This plant is the exception to the usual rule governing flowers for drying, which is to pick them just before they peak. Celosia plumes can be picked at any time — they're fine all season long. If you're picking during the summer and you want the plant to continue to be good-looking, pick the smaller side plumes; the large plume in the middle will leave a crater in the plant, so it's best to leave this one growing until the end of the season.

A **Chrysanthemum (Annual)** There isn't enough demand for these plants to bring them onto the list of top-selling annuals, which means that many garden centers probably won't carry the seedlings in the spring. The plant deserves a better following, but for now gardeners will have to order seeds and start them in advance themselves. This is what we do in the Victory Garden, sowing the seeds in the spring (see the March entry) for garden-size plants on our set-out date of May 1. We sow mixed-color seeds, so we can't be sure exactly what the resulting plants will look like until after they're planted and the flowers appear, but the color range within the mixes is harmonious, so the surprise is always pleasant. Annual chrysanthemums are good, long-lasting cut flowers, too.

The plants are a trifle sensitive to hot weather if they're not kept well watered, so while they do well in full sun, they seem to hold up a little better through the summer if they're grown in half-day sun or shaded for an hour or two during the hottest part of the day, especially if they're pot-grown. If you can't provide them with this selective shading, make sure you attend to their watering needs through mid-summer heat. As I usually do when planting the annual bed, I set 3 plants together, spacing them 12 to 15 inches apart. (For ongoing care, see the July feature.)

Annual chrysanthemums, like the variety Rainbow, make excellent cut flowers

P **Chrysanthemum (Perennial)** If you winter-over your hardy chrysanthemum plants and divide them in the spring (see the April entry), then only one chore remains: pinching back the stems. This isn't a big job but it's an important one if the resulting plants are to be well shaped and densely flowered.

Each pinch will encourage the plant to send out new stems, resulting in a full, well-shaped plant and dozens of stems to bear flowers. Because chrysanthemum flowers are borne only on the tips of the stems, more stems mean more flowers. Two pinches will be needed. The first should be done when the young division is 4 to 6 inches tall. The new branches that result from this pinch should also be pinched when they're 4 to 6 inches long. The important thing is to pinch evenly around the plant so its shape is well rounded. Don't pinch at all after July 15, or you will be pinching out flower buds. This date holds true across the country because hardy chrysanthemums everywhere blossom in late August or September; their flowering season is responsive to day length, not weather.

After each pinch, I give the chrysanthemum plants a feeding of liquid fertilizer to nourish them through the period when they are developing new branches.

A bed of cleome

A **Cleome** Cleome are recommended by a somewhat unusual combination of traits: they grow very quickly, and manage to be both delicate and large at the same time. At maturity, they are 3 to 4 feet tall and 2 to 3 feet across, so they need a spot toward the back of the garden, and a space 2 to 3 feet around so they have room to spread. Because of their size, I put only one seedling to a site; in a cluster, they would be overwhelming. As is true of many annuals, cleome do best in full sun, but they'll grow with less as long as they have at least half-day sunlight.

Cleome plants send up a dominant stem from which other stems grow. In the best conditions, all these stems bear flowers, and while the flowers are noteworthy for their airiness, the total weight of the plant is considerable and there is the possibility that the plant will become uprooted in strong wind or rain. So in June I stake that dominant stem, and that's all the help the plant seems to need to withstand harsh weather.

It is difficult to deadhead a cleome without sacrificing maturing and future flowers. So I just let the fading flowers take care of themselves. For this reason, there is often a self-sowing problem with cleome. I usually pull these volunteers out, because there is no guarantee that they will produce plants as good-looking as the parent. (For more about

deadheading and other aspects of flower-garden maintenance, see the July feature.)

A   **Coleus** Coleus is a great plant for a large bed; planted in quantity, it functions as a multicolored annual groundcover. I've also done smaller plantings, clustering 3 or 5 or 7 together in the annual border for some bright foliage. The dwarf varieties we grow in the Victory Garden — less than 12 inches tall with a spread of 6 to 9 inches — are good choices for window boxes, too (see the June feature). Regardless of how they're handled, the dwarf varieties need to be planted at intervals of 6 to 9 inches so they have room to spread without crowding.

     We start our coleus collection from seed (see the February entry), but the seedlings are one of the mainstays of the bedding plant business, so they're easy to find in garden centers in the spring. After conditioning the seedlings (see the August feature), we set the plants into the garden on the first of May; coleus are among the most frost-sensitive of garden plants, so make sure you don't plant them prematurely in the spring.

Close-up of a frilled-leaf coleus, one of several types available by seed

Coleus look best if they're grown in half-day or filtered sunlight. The standard-size plants benefit from pinching back regularly to keep them shapely; the dwarfs branch well on their own. We also remove the relatively inconspicuous flowers as soon as they appear so the foliage stays attractive all season. If the plants are allowed to flower and set seed, the center of the plant opens up, and the compact shape is lost.

Ⓐ **Cornflower** Cornflowers are vulnerable to mildew, so when they're planted they should be given plenty of space and as much sunlight as possible; if they're crowded or underlit, the mildew has a better chance to become established. So although they'll grow in half-day sunlight, it's better to give them a spot with full sun. (Because of the mildew problem, avoid overhead watering, or water in the morning of a sunny day.) The dwarf varieties we grow in the Victory Garden are 12 to 15 inches in all dimensions, so we give them the full allotment of room in a 15-inch space. Three plants together give the cluster a fuller look than isolated seedlings.

Cornflowers are short-season bloomers. They'll flower from mid-June to August if the dead blossoms are kept picked off; if your attention to this job wanes, the flowers will quit after a month or so. But they're worth growing, even for this brief show, especially if they're given a spot where they can move gracefully in a breeze.

In the Victory Garden, we sow seeds of cornflowers in March and have garden-size seedlings by our set-out date of May 1. But if you want to buy seedlings, you should have no trouble, for these are a popular seedling crop in garden centers in the spring. They may be labeled as bachelor's buttons, or by their botanical name *Centaurea Cyanus*.

Ⓐ **Cosmos** The first of May brings our annual set-out date to the Victory Garden, and the cosmos seedlings begun in March are now ready for the open ground. The tall varieties peak at about 4 feet, with a spread of 12 to 18 inches; among the dwarf varieties, Diablo is no taller at maturity than 18 inches, with a spread of 12 to 15 inches. Diablo is handsome in the garden bed in clusters, or planted singly in an 8- or 10-inch pot (for container culture, see the June feature). We save the taller varieties, including Sensation cosmos, for the back of the border, setting in 3 or 5 together. Once the flowers have formed, the tall varieties need peripheral staking to support their height (see the July feature).

If you are in the market for seedlings, you should have no trouble buying the tall varieties; finding Diablo may

Cosmos Diablo with Victoria, a variety of blue salvia

be more of a challenge. Whichever variety you grow, you'll find they do well in fairly poor soil. In fact they tolerate poor conditions better than most annuals, and can survive without the extra feeding of fertilizer we give our annuals during the season. They need either full or half-day sunshine. All varieties of cosmos bloom right into the fall, providing not only handsome flowering plants for the garden, but good cut flowers as well. Many varieties will self-sow to the point where some gardeners consider the plants weeds. These self-sown plants still bear fairly good flower colors, though, and they're no effort. If you don't want them, deadhead faithfully and pull any volunteers that manage to germinate.

[A]   **Dahlia** Whether grown from tubers, seed, or stem cuttings (see the March and April entries), we set all our dahlias into the Victory Garden in May. These are plants we start ourselves, but garden centers will probably have a wide selection of tubers, potted tubers, and annual seedlings. Our plants are conditioned in the cold frame, but they

A tuberous dahlia flower

are still apt to be nipped by a late frost, so we wait a week or so after our May 1 set-out date to put the dahlias into the garden. All dahlias are best in full sun, tolerating half-day sun, too, but the tuberous and seed-grown types are different in terms of scale and treatment.

Tall dahlia varieties have a rounded shape, 3 to 5 feet in all directions. These are primarily grown from tubers and from cuttings of tuber-grown plants (see the April entry). The cutting-grown plants do not reach quite the size of the original tuberous plant during their first season, but both types will be rather portly, so I put only one plant to a site, setting it in at the same depth at which it grew in the pot. We put the tuberous dahlias into a corner of the perennial border so we can easily lift the tubers in the fall (see the October entry) without disturbing the rest of the garden. They could also be planted in the annual bed. When the flowers form, we stake the plants with peripheral stakes (see the July feature) to help them support their massive weight.

We treat the seed-sown dahlias as annuals, and plant them in the annual bed, 12 to 15 inches apart, in clusters of 3 or 5. The short annual varieties are also good candidates for pot culture, one plant to a 10-inch pot.

If you haven't given the tubers a head start, you can still plant them directly in the garden. The tubers should be covered with 2 inches of soil in a space as wide as the plants will be tall at maturity. One tuber to a site is plenty for these commanding plants.

With the head start we give our dahlias, both the tuberous-rooted and seed-sown plants will come into flower in early summer and continue until frost. That's many a vaseful of one of the best cut flowers around.

[A] **Dusty Miller** In the Victory Garden, we sow our own dusty millers from seed (see the February entry), but garden centers carry seedlings in the spring as well. It's always worthwhile to save money on the seedlings if you can, but if not, buy plants. Dusty millers' silver-green foliage is a wonderful addition to the flower garden, where it both softens the overall appearance and accentuates nearby colors. We put the seedlings into our window boxes (see the June feature) on May 1, our annual set-out date.

Most types of dusty miller are 18 to 24 inches tall and bushy. But they're better-looking if they're kept in bounds, so I let them reach heights of 9 to 12 inches, and then keep them pruned to that size. I find this smaller scale is better when the plants are grown in window boxes — our primary use of dusty millers in the Victory Garden — and it also

The icy-white leaf of Diamond, a variety of dusty miller

prevents them from flowering, which tends to make the foliage coarse. Because of our pruning routine, we set dusty miller seedlings into the window boxes at 6- to 8-inch intervals; when they're grown, the plants have a symmetrical shape that we maintain in the pruning process. If you're growing them in the open garden, you may want to let the plants grow taller and wider, but even so it is important to keep them lightly pruned, and the flowers picked off immediately, so that the plants are always at their finest.

Dusty millers are at their best in full sunlight, but they're versatile plants in that they also tolerate half-day or filtered sun. So they're adaptable to many garden settings, and especially good for cool areas, as they are frost-tolerant and keep their looks well into the fall.

A   Gazania Gazania flowers — excellent both in the vase and on the plant — stand 8 to 12 inches tall over heavy gray-green foliage that is itself only 6 inches tall, with a spread of 9 to 12 inches. The plants can be used as edgers, spaced 9 to 12 inches apart, or in window boxes, where their long season of bloom will keep the display looking beautiful all summer. (For more about window boxes, see the June feature.) Conditioned seedlings will take a few degrees of frost, but we set out plants with our other annuals on May 1, which is our frost-safe date.

Gazanias are desert plants. They do best in full sun, dry soil, and hot daytime weather; cool nights are no problem. Older varieties often close their flowers if not provided with these conditions, but some of the newer selections, including Sunshine, the variety we grow in the Victory Garden, are better adapted to nondesert conditions. Most seedlings sold from garden centers will be tolerant to local weather conditions.

A **Geranium** Geraniums are increasingly grown as bedding plants, but it's more traditional to treat them as container plants and grow them in pots or tubs or window boxes; this is what we do in the Victory Garden. I put one plant to a 12-inch tub, sometimes planting a low hanging plant like lobelia around the soil to cascade over the side of the pot. In the window boxes, I usually combine geraniums with lobelias and dusty millers, spacing the geraniums 14 inches apart along the back of the box. (The dusty millers go in the middle row, in front of the geraniums, and the lobelias at the very front of the box.) Another good three-way combination is geraniums with sweet alyssum and Swan River daisies. Geraniums will flower on half-day sunlight, but they're better if they're grown in full sun. (For more about container culture, see the June feature.)

We set our geraniums outside with our other annuals on May 1, but we condition the seedlings with a few days in the cold frame (see the August feature), so we'd feel safe putting out these chill-tolerant plants any time after the last-expected-frost date.

A window box planting of pink geraniums and dusty millers along the greenhouse in the Victory Garden

Nearly all of the geraniums in the Victory Garden are ones we sow ourselves from seed (see the February entry). If you didn't start seedlings yourself, you will have to buy plants, because it is too late in the season to start seeds of these slow-growing plants. Garden centers should be well-stocked with geraniums in May, certainly by the end of the month since they are favorite cemetery plants for Memorial Day.

A **Globe Amaranth** This plant has problems with moisture-related diseases, so the most important element in planting is giving it a dry, airy spot with full or half-day sun. The standard-size plants reach heights of 18 inches; the dwarfs peak at 12 to 15 inches. All varieties are nearly as wide as they are tall. Because of the need for air circulation, it's best to err on the side of too much space rather than too little, so I'd plant the standard-size plants about 18 inches apart, and the smaller ones 15 inches apart. Three plants together provide a good scale in our space; in any event, clusters should be uneven to avoid boxiness.

Every time we've grown this plant, we've had black aphid infestations on the foliage and flowers. If there's a good native ladybug population, control will be easier. In the Victory Garden, we hose the aphids off weekly.

Globe amaranths, or gomphrena as they're also known, are excellent cut flowers, both fresh and dried. For a fresh bouquet, they can be picked at any time in their ripening phase, but if you intend to dry them, they'll last better if they're picked just shy of their peak, when the flowers are round and about the diameter of a quarter; they're over the hill for drying purposes once the flowers begin to elongate and fade. (For the drying procedure, see the strawflower entry in July.)

A **Gloriosa Daisy** Though it is capable of surviving winter, most gardeners treat this plant as an annual or biennial (see the February entry). In the Victory Garden, we sow seeds in late winter in order to have a full season of blooms the first year; they could also be sown in July and wintered over as we do biennials. Because of their scale, we put them into the perennial border, rather than into our smaller annual bed, transplanting them on May 1. Actually, gloriosa daisies are at home in cool weather and could, if conditioned, withstand cold weather. (Even cool-weather plants are not frost-tolerant in the seedling stage without conditioning. See the August feature.)

As far as weather is concerned, gloriosa daisies are easy to please. Though by nature cool-weather plants, they

Double Gold, a variety of gloriosa daisy

are not damaged by summer heat. So they're a good choice for a large area that bakes in all-day sun; they're also fine in anything more than half-day sunlight.

There are two sizes of gloriosa daisy: the standard, which grows to be about 3 feet tall and 2 feet across; and the dwarf, which reaches heights of 2 feet or so, with a spread of about 18 inches. The dwarf varieties are more popular, but seedlings of both types can usually be found in garden centers in the spring. In the Victory Garden, we don't have the scale to contain a large planting, so we put only one seedling, whether standard or dwarf, to a site at least 2 feet all around. The foliage itself is fairly close to the ground, but the flower stems are tall and somewhat leafy, so by next month, the growing mass of flowers will need the support of peripheral staking (see the July feature). The flowers — cultivated versions of the wildflower favorite, black-eyed Susans — are so numerous that several picked for a vase will hardly be missed.

A   **Hollyhock (Annual)** Annual hollyhocks are not as well known as the perennials, and garden centers are not so likely to carry seedlings. So if you didn't get seedlings started indoors earlier in the spring (see the March entry), you may have lost your chance.

Annual hollyhocks are far less susceptible to rust than are the perennials; we've never had a case in the Victory Garden plants. Even so, it's only smart to plant them with disease problems in mind, as good culture is the best preventive. In this case, good culture means giving them enough space between the plants to keep moisture from accumulating. Summer Carnival and Majorette, with spreads of 15 to 18 inches and 12 to 15 inches respectively, are spaced according to the maximum spread so that circulating air will keep the plants drier. To give a fullness to the planting, we put 3 or 5 plants together — never an even-numbered planting, as it tends to look square, no matter how the plants are arranged. Both these varieties of annual hollyhock will grow tall. At 5 feet, Summer Carnival belongs at the back of our annual border. Majorette, at half that height, can come forward into the intermediate row. Both do well in full or half-day sun, and both need the support of single stakes (see the July feature) when the flowers form.

Majorette, a variety of annual hollyhock

A   **Impatiens**   Here is the ideal plant for that area that most gardeners curse, where the soil is poor and the light low. Impatiens will do beautifully here. In fact, their pastel colors bring a shady spot to life. I've found that most varieties of impatiens do best if they're in filtered sunlight interrupted by about 2 hours of full sunlight a day. This produces vigorous plants of good height and foliage color, and dozens of flowers. But these plants will certainly survive under less-than-perfect conditions. In filtered sunlight, without the direct rays of full sun for any time at all during the day, they'll be a little on the leggy side, but they'll flower. And most of the new hybrids will tolerate several hours of daily sun if they're kept well watered. In a site like this, I'd probably pick a variety with a strong, bright color; the pastels tend to wash out a little in full sunshine.

Impatiens can be planted either in a bed or a container; for the latter, I'd pick one of the trailing varieties. (See the June feature for more about container gardening.) We give all varieties of impatiens intervals of 12 to 15 inches, whether in bed or box, trailer or upright. They'll grow to be about 12 inches tall.

Though we put our impatiens into the Victory Garden on our set-out date of May 1, the home gardener would do well to keep impatiens plants indoors until all danger of frost has passed — a full 3 or 4 weeks after the last-expected-frost date. Impatiens are *extremely* sensitive to frost, even if the seedlings are conditioned. We give them standard soil preparation for annuals but we go light on the fertilizer, as too much nitrogen will produce lush greens but few flowers. This is a plant that will do well on a lean diet.

If you haven't started seedlings of your own (see the February entry), you'll find them by the hundreds in most garden centers, in every available color. I advise against direct-sowing seeds in your garden because their growth rate is so slow. (For information on stem cuttings for indoor plants, see the August entry.)

A **Lobelia** In the Victory Garden, we concentrate on the hanging types of lobelia, one of the key ingredients in our window-box arrangements. Generally, we grow blue-flowered varieties, which is the predominant color; there are also reds, whites, and pinks. We sow our crop in February to have six-pack-size seedlings by the first of May.

No lobelia variety grows much taller than 6 inches or so. Several are in the 4-inch range. Their horizontal growth, whether trailing-type or upright, is 9 to 12 inches. So when we set them into a window box, we allow them spaces up to 12 inches wide. Often we run a line of hanging lobelias across the front of the box, where their growth tumbles out and over the edge. In a hanging pot I'd put 3 or 5 plants together. Lobelias like a site where they receive half-day sun, but filtered or full sun suits them too; in full sun, they require extra watering to keep them doing well.

Toward midsummer, lobelia plants lose steam; they still flower, but the foliage is skimpy. Because there are so many flowers on the plant, regular deadheading is next to impossible. My solution is to shear the plants back by half their height when they show signs of wear and tear. They look spare for a few days but they begin to send out new foliage quickly; they flower again in three or four weeks, and continue to bloom until frost. After cutting, I put a teaspoon of 5-10-5 fertilizer around the base of the plant, 2 or 3 inches from the stem. (For more about fertilizing, see the July feature.)

If they're grown in window boxes by themselves, the midsummer period without flowers can be bothersome. In the Victory Garden combination of lobelia, dusty miller, and geranium, though, the geraniums are full enough so the gap isn't noticeable. (See the June feature for more about container culture.)

A **Marigold** Along with the other annuals, our marigold seedlings are ready to be set out on May 1, after a few days in the cold frame to become conditioned. There are marigolds available in many sizes but we grow only the shorter French types, 6 to 12 inches tall at maturity, and the sterile Nugget hybrids, which at 12 to 18 inches are a little taller. (For the pros and cons of different types of marigolds, see the March entry.) We grow both types in our annual bed; the French are short enough to do well in window boxes, too (see the June feature). To allow for their mature spreads, I set the Nugget types into the bed at 9- to 12-inch spacing, and the French marigolds at 6- to 12-inch spacing. Both also make good pot plants, 3 French marigolds to a 10-inch pot, or one Nugget alone in an 8- or 10-inch pot.

Yellow Galore, a variety of marigold

Marigolds need a spot where they get full sun or half-day sunlight. The tall African varieties are noticeably better when grown in full sun.

French marigolds tend to go to seed if the faded flowers are allowed to remain on the plant, so we keep them deadheaded for the longest possible season of bloom. The Nuggets are sterile (known in horticulture as mules) and are unable to set seed. Nevertheless, it's best to keep the old flowers picked off for the sake of the garden's appearance.

For planting and growing-season maintenance, see the July and August features.

🅐 **Morning Glory** The morning glory seedlings — we sow our own in April — are the last of the spring annuals to be moved to the garden. We hold them until late May, more than a month after our last-expected-frost date, because they will refuse to grow until soil temperatures are above 50°F. Morning glories will live if they're planted earlier — as a matter of fact, if conditioned, these half-hardy annuals will survive a few degrees of frost — but they won't grow well until they're warm enough.

The best site for morning glories is one in full sun with some shade through the hottest part of the day. Half-day sunlight will be enough, though. We've planted morning glories in the soil at the base of the south wall of the house at our suburban site. We've also planted them in pots on a cement-floor patio; as they climb, they obscure a chain-link fence while providing privacy and a wall of bright, living color. They do well in either arrangement, but of course when pot-grown, these large plants will need extra attention to prevent them from drying out and exhausting their supply of fertilizer. (For ongoing care of potted plants, see the June feature.)

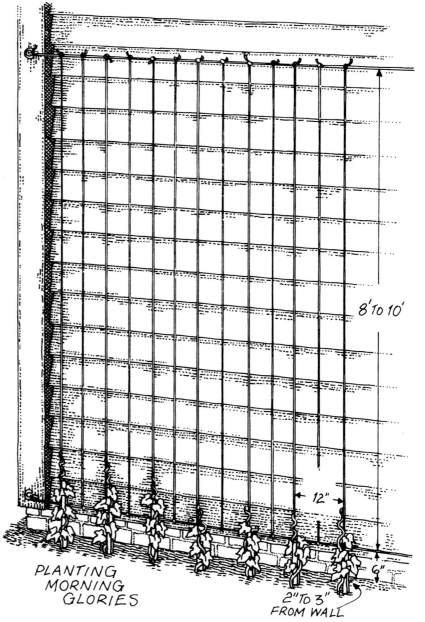

8' TO 10'

12"

6"

PLANTING
MORNING
GLORIES

2" TO 3"
FROM WALL

Morning glories grow quickly to be tall plants, but they don't have much width — 10 or 12 inches is about average. So several plants are needed for a good show of color. For pot culture, you can put one seedling to an 8-inch pot, and line several pots up rim to rim at the base of a fence or support. Grown in a garden bed, they need about 12 inches between them to form a continuous wall of color.

Morning glories are weak-stemmed plants that will climb only if they're given something to hold on to; if they're not given a support, they'll start to creep along the ground. They can weave their way into a chain-link fence, but they can't climb a solid wall, so on the side of the house we had to provide string supports. Our solution to this was 2 lines of wire, running horizontally; the bottom one about 6 inches from planting level, and the top one high enough to accommodate the full height of the plants. We secured the wire with small galvanized hook eyes screwed into the clapboard. Then we provided the vertical climbing structures by running lines of garden twine up at 6-inch intervals (directly above and between each seedling), connecting the 2 wires. Morning glories usually grow without support to heights of about 6 inches. At that point, even if they're still in the pot, the tip of the plant should be gently wound around a stake so the plant can begin to climb upward.

Morning glories flower for most of the summer, letting up as cool weather approaches. As the flowers die, I pick them off to keep the plant looking its best.

Heavenly Blue morning glories

A **Nasturtium** Once planted in the ground, nasturtiums need neglect. If they're overfed or overwatered they send out lush foliage and few flowers. When we put our seedlings into the garden on May 1 (for sowing information, see the March entry), we give them an overhead shower of transplant solution, as usual, but we put no further fertilizer into the soil. We keep even potted semitrailing varieties on this spartan diet. (For more about fertilizers, see the July feature.)

Nasturtiums do their best in all-day sun, but they will grow and flower on half-day and even filtered sunlight. For the upright types, I suggest planting them in clusters of 3 to 5 plants (or more, so long as there is an odd number) 12 inches apart. The semitrailers are fine window-box plants (see the June feature), where they need to be 8 or 10 inches apart. They'll blossom all summer.

Nasturtiums have developed an undeserved reputation as good organic insect deterrents and replacements for insecticides. In fact they are prime targets of aphids, mites, and mealy bugs.

Nicki Rose, a variety of nicotiana

 **Nicotiana** Our conditioned nicotiana seedlings, sown in March, are ready for the garden on the first of May. These half-hardy annuals can withstand 3 or 4 degrees below frost, so they could be put in a week or so earlier — anytime after the last-expected-frost date — without worry. (But *only* if they're conditioned. See the August feature.)

Nicotianas produce some of the most beautifully fragrant flowers known to gardening. Older varieties were heat-sensitive and opened their flowers mostly at night; as a result, they were most fragrant at night. New selections are open and fragrant all day. So put them where you can see and smell them and get to them. They're full-foliaged and densely flowered, and they produce excellent cut flowers right up to frost.

Mostly in the Victory Garden we grow the Nicki hybrids, which are 18 to 24 inches tall, with a spread of 12 to 15 inches; they need a spot 12 to 15 inches across to accommodate their growth. In the garden, we put 3 plants together for a full effect, but this is a heavy-foliaged plant with a dense cover and a single plant is fairly substantial. (Their fragrance also makes them good choices for pot culture. See the June feature.) Ideally the site should be in full sun, but half-day sun will do, too. Deadheading (see the July feature) is necessary more for appearance than to prevent seeding. There are several flowers on every stem, opening in succession. The most practical way to deadhead them is to pick the whole stem after all the flowers have faded. If you should find that, despite deadheading, you have self-sown seedlings, I advise pulling them out. They won't breed true.

Nicotiana seedlings are commonplace in garden centers in the spring, but you may have trouble finding color-separated seedlings in all but the largest centers.

Ⓐ **Nierembergia** At 6 to 9 inches all around, nierembergia are distinguished by neat, short growth that makes them excellent candidates for a number of uses. They're good edging plants, with their profusion of blue-purple flowers, and handsome in a window box or hanger, though their tendency to lose steam in midsummer is a detraction of sorts (see the June feature). In the Victory Garden, we've treated these trailers primarily as edgers lined up along a garden row, or in clusters of 3 or 5 plants in the annual bed, setting in our March-sown seedlings at 6- to 9-inch spacing on our May 1 set-out date. (If you haven't started seedlings on your own, you may be able to buy them at a large, well-stocked garden center.) They need a spot with full or half-day sunshine. They also need moisture — they're not a good choice for a hot, dry spot.

There are so many little flowers on this plant that deadheading single fading flowers would be a full-time job. In the Victory Garden, we let them go until midsummer, when they are beginning to look bedraggled. At that point, I shear off the plants to a height of 3 or 4 inches, and dress the soil lightly with 5-10-5 fertilizer (for more, see the July feature). For 2 or 3 weeks the plants will look unattractive — which is why they're not such good choices for a container unless they're grouped with a full, free-flowering plant — but after that they'll have foliage and flowers again.

Ⓐ **Petunia** Petunias are just on the verge of being hardy in this area. Variously classified as a hardy annual or a half-hardy perennial, they've been known to freeze solid and still survive. Conditioned seedlings can easily withstand several degrees of frost — down to 25°F or so — without damage. So while I tend to group them with the annuals and put them into the Victory Garden on the first of May, in fact they could easily go into the ground earlier. For kindness's sake, I wouldn't put them in before the last-expected-frost date, because there is no reason to subject them needlessly to cold temperatures. But transplanting them a few days early will save time on the set-out date, which can turn into a planting marathon if a quantity of annuals is involved. The plants I set out in the Victory Garden are ones I start from seed myself (see the March entry), but if you haven't sown your own seeds, you will have no trouble finding plants. It's hard to turn a corner in the spring without running into a flat of petunia seedlings. (If the seedlings you buy are leggy, pinch them back to encourage branching. See the August feature for more.)

I've grown petunias in baskets, window boxes, and in the annual bed in the Victory Garden. Regardless of variety, all petunias have a roundish shape, about 12 inches in all dimensions. Most are fairly upright, but there are trailing varieties, too. For the garden bed, the upright varieties are best, but I've grown both the trailers and the uprights in window boxes and hanging baskets; the effect is different, but both are nice. For a 10-inch hanging basket, I plant 3

Plum Pudding, a petunia mixture including several shades of red-to-purple

seedlings together. In a bed or window box, I space the seedlings at 12-inch intervals. (For more about pot and window-box culture, see the June feature.) Where light conditions are concerned, petunias are easy to please. They'll grow and flower in any light other than deep shade. They're at their best in full sun.

Most new varieties of petunia are sterile hybrids that do not set seed; the older varieties, far less common on the market these days, will set seed if allowed. Regardless of which you are growing, it makes sense to keep the flowers deadheaded as they fade, for appearance if nothing else. (See the July feature.) There is a tendency when doing this job to slide the petals off the plant and leave the flower and seed pod behind. This will improve the looks of the plant, but it won't interrupt seed production of varieties capable of producing viable seed. It's smarter to snip the entire flower head and seed pod, either with your thumb and forefinger or with a pair of shears.

Even with regular deadheading, petunias will become leggy in midsummer. The only cure for this is to cut them back to approximately half their original height. After 3 or 4 weeks, they will regain their strength and their looks and continue to bloom until frost. In fact, they'll bloom after frost, but their cool-weather flower production is not much to write home about.

Ⓐ **Phlox (Annual)** Annual phlox are available in two heights: 6 to 8 inches, and taller plants between 14 and 16 inches tall. In the Victory Garden, we've grown two varieties in the shorter range: Crimson Beauty, with clusters of rounded flowers; and Twinkle, an All-America Winner with star-shaped flowers. Annual phlox are not among the more popular bedding plants, but you should be able to find seedlings in larger garden centers if you didn't start your own. (For seed-sowing, see the March entry.)

One of the annual phlox's primary cultural recommendations is that it's a cool-weather plant unbothered by heat — a rare tolerance. Regardless of temperature, it needs a minimum of half-day sunshine. Crimson Beauty has done well for us in the kind of open, sunbaked location that would leave many annuals wilting. This is not to say that the plant withstands drought — it has to be kept watered. All varieties come into flower in early summer and continue until cool fall weather.

There are many colors of annual phlox. Some varieties, including Beauty, are available color-separated, but Twinkle is not, so garden centers will sell seedlings with colors unidentified. If you buy a six-pack of Twinkle, you have a good chance of seeing 3 or 4 different flower colors. Some are solid. Some are bicolors that look a little like pinwheels.

I move our seedlings outdoors along with our other annuals on May 1. We plant them either in window boxes or the garden bed, 6 to 12 inches apart (see the June feature). In the garden bed, I usually cluster 3 plants together for a full effect.

Baby Doll, a mixed variety of pinks

A **Pinks** Old-time varieties of pinks all but stop flowering in summer heat. The newer varieties now on the market are more temperature-tolerant, but even the two All-America Winners we grow in the Victory Garden — Snowfire and Magic Charms — are a little better at our cooler suburban site than in the Victory Garden proper.

Given their reaction to heat, the gardener can help them by giving them a spot out of direct, all-day sunlight. The best location is one with half-day sun, as a few hours of shade during the day will keep them cooler. Given this partly shady spot, pinks do well either in the garden bed or in a window box (see the June feature). In a bed, I cluster several plants together; in the window box, I might be inclined to pair them with dusty miller (see this month's entry). Because Magic Charms is sold only as a mix, it probably isn't the best choice for a window box unless your seedlings have started to flower and you can plant single colors together. The planting intervals are best determined by the mature height of the plant; pinks are generally as wide as they are tall.

The Victory Garden seedlings are started in our greenhouse in February and transplanted to the garden the first of this month, Snowfire at 10- to 12-inch intervals, and Magic Charms 6 to 8 inches apart. As with all our annuals, they are set into well-prepared soil, kept deadheaded, and given a scattering of 5-10-5 fertilizer after the first flush of flowers. (For more on maintaining the flower garden, see the July feature.)

A **Portulaca** We sow seeds for these plants in March. If you're buying portulaca seedlings — they're widely available from garden centers in the spring — the important consideration is the variety's need for hot, sunny conditions. Old-time portulacas closed their flowers in shade or cool weather; the new varieties have been dramatically improved on this score. Afternoon Delight seems to be the best of the new varieties, staying open all day, regardless of temperature. It's available only as a mix, but other varieties, including Sunglo, can be found as color-separated seedlings. Many

garden centers will also offer seedlings of the older varieties, usually as mixtures.

Afternoon Delight, a mix of portulaca

     We use portulacas as edgers, or in clusters in the annual bed. Portulacas are low-growing, some 6 to 9 inches tall, with a horizontal spread about twice that measure. They like a spot with full, or at least half-day, sun. We set them into prepared soil using our standard soil preparation for annuals (see this month's feature), but we go very lightly with chemical fertilizers, or use none at all, as portulacas do well in lean soil. We also forgo the 5-10-5 feeding that we give most annuals after the first flush of flowers.

     As with all our plants, we pick the faded flowers to keep the garden fresh-looking and prevent the plant from going to seed. (And we work carefully, as bees are attracted to portulaca.) These are true annuals, but they often self-sow, in spite of our deadheading efforts. Even in the Victory Garden, where winters are generally fierce, the seeds can survive and sprout the following spring. The resulting seedlings are not likely to be as nice as the original sowing, and

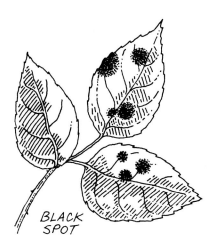

BLACK
SPOT

POWDERY
MILDEW

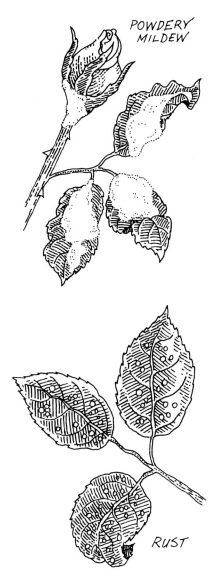

RUST

they will be a little poorer each year. But for a year or two, you may have a satisfactory crop of portulacas for very little effort. If you would prefer the best varieties year after year, pull the self-sown plants and order fresh seeds every spring.

Ⓟ **Rose** As soon as the weather begins to warm in the spring, roses run into trouble. And they run into more trouble than any other plant in the garden, requiring more of the gardener's time and attention.

The greatest danger is from disease. Black spot, powdery mildew, rust, crown gall, and cankers are the most common rose diseases across the country. In the Victory Garden, black spot and powdery mildew have been the major headaches.

You can minimize problems by clearing out old foliage and leaves and by giving plants ample room for good air circulation. Even so, unless you are as lucky as a new copper penny, your roses will be infected at some point. If you keep your eye on the plants, you'll be able to notice problems early.

Black spot is easy to see, and its name is entirely descriptive. Sometimes there's a yellow rim around the spot. This disease takes a foothold in wet foliage; it's most apt to become established after a heavy spring rain or late summer and fall dews.

Powdery mildew, as it advances, appears as a dry white growth on the surface of the leaves and on closed buds. In its early stages, it may be difficult for the amateur rose grower to identify. This disease will survive the winter, so one of the best preventives is good sanitation all year long, keeping dropped stems and foliage cleared away.

Rust also survives the winter, and appears as rust-colored lesions on the leaves or new stems. Plants lose vigor dramatically — and eventually lose all foliage, too.

Crown gall is a bacterial disease that starts out as a swelling near the soil line, which eventually grows into large knobs that weaken plants; it's often spread by infected tools. There is no cure. The only remedy is to dig the plant up and burn it. Crown gall lives in the soil, so the area should not be planted with roses for at least 2 years.

Cankers fungus is spread by wind and water. It's usually a second-string attack, going after plants already weakened by other diseases. The cankers look like dead spots on the canes; often they circle the cane, which dies from the canker to the tip.

Roses are also prey to insects — swarms of them — but in our very humid area, diseases are more troublesome. In the Victory Garden, which is surrounded mostly by buildings, our insect problems have been minimal because we're so far from the nearest garden. But we have had Japanese beetles, aphids, European rose chafers, and rose slugs. The Japanese beetles are large enough to pick off carefully by hand — they bite — and the aphids we can hose off, working in the morning of a sunny day so the foliage dries quickly. Rose chafers are actually brown beetles, about ½ inch long; they're a problem mostly early in the summer. Rose slugs are ½-inch-long larvae that feed on the leaves.

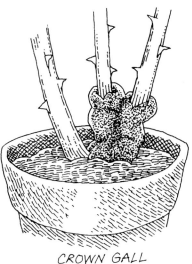

CROWN GALL

There are so many rose insects — varying from one region to another — that a catalogue of them isn't much good. (Your county agricultural agent can help you identify them.) The important thing to know is that rose diseases and pests are rampant, and many are potentially fatal. If your roses are hit, you have two choices: you can treat your collection with a dust or spray or, in very severe cases, you can pull the plant. It was once common practice to treat roses on a preventive basis, every 10 days. Now, in an effort to cut down on pesticide and fungicide use, the accepted line of thinking is to respond at the first sign of a problem, repeat as needed, and give an insurance dose after heavy rain.

If you go into a garden center looking for insecticides and fungicides for your roses, you will find a preparation known as rose dust. It's available as a liquid or wettable powder (these are meant to be sprayed on) or as a dry dust. Regardless of their form, all are known as rose dust, and all contain several insecticides and fungicides, packaged together because many rose pests and diseases tend to strike together. My feeling about this is that there are more chemicals in the rose dust than you would ever need at once. I prefer to examine my plants carefully, identify the insect or disease causing the problem, and respond with only the necessary chemicals. For the inexperienced rose grower, this approach will require time and attention, as well as trips to the county agricultural agent armed with mushy leaves and dead bugs, but in time you will recognize your enemies yourself, and know which chemicals will eradicate them.

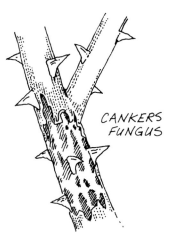

CANKERS FUNGUS

Because May is the first of the warm months in the Victory Garden, this is the time when we have to begin watering the roses. A constant supply of moisture is essential to these plants because their growth is checked if they dry out, and this can cost them both flowers and foliage. Roses need more water than most plants; the rule of thumb is 2 inches a week. If less than this amount falls from the skies, the gardener has to provide irrigation.

Many rose diseases are spread in water, so it's best to water at ground level and leave the foliage dry. If you do use overhead watering, the best time is in the morning of a

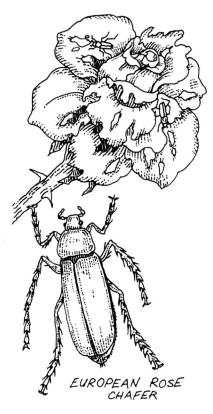

EUROPEAN ROSE
CHAFER

sunny day so the leaves dry quickly. In the large rose garden at our suburban site, we use a drip irrigation system (see the July feature). If you have only a few roses, and if your watering arrangement makes this convenient, you can simply use the hose end, with a breaker attached to soften the stream, and water each plant individually. As a rule, the plants will be watered deeply enough if the bed is flooded, allowed to drain, and then flooded again. For 1 or 2 plants, you might prefer just to leave the hose end at the soil line with only enough pressure to provide a drip. A good saucer of soil around the plants is helpful here. After a couple of hours the soil should be well watered.

One of the best ways to keep the moisture in the soil is with a warm-weather mulch (see the July feature). A coarse mulch, such as bark chips, cocoa hulls, or wood chips seems to work best, and it's easily removed in the fall so the soil can be mounded for winter protection.

In addition to all this attention to watering and pests, there is a small but important job to do this month: rose bushes newly planted this spring need a feeding of 5-10-5 fertilizer when the leaves first appear.

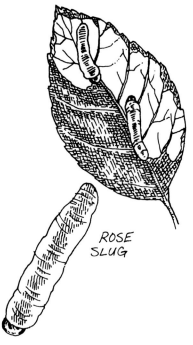

ROSE
SLUG

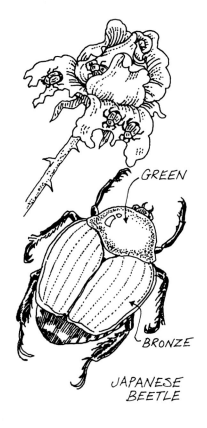

GREEN

BRONZE

JAPANESE
BEETLE

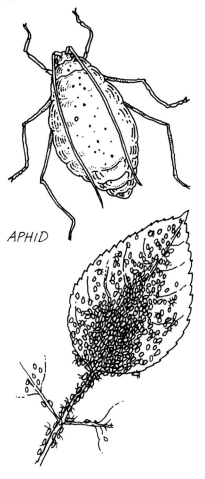

APHID

A   **Salvia** In the Victory Garden, we've grown two varieties of salvia. We start ours from seed in March, but if you're buying seedlings, scarlet sage will be easy to find, blue sage somewhat less so.

Scarlet sage (*S. splendens*) is popular for its red-hot flowers. Although there are some taller varieties on the market too, in most of the varieties we've grown the flowers are about 12 inches tall, over 9-inch foliage; the plants are 12 to 15 inches across. I've often seen these as a border plant, but in the Victory Garden I usually put a 3-plant cluster into the annual border, following our springtime soil preparation for annuals (see this month's feature). They're not demanding plants, and their flowers are long-lasting. The plants stay in flower for most of the season. When the flower stalks begin to fade, I remove them from the base so the foliage obscures the cut.

Blue salvia (*S. farinacea*) is a little easier on the eye than scarlet sage. It's a tender perennial grown as an annual. Victoria, the variety we grow in the Victory Garden, reaches a height of 18 to 24 inches, with spreads of 15 to 18 inches. Because of the strong spikes that bear the flowers, no staking is necessary. For the same reason, blue sage makes a nice cut flower, too. I plant them in clusters, at least 3 plants to a site, all 15 to 18 inches apart.

Both sages are best in full sun, but will grow on half-day sunlight. Both are best deadheaded by removing the whole flower stalk as it fades, rather than trying to pick off individual florets.

A planting of Victoria, a variety of blue salvia

A   **Scabiosa** Annual scabiosa is widely available from seed — we sow ours in March — and can be found in large garden centers as springtime seedlings. To date, none of the varieties is color-separated, but the mixes make a handsome planting because the various colors are compatible; there are subdued shades of red, pink, salmon, and white, as well as one that is close to black. (If you're buying seedlings, look for the botanical name *Scabiosa atropurpurea*, or for the common name, pincushion flower. There are a couple of other scabiosa species on the market, including a perennial, which are quite different from the annual.)

Annual scabiosa is available both in full and dwarf sizes but we've concentrated on the dwarf, which is usually taller than it is wide, reaching heights of about 18 inches, with 12-inch spreads. When I set seedlings into the garden on May 1, I cluster them, 3 or 5 together, at intervals of 12 inches. They need a spot with at least half-day sun, preferably more. As the season progresses, they receive regular ongoing care (see the July feature).

A   **Snapdragon**   If the seedlings are conditioned (see the August feature), snapdragons are among the most frost-tolerant of annuals. In fact, they'll live over winter if temperatures stay above 10°F. So while we hold our seedlings out until our May 1 set-out date, the home gardener may want to spread the transplanting job over a few days, and move the cool-weather plants into the garden anytime after the last-expected-frost date. (Make sure, if you do this, that the seedlings are conditioned; if they're not, they'll be very tender.)

In the Victory Garden, we grow the dwarf varieties of snapdragon, 8 to 12 inches tall, and the 12- to 24-inch intermediates; we put both types into the annual border, in a spot where they're easily reached. They produce such delightful cut flowers that I like to have them nearby. They're sun-lovers, but because of their sensitivity to hot weather, they do well planted in a site protected from midday sun, or under deeply rooted, high-canopied deciduous trees; they'll do well in half-day sun, too. When I put them into the

Yellow snapdragons, from the mix Little Darling, with red geraniums and Plum Pudding petunias, in the Victory Garden window box

ground, I arrange the plants in clusters of 3 or 5, spacing the dwarf varieties 6 to 12 inches apart, and the intermediates at 12- to 18-inch intervals. As with all our annuals, they are put into well-prepared soil and maintained regularly throughout the growing season (see the July feature and After Frost).

If you haven't started seedlings of your own, you should still find quite a variety at your local garden center. You'll probably find both singles and doubles for sale; the doubles are larger and longer-lasting, but the singles look more like traditional snapdragons, and the petals will have the snapping reflex for which these plants are named. I don't advise direct-sowing flower seeds for any plants (see the August feature), but it's a particularly poor idea with snaps because they are so sensitive to midsummer heat. Even the new hybrids produce fewer flowers through July and August than during the spring and fall; so direct-sown plants would come to maturity just when the weather is most difficult for them.

Ⓐ **Statice** The foliage of notchleaf statice lies mostly along the ground. It spreads out 12 to 18 inches while reaching heights of only a few inches; the flowers climb above the foliage on 18-inch stems. With this characteristic, they can be grown either in the front of the border or in the center row. I cluster 3 plants to a site, 12 to 18 inches apart. Full sunlight is best; half-day sun is acceptable.

After a few days in a cold frame, our conditioned seedlings are ready for our prepared garden soil on May 1. In the Victory Garden, we sow our own statice seeds in March, but larger garden centers may sell them if you are looking to buy seedlings. It's a fine garden plant, but notchleaf statice is more commonly grown as a flower for drying; in fact, it's one of the most familiar of all the many dried flowers. (For drying directions, see the strawflower entry in July.) If you plan to dry the flowers, pick them when there is a good show of color, but before they're fully open; they tend to hold up better, and to retain more color, if they're not quite ripe when they're dried.

Purple statice, just about to open

Ⓐ **Strawflower** It's possible to buy seeds of single-colored strawflower varieties, but this is one case where I actually prefer the mixes. The colors are glorious together, with their reds and oranges and yellows. If you would like to buy seedlings, try a large garden center, as strawflowers are not the most common of springtime seedling crops. Some varieties of strawflowers are as much as 3 feet tall, but the mixture we grow — Bright Bikinis — is valued for its com-

A bee at work in a bed of strawflowers

bination of large flowers and short stature, standing only about 18 inches tall.

Our seedlings, begun indoors in March, are ready for prepared soil in the annual bed on the first of May. They're nice in clusters of 3 or 5 plants in the annual bed, or in larger plantings. They'll bloom all summer, sending up flowers 18 inches tall over leaves that peak at about 12 inches. They need full or half-day sunlight.

Strawflowers will yield a steady supply of flowers for both fresh and dried bouquets (see the July entry). As is true of most flowers intended for drying, the best time to pick is before the flowers fully ripen, just as the outer petals are opening. They may flatten out some as they age, but if they're picked at or beyond their peak, the petals sometimes turn downward, and the colors fade.

Swan River Daisy These annuals have been popular with gardeners for some time, but if they were even better known, it would be easier for gardeners to buy seedlings in the spring. As it is, only large garden centers carry them.

If you do find seedlings, you are more apt to find mixes — white, pink, and blue — than separate colors. In the Victory Garden, we plant our seeds in March so the seedlings are large enough for the garden on our May 1 set-out date. If given full sun and cool temperatures, Swan River daisies will bloom abundantly all summer and into the fall, producing so many flowers that the leaves can hardly be seen. But full sun and cool temperatures are a difficult combination to provide. They'll grow in half-day sun, too, and in hot climates if they have a few hours of filtered sunlight or shade to keep them cool. Otherwise, they respond to the heat of summer — temperatures in the mid-80s and upward — by not flowering freely. Even when there are few flowers, the foliage is very good-looking. And if the plants are sheared back to a height of 4 to 6 inches when flower production drops off, they'll send up new growth and flower well through the cool fall months.

Swan River daisies are somewhat weak-stemmed. They can have a crisper look if they're given a bit of brush to climb — just leafless branches of deciduous trees, put into the ground around the plants after set-in. The brush should be no more than 10 inches tall so that the full-grown plants obscure it. If you leave the plants to grow with no support, they will look more casual. Despite the weakness of their stems, Swan River daisies make good cut flowers for a casual bouquet.

Swan River daisies, given their mounded shape, are adaptable to a number of different planting sites. At 12 inches all around, they're a good scale for a container (see the June feature) or a rock garden. In cool climates, their slightly trailing habit will do handsomely in a window box. The Victory Garden summers are too warm for this, so we grow them in the annual bed, clustering 3 plants together at 12-inch intervals, or lined up along the perennial border, where the weak stems curve gently over the raised bed.

A planting of pink Swan River daisies, grown from a mix that includes blue flowers as well

A   **Sweet Alyssum**   Our sweet alyssum seedlings, sown in March, are ready for the garden along with our other annuals on May 1. Actually, these plants are very cold-tolerant, and if conditioned, could go into the garden a few days in advance of other annuals. They're hardy annuals that can survive temperatures down to the mid-20s. They want sunlight for at least half the day; full sun is best.

We use sweet alyssum plants primarily as edgers; I usually put 3 together in a row, giving each plant 9 to 15 inches to spread into. At 4 to 6 inches tall, they're one of the shortest flowering plants available. They're also extremely heavily flowered. Their only drawback is that they lose

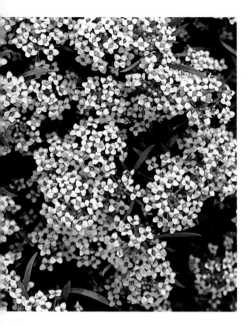

Sweet alyssum, Carpet of Snow

steam after a couple of months of growth. It's impossible to deadhead them, so at that point I shear them back to 2 or 3 inches, taking the flower heads and a bit of stem, but leaving as much of the plants behind as possible. They recover through the summer and are fully revived by fall.

If you are in the market to buy sweet alyssum seedlings, the most important thing is to make sure you're buying the annual sweet alyssum *Lobularia maritima*. (There is also a perennial alyssum — see the July alyssum entry — with a somewhat similar low creeping habit of growth. The two don't resemble each other at all, but the names are similar enough to be confusing.) You should have no trouble finding sweet alyssum seedlings at garden centers, both in white and purple; the white varieties are more freely flowered. Ordinarily I advise against buying seedlings that are already in flower (see this month's feature), but in the case of sweet alyssum this is not a warning I need to give. They're such eager bloomers that they commonly pop into flower while still in the six-pack.

Tulip After the flowers go by, tulip foliage enters a period of decline that lasts for about a month. It is not an attractive process, but it is a necessary one if the tulips are to blossom again; the bulb is actually drawing strength from the leaves as they wither and brown. If you have no intention of saving the bulbs for another year, you can just pull them out when the flowering season ends and throw them away. If you have only a few bulbs planted in your perennial border, you can probably leave them where they are; if the growing perennials do not obscure them, add a few well-placed annuals. But if you want both the bulbs and the garden space they occupy, the solution is to heel them in — that is, to move the bulbs to another site and let the foliage ripen out of view.

Digging the bulbs sacrifices some of the roots and shortens the ripening period. From the plant's point of view, this is not good — if the period is too short it can affect the next year's blossoms — so I advise you to wait until the leaves look ragged, half-green and half-brown. The longer you wait, the better for the bulbs. I use a spading fork for this job, working very carefully so as not to puncture the bulbs. I always loosen the soil well so the bulbs lift out easily, and I handle them by the bulbs, not the foliage. They will have begun the process of splitting — each bulb multiplies during the growing season — but they should be left intact for now. Partway through this job, gardeners sometimes realize they don't know which bulbs are which, so I urge you to work out a labeling system before you start.

Opposite: Oriental Splendor tulips, a variety of Greigii hybrids

For heeling in, tulip bulbs need only a spot with half-day sun and well-drained soil. They can also be grown in filtered light. If they're put in full sun, the foliage should be covered with hay or straw, or some other mulch, for a couple of days so they don't ripen too quickly. I give them a trench about 4 inches deep and lay the bulbs on their sides, pulling the soil over them but leaving the foliage exposed. The distance between the bulbs is not important; they can even touch. After they're heeled in, I water them well, and every other week I feed them with half-strength liquid fertilizer. For the next step in the process of saving the bulbs, see the July entry.

Blaze, a variety of verbena

△ **Verbena** The ideal site for verbenas is one with full sun, where the soil is sandy and the temperatures cool. These plants have done extremely well for us, their flower production dropping off only slightly in the hot weather. And if we could provide them with only half-day sun, they would still do well. Because they stand up well to drought, they're a good low-maintenance annual. Their adaptability to different garden conditions no doubt helps explain why they have become such popular plants.

In the Victory Garden, we sow our verbena seeds in March to have garden-ready seedlings by our May 1 set-out date, but you'll probably be able to find seedlings if you're in the market to buy. Most of the varieties available are 8 to 10 inches in all directions, but Sangria, a wine-colored verbena, has a spreading habit of growth and will reach spreads of 12 to 18 inches; like other varieties, Sangria is about 8 inches tall at maturity. Sangria is also better able to stand up to summer heat than other varieties, which is of special concern if you are in a particularly warm part of the country. If you're buying seedlings, you're apt to find both mixes, containing a range of colors from strong reds to soft pinks and blues, and color-separated plants. In the Victory Garden, we've grown a good-looking red variety called Blaze.

All types of verbena are good for edging and rock gardens. They're also among the best choices for window boxes because, in the Victory Garden at least, they are able to flower all summer, which is something many of the most popular window-box plants cannot do (see the June feature). The upright varieties should be planted 8 to 10 inches apart, whether in a bed or container; in a bed, I cluster 3 together. Sangria needs a larger space, 12 to 18 inches in all directions.

△ **Vinca** Vincas are real favorites in the Victory Garden, not only for their friendly, plentiful flowers, but for their ability to put up with all sorts of weather conditions.

Their preference is for full-day sun, but they'll grow and flower in half-day or filtered sunlight. Like impatiens, they do well even with little direct sun. They're resistant to many diseases and relatively unbothered by pests. They do have one sensitive point — they don't flower well if night temperatures fall below 60°F — but throughout most of the country this isn't much of a problem. All in all, they're excellent, low-maintenance plants.

Vinca plants are slow-growing, so we start our Victory Garden seedlings very early in the spring (see the February entry) to guarantee garden-size plants by the time we set out our annuals on the first of May. If you did not get your seedlings started in advance, you should be able to find them on the market in garden centers, as these once-obscure plants are fast gaining in popularity. Garden centers are most apt to carry one of the "Little" series, representing a range of colors from pure white through several shades of pink. The Littles are about 12 inches tall at maturity, with an approximately equal spread. The name vinca is the old-time botanical name for this plant, and it has held on despite a formal name change to *Catharanthus roseus*. The plant is also commonly known as Madagascar periwinkle. So you may have to look in several places to find seedlings at your local garden center.

Our vincas are planted on our annual set-out date, along with the bulk of the Victory Garden annuals. We've always added them to the prepared soil of the annual bed, clustering 3 plants together 10 to 12 inches apart. An additional low-maintenance quality of this plant is that it is largely self-cleaning: the flowers tend to fall off and blow away, saving the gardener the trouble of clipping off fading flowers. And they don't set seed to the point where it interferes with flower production, so there is no need to deadhead the seed pods.

Vincas will bloom all summer long, until the weather turns too cool for them. Because they are tender perennials, cuttings can be taken toward late summer, and the resulting plants grown inside all winter long.

Little Bright Eyes, a variety of vinca

Wax Begonia We sow the seeds of this versatile, well-known plant in February, but seedlings are readily available in the spring. The popularity of wax begonias stems partly from the fact that they are one of the few and better flowering plants for shady areas. They're at their best in half-day sunlight, but they will grow quite well in filtered sun; they will even grow in nearly full sun if they're well watered and kept shaded through the middle of the day, when the sunlight is at its most intense.

There are many varieties of wax begonia on the market, with flowers in whites and a range of pinks and reds. Depending on the variety, the heights range from 6 to 12 inches; these are roundish plants in which the spread is roughly equal to the height of the plant. In a garden center of any size, you will probably find a number of varieties available as seedlings, both in color-separated selections and mixes. Because the color range is limited, the mixes make for a handsome planting, but I generally concentrate on clustering 3 like-variety plants in the annual border. At our suburban site, we have planted larger areas, massing the wax begonias for a carpet effect that is very appealing.

Wax begonias are slow growers. Our seedlings, begun 2 to 3 months before they're to be set into the garden, are still small — 3 to 4 inches tall — by set-out date. They grow slowly after they're transplanted to the garden, too, but they blossom early and continue to flower as they grow. For a new generation of plants, wax begonias can be propagated by cuttings of nonflowering stems, just as impatiens are (see the impatiens entry in August).

Ⓐ Zinnia Some zinnia varieties reach heights of 3 feet, but in the Victory Garden, where our relatively small, square site demands smaller-scale plants, we have concentrated on the shorter varieties 12 to 18 inches tall. These short plants, especially the excellent Peter Pan strain, have the same extensive color range as the taller zinnias, and they have the added advantage of standing straight without staking. We've grown them mostly in the garden bed, but they're a good scale for a container, too (see the June feature). The taller varieties once dominated the market, but the dwarf varieties, including the Peter Pan strain and the slightly taller Lilliput and Old Mexico zinnias, have now assumed the lead. The dwarf types are shorter stemmed and often smaller flowered, so they're not as appealing to cut-flower enthusiasts as are the taller varieties. You should have no trouble finding seedlings if you did not sow seeds yourself (see the March entry).

Zinnias have some mildew problems, so when they're planted they need plenty of air circulation and sunlight. They'll grow in half-day sunlight, but they're better in full sun because the more shade they have, the more susceptible to mildew they are. The dwarf varieties of the Peter Pan type have spreads of 9 to 12 inches, so I space them a full foot apart, which is close enough for them to look related, and far enough apart for air to move easily around them. Three or 5 plants together makes a good-sized planting in the Victory Garden.

Peter Pan Scarlet zinnias

Zinnia flowers have a tendency to fade quickly, though new varieties last longer than the old. For this reason, it's a good practice to keep the fading flowers picked off. This is especially important with the tall varieties, which tend to go to seed quickly. Better yet, pick a few flowers for fresh bouquets when they're just about to peak. They have a long vase life, and picking the flowers will prolong the plants' flowering period. In the Victory Garden, zinnias bloom right up to frost.

Tall-growing zinnias should be planted at intervals of 12 to 18 inches. They will branch best if they're pinched back once when they have 2 or 3 sets of true leaves. Garden centers are not likely to have done this, so I'd suggest pinching the tips of the tall varieties once, immediately after planting. This will delay flowering, but it results in fuller plants and more flowers later in the season. When the flower buds form, tall-growing zinnias may need staking to help them maintain their stature (see the July feature).

ANNUALS

Annuals are plants that go through a lifetime in one year, from germination to maturation to reproduction and death. During this short time, their obsession is the survival of their kind. Because an individual plant is programmed for a brief life, the species' survival depends on seed production in enormous quantity. In the wild, where the weather conditions are right, most annuals produce thousands of seeds which nestle into the soil and germinate. Thus the species survives and increases year after year and is able, by sheer number alone, to withstand most of nature's periodic catastrophes. In the process of seed production, annuals produce flowers, also in great quantity, but the fact that these flowers are beautiful matters more to us than it does to the plants.

Some plants that we know as annuals do not fit this description precisely. In fact they are perennials, but they are native to parts of the world where the weather is warm year-round, and when they're grown in temperate climates (that is, most of the United States), they die with the approach of cold weather. The phrase often used to describe these plants is that they are "treated as annuals." Many of the most popular garden flowers, including impatiens and petunias, are in fact tender perennials.

Annuals have a great deal to recommend them. They're very easy to propagate from seed. The rate of germination is predictable and speedy. As a rule, they are subject to very few problems with insects and diseases. Most have a very long flowering season; in fact, nearly all the annuals in the Victory Garden blossom from early summer to frost. Blossom colors among annuals include hot reds, bright yellows, and velvety purples, as well as soft pastels. Among some species of annuals, the full color range is represented. All in all, annuals are excellent plants for the novice and veteran gardener alike.

Using Annuals Because they are, essentially, single-season plants, and because the root systems are shallow, requiring a bed of prepared soil only 4 to 6 inches deep, there are more choices for ways to use annuals than any other class of garden flowers. In the Victory Garden, we've used them in the vegetable garden to add beauty to function. We've planted window boxes with them, inventing new combinations to bring variety to the somewhat predictable choices that dominate window-box culture. We also add annuals to the perennial border, an arrangement that brings the long-season color of the annuals to the changing pattern of the perennials. In the Victory Garden, though, the primary use of annuals is in the border alongside the greenhouse, a border they share with the spring-flowering bulbs. After the bulbs fade in the spring, we can plant the entire area with annual seedlings, producing a bed of color stretching the full life of our growing season.

Annuals can be grown in almost any garden site. For most, full sun is best, but half-day sunlight is acceptable. There are several genera of annuals that do best in filtered light or shade. Any size annual bed is all right, too, as long as it's not so large that you can't reach the plants easily to maintain them. At our suburban site, annuals are used in a garden by themselves. This garden functions not only as a beautiful outdoor spot, but as a cutting garden as well, providing endless bouquets for indoor summer arrangements. At this site, the annuals are grown as bedding plants, meaning that several plants of one variety are clustered together. We always plant uneven numbers of plants, to avoid the squared-off look that comes from even-numbered clusters.

When you are planning your garden, read through the individual entries for annuals (especially those in May) so that you can select the flowers that will give you the most for your efforts. If you are looking for particular traits, use the index to this book. For instance, there are several excellent cutting flowers — those that yield sturdy-stemmed flowers for bouquets — in this book, among them: annual scabiosas, zinnias, snapdragons, pinks, gloriosa daisies, cosmos, cornflowers, calendulas, and annual asters. These annuals thrive in filtered sunlight: browallias, coleus, fuchsias, impatiens, lobelias, and wax begonias. These do well in very hot weather: portulacas, vincas, verbenas, geraniums, gazanias, and marigolds.

Annuals Culture

Set-Out Date Whether you buy seedlings or grow them from seed yourself, the most important first step is to establish your garden set-out date; the rest of the schedule for annuals works backward from there. This date is simply the date when the garden is warm enough. It's not only a question of air temperature — cold soil is as much of a problem as cold air — but the set-out date is usually calculated by adding 10 days to the date of the last expected spring frost; the 10 days are the margin of safety. In the Victory Garden, the last-expected-frost date is April 20, so our set-out date is May 1. There is little to be gained from setting plants out prematurely, as they will grow slowly through cool weather. Plants set out later will develop more quickly, thanks to the milder temperatures, and often mature at about the same time as those planted even 2 weeks earlier; this phenomenon is usually known as catch-up.

The U.S. Department of Agriculture publishes maps indicating spring and fall frost dates. These maps will help you determine your last-frost date, but there is a great deal of variation within areas, so I would also advise you to contact your local agricultural agent, who will have a more detailed map of your area. In addition, I would talk to neighbors who garden. Believe me, this is worth doing, as regional differences can be dramatic. Our suburban site, for instance, is only about 10 miles from the Victory Garden, but the last-frost date is mid-May, and the annuals can't go into the ground until Memorial Day weekend, a full month after the Victory Garden seedlings.

Annuals differ in their ability to withstand cold weather. Tender annuals can't tolerate frost at all; some will die if the temperatures fall below 40°F. If the seedlings are conditioned (see the August feature), half-hardy annuals can take a few degrees of frost, to temperatures in the high 20s. Hardy annuals will live even if the readings fall below 25°F. These temperature limits apply to conditioned seedlings only; few young plants would survive cold temperatures if they were moved suddenly from warm indoor temperatures to the harsher outdoors.

Seed Sowing Annual seeds can be direct-sown, that is, planted directly in the garden, but this may delay the flowering season, so I don't usually advise it. (See the August feature.) In the Victory Garden, we sow all our annual seeds indoors in advance of the set-out date, scheduled so that the seedlings are just filling their six-pack compartments by the set-out date. The seedlings will not all be the same size by this time; vincas and wax begonias, for instance, will be much smaller than marigolds or geraniums. The advance time during which the plants grow indoors is designed to give them time enough to grow to a sturdy size. Following is a chart of the annuals covered in this book, and the amount of lead time they require. Tuberous annuals are also included here, according to the schedule for starting the tubers into growth.

Annuals' Lead Time

8 to 12 weeks (See February)

Browallia	Impatiens
Coleus	Lobelia
Dusty miller	Pinks
Geranium	Vinca
Gloriosa daisy	Wax begonia

4 to 8 weeks (See March)

Ageratum	Nierembergia
Aster (Annual)	Petunia
Caladium	Phlox (Annual)
Calendula	Portulaca
Celosia	Salvia
Chrysanthemum (Annual)	Scabiosa
Cornflower	Snapdragon
Cosmos	Statice
Dahlia	Strawflower
Gazania	Swan River daisy
Globe amaranth	Sweet alyssum
Hollyhock (Annual)	Sweet pea
Marigold	Tuberous-rooted begonia
Morning glory (see April)	Verbena
Nasturtium	Zinnia
Nicotiana	

Less than 4 weeks (See April)

Cleome

If you have a greenhouse, you can give your seedlings more time indoors than we have recommended here; actually, we often do this ourselves in the Victory Garden. An earlier sowing will produce larger plants by set-out date, which means they will flower sooner. Of course, they will also outgrow their six-packs and will need to be moved to larger individual pots to keep them from crowding. In a greenhouse, the conditions for growth are excellent, and the seedlings will be both large and healthy, even after several weeks growing indoors. For the home gardener who must rely on artificial lights or windowsills, which even under the best of circumstances are sunny only part of the day, a long period growing indoors is apt to produce weak, leggy plants that don't adjust well to harsh outdoor conditions.

The August feature contains complete information on sowing seeds, and caring for and transplanting seedlings.

Buying Seeds We buy most of our seeds through mail-order catalogues because they offer more variety than garden centers. It's best to have several catalogues on hand when ordering so you can compare prices and find the varieties you want. Most seeds sold these days are hybrids, and as a rule they are improvements over their species' ancestors, being more vigorous and often having other selling points as well. The All-America Winners are especially good choices, having won this designation from a jury of exacting judges after several years of nationwide trials.

We buy single-color varieties whenever we can because, in the Victory Garden, we like to mass color for maximum effect. In some varieties only mixes are available and in this case there is no way to know, from the individual seedlings, what color the flowers will be. There is no solution to this. If we like a variety that comes only as a mix, we buy it and plant a mixed-color bed. Some mixes contain different colors all in the same range — like shades of pink and red — and these are usually very handsome planted together.

Buying Plants You may want to buy seedlings from your local garden center, rather than start your own. The selection won't be as extensive as that offered by seed houses, but the larger centers offer an impressive array of choices nonetheless.

One of the temptations when buying seedlings is to buy flowers, not plants. Because the average consumer is set on buying plants already in flower, the bedding plant (that is, annual seedling) industry does its best to produce what is known as "color in the pack," in other words, seedlings in flower. The temptation is understandable. After all, if the flowers already show, then the color is no mystery. And there's something reassuring about plants that can flower even when young and not yet in the ground. But if you can, resist. With very few exceptions, flowers on a young seedling are not a good sign. Usually they indicate that the plant is stressed in some way, by tight quarters or restricted diet, for instance. It's far better to look for seedlings with good foliage color, and full, sturdy growth. As for the color of the flowers, you can usually trust the color guides the garden centers provide. If the seedlings you buy are not quite as sturdy as you would like, pinch the tips back once. This will delay flowering, but the plants will be bushier and the flower show, though later, worth the wait. (Some plants should not be pinched at all. See the August feature.)

The Victory Garden annual bed in midsummer

The annuals along the main path of the Victory Garden

bulbs' flowers have faded, we pull the bulbs and either discard them or heel them in. At that point we rake the bed with a steel rake to level out the surface, and we're ready to plant our annuals. If you don't have bulbs to worry about, and if you prepared the soil in the fall, all you need do now is rake the soil to open it and smooth out the lumpiness that tends to develop over winter. (For planting, see the August feature.)

Ongoing Care Annuals are largely trouble-free through the season. Many annuals that reach mature heights of 18 inches or more need staking if they're to stand straight (see the July feature). And most annuals benefit from a little 5-10-5 fertilizer — no more than a teaspoon per plant — after the first flush of flowers. Beyond this, and watching for insect and disease problems, the only significant task is keeping the flowers picked off as soon as they fade. If this job isn't done regularly, the flowering season may be shortened considerably on some species.

For more about all these procedures, see the July feature.

Soil Preparation One of the advantages of growing annuals is that they do not require much in the way of soil preparation. Their roots are shallow, so the bed of prepared soil need be only 4 to 6 inches deep. Because the plants are so undemanding, soil preparation for annuals can be left until the spring, unless you're putting in a new garden or have sod to contend with. In the Victory Garden, we do all soil preparation in the fall (see After Frost) because we plant spring-flowering bulbs in our annual border. In the spring, after the

178 **MAY**

Planting the Annual Garden

(Reading top, left to right, then bottom, left to right) In planting the garden of annuals at the suburban site, we began by charting the garden on paper. Then we made plant labels, using indelible ink so the information wouldn't be lost in a rain. The next step was to till the soil, which had not been done the previous fall. After the soil was turned, we raked the bed smooth. Then we transferred the chart to the garden bed, and as a last step we marked the planting sites with ground limestone.

Monthly Checklist

Fuchsia
Gladiolus
Iris
Rose

A floribunda rose (see page 186)

JUNE

June is something of a payoff month in the Victory Garden. The work load is relatively light and there are many new flowers making their first appearance, among them baby's breath, balloonflower, bee balm, Canterbury bell, Carolina phlox, Carpathian harebell, clematis, coreopsis, delphinium, English daisy, flax, foxglove, gaillardia, perennial hollyhock, iris, early lily varieties, lupine, Maltese cross, Oriental poppy, painted daisy, peach-leafed bellflower, shasta daisy, and sweet William. We also have the late-flowering bulbs still, including the commanding giant allium. The roses are in. And while the annual garden has another few weeks to go before it peaks, some of the cool-weather annuals, like sweet peas and snapdragons, are still with us for as long as the weather stays on the cool side.

Most of the work this month in the Victory Garden is concerned with maintaining the garden's appearance and good health. This is the time I put a warm-weather mulch on the annuals and perennials, which helps keep moisture in the soil and weeds under control. Mulches are handsome as well. This is also the month when weeding must begin; my philosophy on this chore is to do it early and often so that the garden looks its best and grows without competition from unwanted visitors. (For more about maintaining the flower garden, see the July feature.)

There are a couple of other small jobs. Inside, I like to sow some of the quick-growing annuals, such as ageratum, marigold, and sweet alyssum, so they're garden-size by the time the spring sowings lose steam, toward midsummer. Because the sun is warmer and brighter at this time of year, these plants will need less time to mature than did the earlier sowings, a phenomenon known as the catch-up effect (see the May feature). This is also the month when established rose plants should be given a feeding of 5-10-5 fertilizer in a ring about 6 inches from the plant's crown. And looking ahead, if you intend to divide your Oriental poppies this year, mark the plants' location clearly now so you'll be able to find them later in the summer, when the foliage will have disappeared completely (see the August entry).

A   **Fuchsia** Fuchsias are among the best loved of summer-flowering plants. There are upright varieties that are grown as bed plants, but the hanging types are more popular and it's these we've concentrated on in the Victory Garden. Both types produce remarkable, pendulous flowers in great number. Most gardeners buy plants already potted in hanging baskets. You could save a little money by buying 3 smaller plants and potting them yourself in a 10-inch pot; if you do this, buy the trailing varieties, not the uprights. Botanically, all varieties are *Fuchsia x hybrida*.

    Given a spot that is shady, moist, and cool, fuchsias will bloom all summer. They're an excellent porch plant for this reason; besides, it's wonderful to look up at those astounding pendant flowers while sipping an afternoon lemonade. The shade is particularly important to fuchsias. They can take full sun through May, but after that they will burn in anything stronger than filtered light. The soil must be constantly moist, which is sometimes a problem for gardeners who tend to forget hanging plants during their regular

One of the several varieties of cascading fuchsias

tours with the watering can. In the case of fuchsias this neglect is expensive because the leaves will yellow and wither fairly quickly if the soil dries out. The plants also need regular feeding with a standard houseplant fertilizer. Because newly purchased plants have probably been potted with slow-release fertilizer in the soil, I usually feed new fuchsias with half-strength fertilizer every third or fourth watering until I've had the plant about a month. At that point the slow-release nutrients are likely to be spent and the plant is better established, so I begin full-strength summer feedings with every third or fourth watering.

The only other care fuchsias need through the growing season is to have their seed berries removed (the flowers drop as they fade) and the branches trimmed occasionally to keep them from becoming leggy. At the end of the season, they can be cut back and held through the winter (see the October entry).

Standard-size gladiolus

A   **Gladiolus** In the Victory Garden, we plant the first of our gladiolus corms in April, so we have our first flowers for picking in June. They can be picked as soon as there is color in the bottom florets, but I prefer to wait until 5 or so of the lower florets have opened; this way I can enjoy them both in the garden and in the house.

Glads are such popular cut flowers that I'd like to pass along some hints that will give you the longest-lived bouquet. First, take a vase of warm water into the garden with you and put the flowers in as soon as you cut them. You don't have to arrange them at this point, just protect them from the drying air. When you cut the flowers, leave as much foliage on the plant as possible without compromising the length of your cut flowers. Take only as much stem as you need, because it is part of the plant's food manufacturing element, and the corm draws strength from the ripening foliage. After you pick the flowers, break off the top of the stem and 2 or 3 florets. These top blooms won't open anyway, and removing them seems to help the lower flowers open more fully. Finally, make sure you cut the bottom of the stems at an angle so the water can move up easily.

P   **Iris** The only irises that need attention in June are the bearded irises that have been in the ground 3 to 5 years and are ready for dividing. Now is the best time to do this, because the plants rest after flowering and they are less stressed by being dug and cut. With several seasons of growth behind them, bearded irises will have spread beyond their original site, but the centers of the plant will have lost vigor; all the healthiest growth will be at the outer periphery of the root mass, and it's these sections that should provide the new divisions.

Bearded iris roots are fairly shallow, so I dig up the whole clump at once, and shake off the soil. It's easier to work with these plants if some of the foliage is cut back; this is a smart idea anyway because there is bound to be root loss in the digging process and the top growth should be pruned accordingly. However, the foliage is the plant's food manufacturing element, and it should not be pruned more than necessary; I usually cut it back by about a half to two-thirds.

The best divisions are those known as double fans. These are Y-shaped, with two small rhizomes growing at an angle from a larger one; these are best because they will produce a good show the first year. Single fans, with one limb (and sometimes the stem) of the Y missing, will also develop into handsome plants, but they will take longer to do so. Unlike their beardless relatives, bearded irises are easy to divide. The roots are fleshy and simple to cut with a sharp knife.

Fans of bearded iris are also available on the market in early summer. You'll find that the double fans are more

A white-flowered bearded iris with an orange beard clearly visible

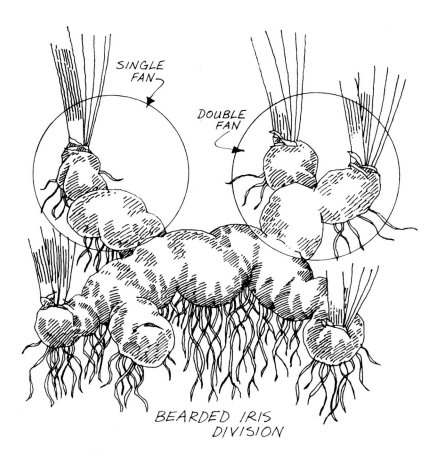

SINGLE FAN

DOUBLE FAN

BEARDED IRIS DIVISION

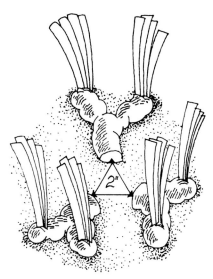

PLANTED RHIZOMES

expensive because they will produce a good show of color the first year; the singles need another season of growth before their flower show is impressive.

Whether you divide your own plant or buy rhizomes from a garden center, the planting technique is the same. The first step is to find a site with full or half-day sunlight, and then dig a hole about 18 inches wide and 12 inches deep. In the Victory Garden, the soil in the perennial border is well worked, but we add more organic material and bone meal to the excavated soil. We also test for acidity, adding lime if needed to bring the pH close to 7.0. Then we refill the hole and firm the soil.

Individual bearded iris rhizomes can be planted in an open bed, 6 to 8 inches apart, but I think the best-looking iris display is produced if the rhizomes are set 3 together in a triangle. They should be no closer together in the center than 2 inches; the ends with the vigorous young rhizomes should be pointed outward, and the feeder roots should hang down. The rhizomes should be covered by 1 to 2 inches of soil at planting time; as they become established, rain will wash some of this soil away, and the rhizomes will seek their own depth. So I scoop out a spot for them and then spread out the feeder roots so they aren't crushed under the rhizome. If the soil is dry, I water after planting.

Rose June is the month when roses are forgiven for all the trouble they cause. Across much of the country, this is the time they begin sending up those incomparable flowers. There's just nothing like them.

I like to pick a few roses for a bouquet and leave most of them on the plant. Cutting the roses is also a pruning process that establishes the plant's future growth pattern, so I make it a practice to distribute the cuts around the bush. If several roses are taken from one spot, the plant may lose its shape. Whether you want flowers for a bouquet or not, it's critical to prune flowering canes when the blossoms fade in order to guarantee that the plant will continue to flower.

The leaves of rosebushes are composed of either 3 or 5 individual leaflets; these are called either 3-leaf or 5-leaf eyes. The 5-leaf eyes are the important ones, as the buds at the base of these eyes produce the next flowering stems, which will aim in the same direction as the eye. The 3-leaf eyes are "blind"; they produce no flowering stems. For this reason, when flowers are cut from a rosebush, and when canes are pruned, they should always be cut just ¼ inch above a 5-leaf eye. The bushes need as much foliage as possible, so I never take more of the cane than I need when I

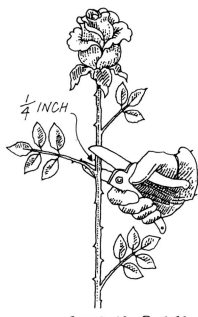

¼ INCH

CUTTING ROSES

A hybrid tea rose

cut. If possible, I leave at least two 5-leaf eyes on the cane, and cut just above one of them. It's important to use a sharp instrument to cut the canes, as the wood is tough and will be crushed by a blunt tool; there are special cutting shears designed just for roses.

The 5-leaf rule also holds when you are pruning away damaged or diseased canes. This is an important thing to do. Many diseases will spread quickly through a rosebush if they're allowed to take a foothold in unhealthy canes. For the same reason, make sure you keep fading flowers picked off, and clear fallen flowers and leaves from the ground around the plants. The cleaner the area is, the less chance for problems.

FLOWERS IN CONTAINERS

Growing flowers in containers — window boxes, pots, hanging baskets — has several things in its favor. For one, there is more effect per plant. A few marigolds in a garden bed are apt to look sparse and forlorn, but the same number of plants growing in window boxes can look bountiful and complete. Another advantage, and an important one for many gardeners, is that it may be easier to provide the correct light conditions to a container-grown plant than to a bedded plant. Because of their height above the ground, for instance, window boxes often enjoy more sunlight than does the ground below. Pots and hanging baskets have the added virtue of portability; they can be moved to spots where the conditions are right. Best of all, container culture brings gardening to people who have no more space outdoors than a balcony or window ledge several stories up.

There are more good things to say about container gardening than bad, but there is an important drawback: increased maintenance. Because there is a limited amount of soil, and because the sides of the container are exposed to the air and hot sun, the soil dries out and loses its nutritive supply very quickly. So containerized plants need both water and fertilizer more regularly than plants growing in a garden bed.

The Containers The most commonly seen containers for flower gardening are window boxes, pots, large tubs, and hanging baskets. There are also tall standup containers, shaped something like a pyramid of steps, that are designed to make the best use of limited floor space. (In my opinion, these are more efficient than they are beautiful.) Most of our containers in the Victory Gar-

den are purchased from garden centers, but with a little ingenuity containers intended for other uses can be adapted for growing flowers, and the cost of buying containers saved.

In the Victory Garden, a line of five redwood window boxes stretches the length of the greenhouse, where they are visible from both inside and out. Redwood is the most expensive material available for window boxes, but it's the best because it does not conduct heat (no wood does), and because it does not need to be treated with a preservative (as many woods do). Metal boxes, usually painted green, are commonplace and inexpensive, but a better alternative is a fiberglass or heavy plastic box or box liner that will not rust and will last much longer. Unfortunately, many of these commercial window boxes have no drainage holes; if I bought one of them, I'd drill the bottom so water can drain through (see below). If you make your own window boxes, and if you're willing to take them down in the fall and store them for the winter, you can treat pine with copper naphthanate, then paint or not, as you wish.

A good depth for a window box is 8 inches; the length and width can vary. Most window boxes are designed so the front wall slants outward slightly from the top to give trailing plants a full and graceful fall. The Victory Garden boxes are about 8 inches across the top and 6 inches across the bottom. Drainage holes are absolutely essential in window boxes and in all containers. Our boxes have holes an inch or so across

A tub of annual phlox, the variety Beauty

at 6-inch intervals on the bottom. We have patches of window screening over the holes to prevent loss of soil.

We've made extensive use of pot- and tub-grown plants, both in the Victory Garden itself and at our suburban site, where the wooden deck patio has been brought to life with a variety of flowers growing in containers. The important considerations in selecting pots are size and material. Because there is a problem with the soil drying and losing nutrients, large pots are necessary. There is no rule of thumb here, as the size of the pot needed will depend on the particular plant grown, so I've given specific suggestions in each of the entries where it's appropriate.

I have always veered away from using clay pots alone for container culture. The traditional clay pot is porous, which contributes to the drying-out problem. However, if you are devoted to the appearance of the old-fashioned clay pot, you can use a plastic pot as a liner. In addition, some of the newer glazed pots are better able to retain water, and they're very handsome; they're also heavier than plastic pots, so they're more stable in wind. (Clay pots often develop a white film around the outside from fertilizer salts leaching through; there's no way to prevent this.)

The advantage of plastic

A window box with deep purple nierembergia, lavender petunias, red geraniums, and yellow and pink snapdragons

pots is that they hold water and nutrients in the soil. We use plastic hanging pots, 8 or 10 inches across, for our basket displays. And generally we use plastic pots for floor or ground containers too. However, the largest standard plastic pot in the trade is 12 to 14 inches across; that's large enough for many kinds of container gardening, but not for all. If larger containers are needed, redwood, fiberglass, or special concrete composition tubs are the most available.

Soil Container gardening demands special soil, one able to hold water and nutrients well even through hot, dry weather. In the Victory Garden, we mix our own. Our basic recipe calls for 1 part peat moss or compost, 1 part garden soil, and 1 part builders' sand. (If I use compost, I screen it through ½-inch mesh screening.) The organic material gives this mixture body, and the sand will improve drainage. Then we add a slow-release fertilizer to the soil so the plants are given gradual doses of nutrients as they develop. I suggest a balanced fertilizer at this stage; in fact, most slow-release fertilizers are balanced, containing equivalent portions of nitrogen, phosphorus, and potassium. If

you are growing only a few plants in a container or two, you may prefer to buy packaged soil. If you do, make sure the mix is not entirely soilless. It should be at least ⅓ soil. The ingredients may not be listed on the package, but your garden center should be able to tell you which packaged mixes contain soil. (For more, see the August feature.)

Selecting Plants The best candidates for container culture are annuals and tender perennials, which usually have shallow roots and long flowering seasons. The most popular flower for container growth is the petunia, and while it's hard to argue with its popularity from an aesthetic point of view, the truth is that there are bet-

ter choices. Petunias often become leggy and ragged-looking by midsummer. They will revive if cut back, but there will still be a few weeks without color, and if they're planted in containers by themselves, this is conspicuous. Other well-liked plants, including ageratum, coleus, browallia, lobelia, and sweet alyssum, share this trait. One way out of this is to combine these plants with others that flower predictably all summer. If these are full-foliaged plants, they will obscure the sheared-back plants while they recuperate. If you want a one-variety container, the best

White sweet alyssum, red and white pinks, red geraniums, petunias, and dusty millers in the Victory Garden window box

choices are geraniums, dwarf marigolds, dusty millers, wax begonias, impatiens, verbenas, vincas, and dwarf zinnias.

Hanging baskets are best looking if they contain only matched plants, so the effect is of one large plant. (Three to 5 individual specimens may be needed to give this full look; one plant can rarely do it on its own.) Impatiens are good choices for hanging baskets; so are fuchsias and petunias.

When we plant either large pots or window boxes, we lean toward variety. For instance, one of the favorite Victory Garden window-box combinations is geranium, dusty miller, and lobelia. In a large pot or tub, where there is more soil available, you can combine vegetables or herbs and flowers, for instance a bell pepper, parsley, or rosemary in the center of a pot, surrounded by cascading lobelias. If you've never tried this, be sure to use a big container and be conservative with the number of flowers you add. The danger is that the flowers will overwhelm the vegetables.

Planting The first step is to add about an inch of drainage material, such as gravel or clay shards (a clay pot broken into pieces about 1 inch across), to the bottom of the container. This improves air and water circulation through the soil. Next, fill the container with the soil mix. I usually fill the container to the rim, set the plants in, and then firm the soil, bringing the finished soil line to about 1 inch below the rim of the container. When planting window boxes, the tall plants should go along the back, and the shorter toward the front. Cascading plants should be at the front edge; they can be tipped forward slightly as they're set in so

they immediately aim out and over the edge.

The display will look fullest if the plants are set in at the minimum recommended spacing (see the April feature), but they will also become overcrowded quickly and require more maintenance. I recommend planting at the maximum spacing, and letting the plants fill out through the summer.

Care It's an axiom that containerized soil dries out quickly and needs frequent watering to support plant life. This is especially true in midsummer, when the days are hotter and the root systems nearing maturity. In the spring, though, when the seedlings are small and the weather gentler, there is actually a danger of overwatering. The best gauge, all season long, is to water when the top ½ to 1 inch of soil dries out. Be sure the soil mass is completely moistened; don't stop watering until the water starts to come out the bottom of the container. If you use a packaged soilless mix for your containerized plants, you will have to water very carefully. These mixes tend to

Coleus and upright tuberous-rooted begonias, an excellent combination for container culture in a shady area

pull away from the sides of the container when they become dry, and water runs right out along these spaces without penetrating to the roots.

Because they grow in a limited quantity of soil, containerized plants need fertilizing more frequently than bed plants. In the Victory Garden, I feed them every other week with a solution of water and a water-soluble fertilizer. This is the same mixture we use as a transplant solution.

Containerized plants tend to draw attention because they are isolated and framed by the container. So they need special watching to keep them looking their best. They should be pruned if they start to lose their shape, if stems break, or if the plants suffer insect or disease problems. Fading flowers should be removed, both to improve the appearance of the plant and to prevent a loss of vigor. (For more, see the July feature.)

JUL

Monthly Checklist

Alyssum
Balloonflower
Bee Balm
Canterbury Bell
Carpathian Harebell
Columbine
Delphinium
English Daisy
Flax
Forget-Me-Not
Foxglove
Gaillardia
Hollyhock (Perennial)
Lupine
Maltese Cross
Painted Daisy
Pansy
Peach-Leafed Bellflower
Purple Loose-Strife
Rose
Shasta Daisy
Strawflower
Sweet William
Tulip

Long-spurred columbine (see page 199)

JULY

July brings hot, dry weather to the Victory Garden, so this is the month when a good reliable watering system is a must. In order to avoid spreading diseases, which take a foothold in moist foliage and flowers, I recommend an arrangement that works at ground level, watering the soil but not the plants. As an alternative, you can use one of the overhead sprinklers if you water in the morning of a sunny day and give the garden several hours to dry before nightfall. Where moisture is concerned, most annuals have to be watched particularly closely, as their root systems are too shallow to probe for deep water. (For more about watering, see this month's feature.)

Annuals need other attention this month as well. Most of them come into flower in the Victory Garden early this month, usually producing a good flush of blooms, then dropping off slightly. I like to scatter 5-10-5 fertilizer on the soil just after that first flush, to provide the plants with some quick energy for the remainder of the season. With the hot weather, some of our annuals lose steam this month, particularly petunias, sweet alyssum, ageratum, and (the biennial) English daisies. Petunias and sweet alyssum can be cut back now and allowed to grow back and flower again later in the season, but ageratum and English daisies have little future and are better pulled and replaced with healthy, young plants.

Most of the work this month is devoted to perennials. Next year's plants can be sown now, giving you an inexpensive way to grow precisely the plants you want, without paying garden-center prices in the spring. Established plants need some attention, too. Late-blooming irises can be divided now (see the June entry). Early-flowering daylilies are also division candidates, as soon as they're finished flowering, but we usually leave this job until later (see the September entry), when we're less busy. Carolina phlox and painted daisies, if cut back after flowering, will come back into blossom later in the season. And several perennials, including Carolina phlox, can be propagated vegetatively this month by root cutting (see the August Oriental poppy entry); gaillardias, bee balms, and Marie's balloonflower can be propagated by stem cuttings. These vegetatively grown plants, once rooted, can be treated as the seed-grown plants, and set into the nursery row for the winter.

P **Alyssum** Through the 4-week blossom period in May and June, this low-growing perennial bears so many yellow flowers that the foliage is nearly hidden. This dense show of color is rather unusual for a perennial, but it's certainly welcome. Most varieties of alyssum are less than 12 inches tall and do well in full or half-day sunlight. In the Victory Garden we've grown a buttercup-yellow variety called Basket of Gold; depending on the growing conditions, it reaches heights of 6 to 12 inches and spreads 12 to 18 inches. Regardless of variety, alyssum is an excellent cold-weather perennial, hardy in Zones 3 through 8 (see the Appendix for the zone map). It makes a fine edging plant, and I have a few beautiful specimens in my rock garden at home.

A rock garden planting of alyssum, the variety Basket of Gold

Alyssum plants are fairly easy to find in garden centers in the spring, but they're also easy to start yourself, from seed. This can be done in late winter (February would be the month in the Victory Garden) so the seedlings could be moved to the open garden in April, after conditioning. These plants probably will not flower for another year.

I think, though, that it's a better idea for the home gardener to sow seeds in summer, winter the plants over in a nursery bed outdoors, and then move them to flowering locations in the spring (see the September feature). The seeds are sold by many mail-order catalogues; make sure when you're ordering that you're buying the perennial and not the annual seeds (unless you want the annuals, too). The botanical name for the perennials is *Aurinia saxatilis*, but they are apt to be labeled by their older name, *Alyssum saxatile*. The sowing technique is the standard one (see the August feature). In September, we move these young seedlings to a nursery row at 4- to 6-inch intervals; this is where they spend the winter, under a protective layer of mulch. For more about this nursery bed arrangement, see the September feature. Then in the spring (see April) they're ready to be moved to their permanent locations. They may or may not flower the first spring. (For alyssum that will flower the first year, barring unforeseen problems, you are better off buying a division in the spring.)

P **Balloonflower** As perennials go, the balloonflower enjoys a particularly long flowering season, from late June through late summer. In most varieties the flowers are white, purple, pink, or blue; just before the flower buds open, they swell into a rounded shape, and this is the balloon for which the flowers are named. Their botanical title is *Platycodon grandiflorus*.

In the Victory Garden I have concentrated on a variety called Marie's balloonflower, which has some unique traits. It is shorter, at 18 to 21 inches, than most varieties of balloonflower and it is propagated vegetatively rather than by seed. For this reason, I buy cutting-grown plants of this variety in the spring (see the April entry).

Most varieties of balloonflower, by contrast, are 2 to 3 feet tall. However, they have tidiness in their favor. They are able to support their own weight without staking, and once they reach a spread of 12 to 15 inches, they stay in bounds and do not need division. What this means to the gardener, of course, is less work.

Seedlings of tall varieties of balloonflower are sold by garden centers in the spring, but they're easily sown by the home gardener in midsummer, carried over winter in a nursery row, and then moved to the open garden in April. The seed-sowing routine is the standard one, described in the August feature. The only oddity worth noting is that the wintered-over plants will be very slow to send up growth in the spring; in fact, gardeners often assume that the plants have suffered winterkill. My advice is to mark the planting site well in the fall when you set the plants out, and then wait patiently in the spring for these latecomers to show their heads.

Because these plants are rarely divided, I usually start new plants of the standard varieties by seed. Marie's balloonflower can be propagated by stem cuttings in July (see the August feature), then wintered-over in a nursery row with other seed-sown perennials.

🅿 **Bee Balm** There are several important things to know about bee balm. It draws both bees and hummingbirds to the garden. It's very easy to grow, and tolerant to cold as

Adam, a variety of bee balm

low as Zone 4 (for zone information, see the Appendix). It does well in either full or half-day sunlight. It comes into bloom in June and continues through August with the right treatment (see the April entry). If cut back after flowering, it blossoms again in the fall.

Bee balms grow quickly. They reach a height of 3 to 5 feet their first year, and after 3 years in the ground, they'll be nearly the same distance across. So they need to be planted in a spot where their size is an advantage and not a drawback. And they need a good, big site with plenty of air movement allowed, because they're vulnerable to mildew problems. Regular division is necessary to keep them in bounds (see the April entry).

Divisions of bee balm are readily available from garden centers in the spring, and once you have a plant, you can multiply your collection by division in the spring or by stem cutting in midsummer. But for the first plant, it's easy to sow seeds in July, winter-over the plants in a nursery row, and then move them to flowering spots in the spring (for more, see the September feature). You could also sow seeds in February and probably have a few flowers the first year.

The seeds are somewhat out of the ordinary for the catalogue houses, especially in separate colors, but if you look around you'll find them. The botanical name is *Monarda didyma*. Most varieties are white or shades of red. In the Victory Garden we've grown Cambridge Scarlet, a bright cherry-colored variety known as Adam, and Croftway Pink. (Cambridge Scarlet cannot be propagated by seed, so we bought a division one spring.)

The sowing technique is the standard one (see the August feature). When the plants are 4 to 6 inches tall, I pinch the tips once to encourage branching. Some gardeners pinch the tips back through the spring, too, to control the plant's height, but we've never made a practice of this at the Victory Garden because bee balm is one of the perennials we count on to provide mass in the border.

ⓑ **Canterbury Bell** When I was a child, this biennial was one of my favorite flowers. It blooms only for 2 or 3 weeks, but it comes in June, a transition month between the spring and summer flowers. The flowers themselves are unique: bell-shaped with rolled edges, the colors muted and soft. The plants stand 2 to 2½ feet tall, with spreads of 12 to 18 inches. They like full or half-day sunlight.

Canterbury bells demand a fair amount of effort for a very short season — we pull them out entirely after flowering — but they have so much to recommend them that I

Canterbury bells grown from a mix

don't begrudge the work or time. Along with the rest of the biennials, I start them from seed in July. The seeds are sold through most of the major catalogue houses. Most of the varieties are simply identified by color; there aren't many differences otherwise. The various colors of soft blue, pink, and white are wonderful together, so the mixes are every bit as good-looking as the color-separated varieties. The botanical name is *Campanula Medium*. Sometimes they're known as cup-and-saucer plants, after the formation of the flowers. (For sowing information, see the August feature.)

In September, I move the seedlings to nursery rows at 4- to 6-inch intervals and later mulch them for the winter. Canterbury bells are hardy in Zones 4 through 10 (see the zone map in the Appendix), so they will live through the winter in most parts of the United States. Then in the spring (see the April entry), I move them to their permanent locations. I usually put Canterbury bells into the perennial border, where the soft colors blend well. But they would do well in the annual border too.

Carpathian harebells, the variety Blue Clips

P **Carpathian Harebell** Carpathian harebells are low-growing, long-season perennials. At maturity, the foliage is 4 to 6 inches tall; the flowers sit 1 or 2 inches above this. They spread fairly slowly, but after 3 or 4 years in the ground they'll be 9 to 15 inches across. (At that age, they need dividing. See the April entry.) They don't bear many flowers at once, but they have a long season, coming into bloom in June and continuing into September or October.

For new plants, sow these perennials in July, following the standard routine outlined in the August feature. Seeds are easy to find in garden catalogues. We've grown both Blue Clips and White Clips, which cover the entire available color range. The botanical name for Carpathian harebell is *Campanula carpatica*. When you're looking for seeds, it will be easy to be confused by the various types of *Campanula* that are available. Some are biennial (see this month's Canterbury bell entry). Several, Carpathian harebell among them, are perennial. All the species of *Campanula* bear soft-colored bell-shaped flowers, but the habits and shapes and hardiness vary from species to species. The message is: Make sure you're buying what you want.

Along with many of our other perennials, Carpathian harebells are started into growth from seed in July. (They will also flower the first year from seed sown in February.) The sowing routine is described in the August feature. Then, in September, I move the seedlings to the nursery bed at 4- to 6-inch intervals. After the ground freezes, they're mulched for winter protection along with the rest of the Victory Garden perennials. They're hardy in Zones 4 through 10. In the spring (see the April entry) I move the young plants to permanent locations along the front edge of the perennial border or in the rock garden. They're best in full sunlight, but they'll grow in half-day or even filtered sunlight.

P **Columbine** This is a spectacular plant that has always done well for us in the Victory Garden. The flowers, which appear for 2 to 4 weeks in June and July, are uniquely shaped and colored, with unusual long spurs. (The spurs are long, spidery petals that give the flowers a distinction all their own.) There is an extensive array of soft colors available, and many varieties are two-colored, the outer petals one shade and the inner cup another. The foliage is very appealing and tends to soften the looks of the garden. The plants are easy to care for as well. They're at their best in half-day sunlight, but they will grow in full or filtered sun too. They survive quite cold winters, being hardy from Zone

Long-spurred columbine in the perennial border at the Victory Garden

3 to Zone 10. (For the zone map, see the Appendix.) As a bonus, they attract hummingbirds to the garden.

There are many species of columbine available. The nicest are the tall ones — they mature at 3 to 4 feet tall and 18 to 24 inches across — especially the long-spurred hybrids (*Aquilegia x hybrida*). We have a beautiful specimen in the Victory Garden. We also have a dwarf plant called Nana. It bears purple flowers and grows 12 to 18 inches tall and 10 to 15 inches across; during the early summer blossom period, the flower spikes top the greenery by 6 inches or so. The botanical name for Nana is *A. flabellata*.

Columbines do not have an especially long life. They do self-sow, and can be treated as self-renewing biennials, but in the Victory Garden we pull seedlings, leave the original plant growing for a period of about 3 years, and then start new plants from seed in midsummer. The seed-sowing technique is described in the August feature; columbine seeds need light to germinate, so they should not be covered after sowing. In September, we move the young plants to the nursery bed with 4- to 6-inch spacing, along with our other summer-sown perennials.

P **Delphinium** Delphiniums are among the most familiar of perennials. The best known are the bee delphiniums (*Delphinium elatum*) and the most familiar of these is the hybrid strain Giant Pacific; in flower, they stand 4 to 6 feet tall, and as much as half of that height is in the tall pale flowers. The colors are lovely soft shades of pink, lilac, and blue, as well as white. In addition to these tall beauties, there are new shorter varieties worth attention, too. They're good-looking, a better scale for many gardens today, and they often don't need staking. Connecticut Yankee is a new strain of delphinium, and an All-America Winner; it stands about 3 feet tall, and bears shorter, looser flower heads than Giant Pacific, but in the characteristic colors. Blue Fountains bears large spiked flowers on plants only 18 to 24 inches tall. No variety of delphinium has much of a spread, no matter how long it has been in the ground. Giant Pacific varieties will be 18 to 24 inches across, and the shorter plants are in the range of 12 to 15 inches. Established plants will send up several flowering stems each.

In the Victory Garden, we've grown all these types at one time or another. They're all best in the full sunlight of the perennial border, but they'll do well in half-day sunlight, too. Hardy in Zones 3 through 7, delphiniums are very good in cold weather, not so good in hot. (For more zone information, see the Appendix.) They flower in June and July, and if they're cut back after they flower, they'll send up another,

Opposite: Pale and deep blue Giant Pacific delphiniums, with pink and red foxgloves in the background

less-vigorous, show in August and September. All that's involved, for both the tall and short varieties, is cutting off the flowering stem about 12 inches from the ground after the flowers fade.

Delphinium seedlings are commonplace in garden centers in the spring. Greenhouse gardeners can sow seeds in February for blossoms the same year, but it's simpler for the gardener without access to a greenhouse to sow seeds in July and mulch the plants for the winter; this will result in a sturdier, better-developed plant. All the major seed houses carry the seeds, usually in quite a wide selection. The general seed-sowing technique is given in the August feature, but delphiniums need just a bit of special attention to increase the rate of germination: the seeds should be put in the freezer for 5 to 7 days before planting. The seed company may do this before shipping, but I always play it safe and freeze the seeds myself before sowing them directly from the freezer.

ⓑ **English Daisy** This is the original daisy. Given the right weather and culture, it's actually a perennial (the botanical name is *Bellis perennis*), but in most northern gardens, including the Victory Garden, it's treated as a biennial (see the September feature).

At 6 to 9 inches all around, English daisies are good plants for the annual bed, or for any site where they're in full or half-day sunlight. They bloom for 4 to 6 weeks during June and early July, but they stop when the weather heats up, so we pull the plants after flowering and replace them with petunias or verbenas, or a small edging plant such as ageratum or alyssum.

English daisy seeds are very widely available, both from garden centers and seed houses. The flowers are white, red, or pink; otherwise there isn't much difference from variety to variety. It's usually possible to find both mixes and color-separated seeds. Like all our biennials, English daisies are sown in July for next summer's flowers. (The seed-sowing routine is described in the August feature.) English daisy seeds are very small, and quick to germinate. They have a tendency to damp off as young seedlings, so it's important to use a sterile soilless mix for sowing the seeds. The seeds need light for germination, so they shouldn't be covered after sowing. The seedlings are ready for transplant to six-packs in August, and for the nursery bed, spaced at 4- to 6-inch intervals, in September, along with other young biennials and perennials. After the ground freezes, all the plants are mulched to see them through cold weather (see After Frost for more about mulching).

Seed-sown blue flax

P **Flax** This beautiful perennial is tougher than its delicate looks would indicate. While it's best in full sun, it will grow in half-day or even filtered sunlight. The plant is neat, with small flowers and foliage. The plants are hardy in Zones 4 through 10 (see the Appendix for a zone map).

The most common flax is blue-flowered, 12 to 18 inches tall, and 9 to 12 inches across; the botanical name is *Linum perenne*. (This is not the plant grown commercially as the source of either flax or linseed oil.) We've had this plant in the intermediate position in the Victory Garden from the start. It's lovely with columbine, and with threadleaf coreopsis. It's also a nice choice for the rock garden, or as an edger along the front of the border. Flax blooms in June and July.

If you want to grow flax in your garden, you had better start the seeds yourself, as it's the rare garden center that will sell plants in the spring. Seed houses do sell the seeds, though, identified either as flax or *Linum*. My advice is to sow the seeds in July, winter them over in a nursery bed at 4- to 6-inch intervals, and then move them to their permanent locations in the spring (see the April entry).

Ⓑ **Forget-Me-Not** This biennial is recommended by its dainty blue flowers and by its tolerance for shady, moist conditions. It's at its best in half-day sun, but will grow in filtered sunlight as well. In the Victory Garden, we've put it into full sun in the perennial border, where it has also done beautifully. It's a plant that's easy to please, and very hardy (Zones 3 to 10); it has withstood our New England winters without suffering. (For a zone map, see the Appendix.) It blooms for about 6 weeks in May and June, forming compact plants 6 to 9 inches all around, so it is often used as a carpet among spring-flowering bulbs.

Most forget-me-nots are blue-flowered. There are white and pink varieties too, but they're rarely seen. Seed houses will concentrate on the blues, often several varieties in different shades. One caution when you're ordering seeds: there are several flowering plants called forget-me-nots, some annual, some biennial, and some perennial. The one described in this entry is a biennial; the botanical name is *Myosotis sylvatica*, but it's more apt to be listed as *M. alpestris*.

Biennial forget-me-nots are often available as seedlings from garden centers in the spring. They'll bloom in the summer from seeds sown in pots in February, but the average home gardener is better off sowing seeds this month. Then the plants can be wintered-over in a nursery bed (see the September feature), and moved to permanent spots in the spring. That's my routine for all the biennials in the Victory Garden. The seed-sowing technique is described in the August feature.

Ⓑ **Foxglove** Here is one of gardening's old favorites. The standard varieties of this biennial are straight and stiff-stemmed, only 12 to 18 inches across but climbing to heights of 4 or 5 feet. The Excelsior strain is unique in that it has flowers that circle the stem. As elegant as the tall versions are, the new shorter varieties, especially the All-America Winner Foxy, fill a real need in the garden. With a mature height of 3 feet, they're of a far more usable scale than the full-size varieties. Dwarf foxglove will spread to 12 to 18 inches. Regardless of variety, more than half the mature height of the plant is in the flower spikes.

In the Victory Garden, we plant both types of foxglove in the perennial border, where they receive the full-sun conditions in which they do their best. They also tolerate half-day and, especially in hot areas, filtered sunlight. After their 6-week blossom period through June and July, we pull the plants out and replace them with other tall-growing annuals, such as gladioluses.

Some biennials can be brought into flower if seeds are sown in late winter, but as a rule foxglove is not one of them. Foxy is the only variety that will reach flowering size quickly enough to be handled this way, and even it must be

Two of the colors available in the variety Foxy, a dwarf foxglove

sown in January for June flowers. Through the spring it becomes very large indoors, where it is subjected to long months of poor growing conditions. So without question the best way to propagate foxglove is to sow seeds this month, move the young plants to the nursery bed in September, mulch them for the winter, and move them to their flowering spots in April. (For more about this routine, see the September feature.) All the major seed houses carry seeds, usually in mixes containing many muted colors. Foxy is available only as a mix. Botanically, foxglove are known as *Digitalis purpurea*. The sowing routine is the standard one (see the August feature), with one exception: the seeds should not be covered after sowing, as they need light for germination.

P **Gaillardia** There are relatively few perennials that thrive in hot weather and full sun, but this is one of them. (They'll grow in half-day sunshine, too.) One handsome, tall variety is called Dazzler; it's more than 3 feet tall at maturity. There are also dwarf varieties, such as Goblin, no taller than 12 inches or so.

Goblin, a dwarf variety of gaillardia

In the Victory Garden, gaillardias will bloom heavily for most of the summer and into the fall, bearing numerous red or yellow flowers. In many varieties the flowers are red with yellow-tipped petals, which explains their common name, blanketflower. In some, the contrast between the colors is particularly pronounced. Most seed houses sell seeds for both the standard and dwarf gaillardias. The botanical name is *Gaillardia x grandiflora*.

Gaillardias are fairly quick to grow from seed, so they could be sown in the spring and still bloom the same year. However, I find that the flower show is better if the seeds are sown in midsummer, wintered-over in a nursery bed, and then moved to flowering locations in the perennial border in the spring (see the April entry). Therefore, I sow the seeds this month, following the sowing procedure described in the August feature. The seeds need light to germinate, so they should not be covered after sowing.

Gaillardias, once established, are easily propagated, either by stem cuttings this month or by division of the roots in the spring (see the April entry). The cutting-grown plants should be moved to the nursery bed in September and mulched for the winter; in other words, they should be treated like the seed-grown plants.

A single-flowered perennial hollyhock

P **Hollyhock (Perennial)** When I think of old-fashioned garden flowers, I think first of perennial hollyhocks. The color range is impressive, including red, white, yellow, pink, and shades between. All the colors, pastels included, are clear and strong. During the blossom period, from late June to August, the plants themselves will stand 4 to 6 feet tall, and as much as half this height will be flowers. All varieties of perennial hollyhock reach this height. There are no dwarf strains except among the annuals (see the March and May entries for annual hollyhock). Hollyhocks do have some problems with rust, but it can be managed (see the April entry).

Garden centers will sell seedlings of hollyhocks in the spring, but there's no reason why gardeners can't start their own plants from seed, as we do in the Victory Garden in July. Most seed catalogues will carry the Chater's varieties, either in mixes or by color. The botanical name is *Alcea rosea*. They're sown according to the routine outlined in the August feature, except that they're sown directly into six-packs. In September, they're moved to nursery rows. (The first-year foliage should *not* be cut back to control rust, as is the practice with established plants.) In the spring (see the April entry) these wintered-over plants are moved to their flowering site in full or half-day sun.

208 **JULY**

Lupine These tall perennials have in their favor a beautiful array of rich colors and cupped leaves that will trap a drop of rainwater, glistening afterward in the sunlight. Actually, their height is a factor only during their 4-week June flowering season, when the blooms are 3 to 5 feet tall. By the first of July or so, the long, flowering stalks have gone by and when they're removed, the handsome foliage that's left behind is only about 18 inches tall. The plants spread 12 to 18 inches across during their first season, and don't spread much more. They're at their best in full sun, but they'll grow on half-day sunlight too.

Opposite: Standard-size Russell lupines

Lupines are short-lived plants that will last only 3 or 4 years. They're not good candidates for division, so they have to be resown every few years for a new collection. I suggest sowing seeds this month, and wintering the plants over in a nursery bed. (Those of you with greenhouse facilities may prefer to sow the seeds in February for same-year flowers.) All the major seed houses carry the seeds of the Russell strain, which is the best type available; the botanical name is *Lupinus polyphyllus*. There are both dwarf and standard Russells, but in the Victory Garden we've concentrated on the standards because they are so graceful. The dwarf varieties are stocky and less appealing.

The seed-sowing of lupines follows the information in the August feature, with some important modifications. The germination rate for this plant is poor, so I begin with a technique designed to encourage the seeds to sprout. First I freeze the seeds for 2 days, then I put them directly from the freezer into warm water where they soak for 24 hours. Because lupines are legumes, I dust the seeds with a nitrogen inoculant — available as a powder from most garden centers and farm supply stores — which helps the plants take nitrogen from the air. Then I sow the seeds directly in six-packs, 2 or 3 seeds to a compartment. They're not sown in a communal pot and then moved to six-packs because they do not transplant well. Like many perennials, lupines do not have an especially good germination rate. I find that about half the seeds in the package will sprout.

Maltese Cross The perennial border in the Victory Garden, having been designed as a demonstration site, has undergone many changes in the years since it was first planted. The plants that have survived those changes have done so mostly because they are reliable and beautiful and we don't want to lose them. The Maltese cross has been such a plant. A division of the original still occupies the space at the back of the border where its parent was planted on a rainy spring day many seasons ago.

The colors of the Maltese cross, while limited to red, pink, and white, are vivid and strong. The flower heads themselves are large, so the overall impact of the plant is very dramatic. The stems are stiff, so the flowers are good for cutting. The plants blossom through June and July, and again in September if cut back after the first flowering for another, less dramatic, period of blooms. The plants are 2 to 3 feet tall, and about the same dimension across. There are no dwarf varieties. Maltese cross plants are hardy throughout the country, in Zones 3 to 10. (See the Appendix.)

This is another perennial that can be sown from seed this month, wintered-over in a nursery bed, and moved to its flowering spot in the spring. (For sowing, see the August feature.) The seeds are sold by many of the seed houses. The botanical name is *Lychnis chalcedonica*; the common name Maltese cross derives from the shape of the individual florets.

These perennials need sun, preferably all day, though half-day sunshine is acceptable. I have them in a spot where they occupy the middle and back sections of the perennial border. Their growth rate is such that they need dividing every 3 or 4 years (see the April entry). Established plants can also be propagated by stem cuttings taken in July and wintered-over as you would a seedling.

If you can provide them with the right indoor growing conditions, Maltese cross seeds can also be sown in February for same-year flowers. (In the spring, garden centers are apt to carry both divisions and seedlings.)

P **Painted Daisy** Painted daisies are actually members of the genus *Chrysanthemum*, but they were long known by the botanical name *Pyrethrum*, and this has stayed with them. By either name, this is an excellent perennial. The color range is limited to white, red, and pink, but within this range there are many beautiful shades.

The flowers rise on tall, strong stems, so they're good for cutting. The June blossom period is about 4 weeks long, and the plants will flower again in late summer if they're cut back to the foliage rosette when the first flowers fade.

Garden centers usually sell seedlings in the spring, but you'll probably have better plants if you sow seeds yourself in July and winter-over the plants in a nursery bed (see the August and September features). The seeds are available from most of the mail-order houses, identified as *Pyrethrum roseum* or *Chrysanthemum coccineum*. The most common variety is Robinson's Mix, which we've grown and liked in the Victory Garden. The foliage is 15 to 20 inches tall, topped during blossom time with flowers that are 6 to 9

inches taller. The plants reach horizontal dimensions of 12 to 15 inches and stay there neatly in bounds. Robinson's Mix is a single-flowered variety, but its flowers are larger than even the doubles. If you buy double-flowered varieties, there will still be some singles in the package.

Robinson's Mix, a variety of painted daisy

(B) **Pansy** Pansies will bloom in late spring from seeds sown in February, and for this reason they are increasingly grown commercially as annuals. This saves the professional grower time in producing one of the staples of the bedding plant business. In my opinion, the home gardener is better off treating pansies as biennials, which is closer to tradition. Either way, pansies bloom from spring to frost.

Pansy seeds are as easy to find in garden catalogues as the plants are in the spring, but they're much less expensive. There are many varieties, most with distinctively bi-colored flowers. The old-time varieties gave way in summer heat, but new ones can go all summer. If you live in a hot area, buy one of the varieties singled out for heat-tolerance.

Planting pansies in the Victory Garden

The varieties are categorized by the size of the flower, and many of the categories suggest hugeness — giants, majestics, jumbos. The largest flower on the market now is 3 or 4 inches across, which is certainly jumbo by comparison to the original plant, with flowers an inch or so in diameter. For my own taste, I like pansy flowers when they're no more than 2 inches across; to my eye, the large flowers are a visual burden to the small plants, which range in heights from 6 to 12 inches. Regardless of variety, the spread of a pansy plant is 6 to 9 inches. (For sowing directions, see the August feature.)

P **Peach-Leafed Bellflower** I've always been fond of this perennial. It sends up simple, small blossoms in clear white or blue. It has a long flowering season for a perennial, blossoming for about 8 weeks through June and July. It provides long-stemmed cut flowers. It's a rugged, large plant that can be planted in the middle of the perennial border or given a larger spot and allowed to naturalize. It grows well

White Pearl, a variety of peach-leafed bellflower

in full or half-day sunlight. It's pest-free and long-lived. The plant reaches a height of 2 to 3 feet, and spreads to a modest 12 to 18 inches.

Peach-leafed bellflowers are readily available from garden centers in the spring, both as seedlings and as divisions, but in the Victory Garden we start our own seedlings in midsummer. The seeds are a trifle hard to find, but they are sold by some of the mail-order seed houses. The botanical name is *Campanula persicifolia*. There is nothing demanding about sowing the seeds; the routine is outlined in the August feature. Along with our other perennials, the seedlings are moved up to six-packs when their true leaves develop, and then into a nursery row in the garden in September. After a winter under a thick blanket of mulch, they are ready in April to be moved to their flowering spot. (For more about the timing of seed-grown perennials, see the September feature.)

Peach-leafed bellflowers require division every 4 or 5 years. See the April entry for more.

P **Purple Loose-Strife** Though it is not native to this country, purple loose-strife is so at home here that it has become naturalized along river banks from coast to coast. (According to folklore, the odd name is based on the plants' ability to calm farm animals so that they, and presumably their owners, lose strife.) It thrives in moist areas and will, if saved from drought, tolerate a range of sunlight conditions. It's at its best in half-day sunlight, but it will grow in full or filtered light, too.

Purple loose-strife blossoms from mid- to late summer, sending up deep rose-purple flowers on slim, tall spikes. If they're deadheaded (see this month's feature) so the cut lies 2 or 3 inches down in the foliage, they'll branch and produce more flowers. These plants are both graceful and sturdy — they can stand without staking — but given their size they're better alone or in a large, casual perennial garden.

For a new plant, your choices are to spend money buying divisions in the spring, or to spend only a few pennies and sow the seeds yourself this month. The seeds may not be readily available, but they are sold through many catalogues, particularly those that specialize in wildflowers. Two species are usually available: *Lythrum Salicaria* and *L. virgatum*. There are more varieties available in the latter. The sowing procedure is described in the August feature. Once you have a plant, you can propagate it either by stem cuttings in midsummer or by division in spring (see the April entry).

P **Rose** In midsummer, there are few of us who like to think that there are measures we should take in preparation for winter, but it's true where roses are concerned.

Most of today's hybrid roses have warm-weather roses in their parentage, and for this reason they do not have the inclination to dormancy that makes hardy perennials hardy. Herbaceous perennials die back completely, right to the soil line. In a woody perennial the stiff stems or trunks of the plant live from season to season, but the leaves and flowers die back, and the plant's system slows considerably. So without a tendency to dormancy in their genetic makeup, roses, which are woody perennials, do not respond to cooling weather by slowing their growth. They just keep on sending out tender new green leaves, which prevents the canes from properly hardening and makes the plants vulnerable to winter's cold.

This is where the gardener comes in. There are several things that can be done, beginning in mid-July, to urge the plants to slow their growth. The first is to allow the plants to set seed by leaving some flowers on the plant to ripen. Another step is to reduce the amount of water applied by hose; there's nothing you can do about the rain, but reducing moisture will cause the plants to slow down. I also stop fertilizing the plants completely. And I pull back any

warm-weather mulch from around the stem, so the exposed ground cools early in the season.

For information on mulching roses for the winter, see After Frost.

🅟 **Shasta Daisy** Daisies of all sorts are among the most popular flower shapes in the garden. This is a fondness I share. Those simple, forthright flowers are just irresistible. The shasta daisy is particularly favored because it is white-flowered, like the wild daisy, and very unfussy. It's good for cut flowers, too. In sum, a fine plant.

Shasta daisies are easy to come by, whether you buy seedlings or divisions in the spring, or sow the seeds. The correct botanical name is *Chrysanthemum x superbum*, but *C. maximum* is used, too. Unless you have a greenhouse where you can keep the plants happy through the spring from a late-winter sowing, I suggest following the routine for sowing perennials that is detailed in the September feature: sow the seeds in pots in July, move the seedlings to six-

One of the more double-flowered selections of dwarf shasta daisy

packs when the true leaves develop, then transplant them into the nursery bed in September. When the cool weather approaches, cover the nursery bed with a 4- to 6-inch layer of mulch to see the plants through the winter. Then move the plants to their permanent flowering spots in the spring (see the April entry).

Standard-size shasta daisies are 3 feet tall and 2 feet across, but we've grown only the dwarf varieties in the Victory Garden; most of these are 1 foot tall, with a spread of 12 to 18 inches. All varieties come into bloom in June and continue into August.

A **Strawflower** This flower is among my favorite choices for drying, but there are many others that can also be treated this way with beautiful results. The criterion for good dried flowers is that they hold their posture, flower shape, and color for a long period. As a general rule, the best time to pick flowers for drying is just before they peak, as this timing seems to help them hold their color and shape. However, you can give your arrangement a more varied look by picking flowers at several stages of maturity, some more open than others. (For other candidates for drying, see the March entries for celosia, globe amaranth, scabiosa, and statice, and the April entry for baby's breath.)

Regardless of the particular flower, the drying technique is the same. First, pick the flowers with 6 to 12 inches of stem. Then, strip off all the leaves, and cluster like varieties (or an arrangement of several varieties) together. Wrap a rubber band around the base of the stems; as the stems shrink in the drying, the rubber band will constrict and continue to hold the flowers in place. Then hang the bou-

A Bright Bikinis strawflower, mature enough for a fresh bouquet but too open for drying

quets upside down in a dry shaded place, using a paper clip as the hook. They'll be dried and ready for display in a dry vase in 2 or 3 weeks.

B **Sweet William** This is our favorite Victory Garden biennial, especially in the dwarf sizes that are no more than 6 to 9 inches tall at maturity, with a spread of 9 to 12 inches. The full-size varieties are 12 to 18 inches tall, and 15 to 18 inches across. Both types bloom for about a month in June, sending up flowers that are white or one of several bright shades of red or pink.

If you intend to let your plants self-sow (see the April entry), give them a spot with full- or half-day sunlight. On the other hand, if you decide to pull your plants after flowering, they'll survive their short season in filtered light. In the Victory Garden, we've planted sweet Williams among spring-flowering bulbs. They also contribute to the changing pattern of color in the perennial border; a combination of spring-flowering bulbs, sweet Williams, summer-flowering annuals, and hardy chrysanthemums will provide an overlapping succession of flowers all season long, from early in the spring until after frosty weather arrives in the fall.

Tall Double, a mixed variety of full-size sweet William

Being biennials, sweet Williams must be sown in midsummer of one year for flowers the next. There are several varieties sold by seed from mail-order catalogues; they are all mixes. The dwarf variety we've grown in the Victory Garden is called Pinocchio. Sweet Williams are easy plants to grow from seed (see the August feature). The seeds germinate well and the plants are undemanding as they develop.

Ⓑ   **Tulip**   There are several ways to treat tulips (see the October entry). If you've decided to heel in your bulbs in some inconspicuous spot so you can save them for another year (see the May entry), then July brings the last phase in the process. Usually by this month the foliage has died, leaving no sign of green growth, which means the bulbs are ready to be dug and stored.

The first step is to dig them up and cut off the withered foliage. At this point, the bulbs should be divided; every mature bulb will split into 2 or 3 smaller bulbs that are held together, usually, at the basal plate. Dividing them

A bed of Darwin hybrid tulips at the suburban site

means simply pulling the two halves apart. Make sure you work with one variety at a time so you can keep them separate for your fall planting (see the October entry).

For the remainder of the summer, the bulbs should be kept cool, dry, and dark. I usually store them, variety by variety, in onion bags that I hang from the floor joists in my basement. This also keeps the bulbs away from mice. If your storage area is a little damp, I'd advise using either dusting sulfur or a fungicide such as ferbam or thiram before storage.

MAINTAINING THE FLOWER GARDEN

Where the maintenance of a healthy garden is concerned, the gardener's best friend is a keen eye. If you watch your garden closely, if you look at the flowers and the buds and the stems and the undersides of the leaves at least once a week, you'll often be able to spot problems before they get out of hand. This hardly seems like necessary advice — what is more appealing, after all, than flowers at close range? — but I know well enough that many gardeners like to hope that the garden will take care of itself, which it won't.

Weeding Many gardeners consider this the dregs of gardening, and all too often they postpone the job until the flowers are being choked by weeds as tall as they are. My advice is to weed often, starting early in the season. Once a week, routinely, remove any weeds that have sprouted. Remember that any plant, including a volunteer seedling of a self-sown plant, must be considered a weed if it's growing where you don't want it. If the weeds are very close to your cultivated plants, use one of the hand-weeding tools on the market to slice the weed stem just below the soil line. If you try to pull weeds out of this position, you're apt to disturb the root system of the plant you are trying to grow. You'll find that a warm-weather mulch (see below) will cut down dramatically on the weeding chore.

Watering In most years, and in most sections of the country, the spring is moist enough that gardeners do not need to worry about watering the entire garden. Of course, plants must be watered individually when they're set in, and a direct-sown seed bed must never be allowed to dry out, or germination will fail. But the task of watering the whole garden doesn't usually become necessary until summer, when there is less rainfall, when the sun is blistering hot, and when the plants have developed large, thirsty root systems.

Plants vary in the amounts of water they need. Because their root systems are deep and water-retentive, bulbs and perennials are usually able to withstand dry periods, but if there's a prolonged drought, it makes sense to water them; by all means respond if you see the foliage wilting. (Roses are a special case; see the May entry.)

The plants to watch are the annuals. Because they are shallow-rooted, and because they grow and flower so actively all season long, they need a more constant supply of water than do other plants. The rule of thumb is that they need an inch of water a week; an inch of water will penetrate about 6 inches of dry soil. It is difficult to estimate the amount of water the plants are receiving without some sort of gauge. The simplest gauge is a metal can, but garden centers sell devices designed specifically to measure very small amounts of water, which the can does not do well.

If the heavens do not provide your annuals with the necessary inch of water a week, you will have to do so. The best time to water the garden is in the early morning of a sunny day. If you wait until midday when the sun is hot, you will lose much of the water to evaporation. And if you wait until late in the day, the plants will go into the evening with wet foliage, which is an open invitation to disease. The best way to water is in fairly long periods so the soil is well-soaked occasionally rather than lightly moistened frequently. Light sprinklings don't penetrate deeply enough into the soil; this may restrict the plants' roots to the top few inches of soil, which in turn makes them even more sensitive to drought, while restricting their growth.

If the garden area is small, and if you're willing to make a few trips, you may be able to water successfully with a watering can. You might just spray manually with the nozzle end of a hose; there are some good attachments available to break the stream of water so it is not too harsh for the plants.

Any manual method of watering requires time, and there is the temptation to become tired of the job before it is quite done. In the Victory Garden, we rely on systems that can be left alone to do their work and turned off when they're finished.

There are two main categories of watering equipment, though there are several variations within each. The first is the overhead sprinkler, which sends a fine spray upward into the air so that as it falls on the plants it has the gentleness of rain. This is the cheaper, and in some ways the easier, method, but because many flowering plants are susceptible to moisture-related diseases, I think this type of device is best limited to the vegetable garden, or used only on sunny mornings.

In the Victory Garden, I favor drip irrigation for flowers. In its simplest form, drip irrigators are hoses laid on the ground giving out only a small trickle of water, moistening the soil but not the foliage or the flowers. The gardener can accomplish this by setting up the hose and moving it around the garden so that each section is watered, but to do a garden of any size would take hours, and there is always the danger that one section or plant would be shortchanged. The more efficient move is to buy a soaker hose. In the old days these were canvas, the water dripping slowly through the fabric. Now they're usually plastic, with holes punched at intervals along the length. Any kind of soaker hose must be snaked through the garden carefully so that complete coverage is assured; the hose manufacturers

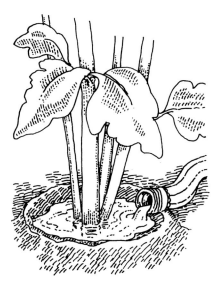

TWO DRIP
IRRIGATION
TECHNIQUES

will provide directions for this. Drip irrigation is much slower than overhead watering, requiring at least three times as long to set down the same amount of water, but the water goes to the roots where it's needed, with a minimum of runoff, evaporation, and wet foliage.

Fertilizing Plants need many nutrients for good growth. In particular, they need three elements in substantial quantities: nitrogen, phosphorus, and potassium. Each makes a contribution to plants' vigor. Nitrogen helps plants grow quickly and develop full foliage with good color. Phosphorus encourages sturdy growth and aids in the ripening of flowers and fruit. Potassium helps plants ward off disease and the effects of cold weather.

Growing plants actually consume the soil's nutrients. In nature, the process of decay replenishes the soil, but in the garden, where plant refuse is cleared away and this natural cycle is disrupted, the gardener must regularly add fertilizer to keep the plants properly nourished and looking their best.

Most plants need a balance of all the major elements. For this reason, commercially marketed fertilizers are rated according to the amount of each that they contain. The rating is written as a series of three numbers, representing nitrogen, phosphorus, and potassium, always in that order; this rating is sometimes known as the NPK scale, after the elements' chemical symbols. Most flowering plants do best if the ratio is 1-2-1 or 1-2-2; in other words, they need twice the dosage of phosphorus as they need of nitrogen, with the amount of potassium matching either one. The reason for the low nitrogen percentage is that nitrogen encourages foliage growth, and too much can result in lush leaves at the expense of flowers.

Several materials will add nutrients to the soil. Organic matter, while more valued for the role it plays in improving the soil's structure (see After Frost), will also increase fertility. In fact, animal manures have traditionally been the farmer's primary fertilizer. The problem with organic material is that its composition is not predictable; with animal manures, for instance, the nature of the manure will vary according to the animal's diet and other factors. Because it is not predictable, there is the possibility — in fact, the likelihood — that the plants will be overfed or underfed one or more elements if the gardener or farmer is not both skilled and knowledgeable.

Marketed organic fertilizers, such as bone meal, blood meal, and fish emulsion, are predictable. Any commercial fertilizer, whether organic or manufactured, must by law describe the composition on its package. The advantages of these materials is that they are natural, they act slowly and last a long time, and they also contribute organic material to the soil.

Manufactured fertilizers may rely entirely on produced chemicals, or they may combine these with organic materials; the label will indicate this. These fertilizers are generally referred to simply by their NPK rating, such as 5-10-5. They have certain advantages over strictly organic fertilizers.

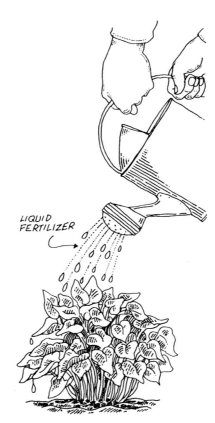

LIQUID FERTILIZER

GRANULAR FERTILIZER

TWO METHODS OF FERTILIZING

For one thing, they're less expensive. For another, they are available in different forms, so the gardener can choose one that acts very quickly or one that is pelleted to release its nutrients slowly.

In the Victory Garden, I use all of these substances, and I think that's the best route for the home gardener, too. The organic matter and organic fertilizers provide both body and fertility, while the chemical fertilizers provide the vigorous start and the quick release of nutrients that plants need. When the soil is prepared in the fall, we work in organic matter and bone meal. We also make sure that the pH of the soil is correct, because this helps release the nutrients in the soil; if the pH is off, many of these nutrients may be chemically inaccessible to the plants. (For more, see After Frost.)

We add more fertilizer in the spring. Just after setting out annual seedlings, we add a teaspoon of commercial fertilizer, usually 5-10-5 or 5-10-10, in a ring around the drip line, that is, the outer periphery of the foliage, of each plant. Before planting perennials and bulbs, we add a dusting of bone meal to the soil. Regardless of the kind of fertilizer used, it's important that it be worked into the soil before the plants are set in, so that the roots are not in direct contact with the fertilizer. Because the danger at this point is overfertilizing, my advice is to be sparing and err on the side of too little rather than too much. An overdose of fertilizer can not only burn roots, it can force the plant to grow too quickly, which produces weak, succulent stems and foliage.

In addition to a fertilizer added to the soil, newly set plants also benefit from an overhead meal of transplant solution. Any water-soluble complete fertilizer, dissolved in water, will do the job. As an alternative, you can use a manure "tea," which is made simply by putting 2 or 3 cups of fresh or aged manure into a cloth sack, and leaving it to soak in a standard 12-quart pail filled with water. By the next day, the tea that results will make a fine transplant solution. And as you use the tea, you can replenish your supply by adding more water, and occasionally changing the manure.

At intervals through the growing season, such as just after the annuals' first major show of flowers, I give the plants an extra boost by applying a manufactured fertilizer, either 5-10-5 or 5-10-10, under the drip line. Over time, water will carry the nutrients down to the plants' roots.

Once the growing season is well under way, it is often necessary to fertilize plants in a mulched bed. In this case, pull the mulch back, put the fertilizer on the bare soil, and replace the mulch.

Pests and Plagues

Along with many other gardeners, we in the Victory Garden are moving rapidly away from the use of manufactured chemicals to control insect and disease problems. Where once we sprayed regularly in order to stop damage even before it became visible, we now wait longer to act. We don't let things get out of hand, but we tolerate a few insects and spotted or discolored leaves. When we do act, we rely on all the time-honored tricks in the bag; it's a case of the old dog learning old tricks. Organic preventives and controls may be less effective in the short run than the all-out punch of commercial insecticides and fungicides, but many work very efficiently, and they have no potentially dangerous side effects.

Some species are more vulnerable to certain diseases than others, and often within species there are differences from variety to variety. Whenever we can, we buy resistant varieties. Most annuals are bred for disease-resistance, but the catalogues do not always note which are best. The best friend in this case is experience; if a particular plant seems to draw hordes of insects or spends the summer with spotty leaves, we just don't grow it again.

Healthy plants are far more able to fight infestations and diseases than are weak ones, so one of the best ways to prevent problems is to provide good growing conditions (see the April feature). In addition, the garden should be kept clean of plant refuse, so that disease spores and insect colonies are not allowed to multiply at their leisure on the surface of the soil. Finally, we scrutinize the plants regularly, looking under leaves, into flowers, and along tender new stems and buds. Thanks to resistant varieties, diseases are now easier to control, but they haven't disappeared by a long shot. Often, the early signs of disease damage are spots or discolorations, followed by mushy-textured leaves and defoliation. Insect damage may appear first as curled or chewed leaves, either with obvious bites or tiny pinprick holes. With very small insects or those that feed at night, these signs of trouble may be visible before the insects themselves. Many insects act as carriers of diseases that are in themselves difficult to control, in which case the solution is to control the insect.

Fungi are responsible for many other diseases that show up in the garden: black spot, powdery mildew, damping off. If we spot the beginning of a disease, we remove the affected parts of the plant whenever we can. This is not always effective in stopping the disease, as it may have spread into the plant's system. If the disease reappears and threatens the plant's life, as well as the lives of surrounding plants, we use an eradicative fungicide, one designed to cure.

There are also preventive fungicides that must be used for certain diseases that cannot be stopped once they take hold. Your county agricultural agent is your best source of information on this score, as plant diseases vary from area to area.

Though the breeders are at work on this, at present most of the progress in plant resistance has been in the area of diseases rather than insects, which are as much of a problem now as they ever were. If organic measures fail and an infestation becomes large enough, they'll eat their way right through the garden. My best advice is to be alert and try to match your response to the level of the problem.

In the Victory Garden, if we see an insect problem starting, we use the manual approach first, picking off large insects one by one and removing them from the garden. Populations of tiny insects, like aphids, can often be washed from the plants with a spray of water. They won't all be killed by this shower, but they'll be knocked down to the soil; eventually they'll climb back up, at which point they can again be washed down. In the Victory Garden, a regular weekly shower is enough to keep aphid damage at a minimum.

As my next line of defense I pull out one or two badly infested plants in an effort to reduce the insect population dramatically. This can be an unhappy task, but it's better to lose one plant than several. Think of it as an opportunity to change the garden a little by adding a replacement plant.

If all else fails and the problem is very serious, I use an insecticide. There's a common misconception that organic insecticides are always less toxic than those manufactured in a laboratory. This is just not true. Nicotine sulfate is organic, and one of the most lethal substances known. Environmentally, the advantage of organic over nonorganic insecticides is that they break down much more quickly; there is a great deal of work being done in laboratories to improve manufactured insecticides on this score.

If you need to buy an insecticide, here is some advice. Do some homework so you're sure what insect you have and what insecticide will kill it; again, your county agricultural agent is the best adviser. Then, buy only the amount of insecticide you need, which usually means buying the smallest package available. Follow the package directions to the letter. Then store unused portions carefully, out of the reach of children and animals. Most insecticides are far more dangerous in storage than they are on the plant.

As a group, fungicides are less potent than insecticides, but they must be treated with the same respect, used in moderation, and very carefully stored.

Deadheading and Pruning Deadheading is the removal of faded flowers. There are two reasons to do this. One is simply appearance. Fading flowers are not attractive, whether clinging to the plants or cluttering up the floor of the garden, where they can create an environment conducive to pests and diseases. All plants, including annuals, biennials, perennials, and bulbs, benefit from this procedure, and if the refuse is composted, the whole garden is the better for it for years to come. (Don't add diseased plant material to the composter, or refuse that has been treated with an herbicide.)

Another important reason to deadhead is to prevent plants from going to seed. In nature, the production of flowers is a necessary precedent to the production of seed, and when the plant reaches its quota for seed production, it stops flowering and loses vigor. In annuals, this is a long process, during which the plants

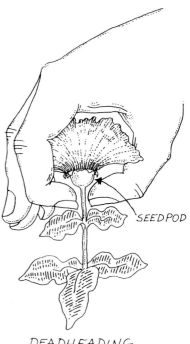

SEEDPOD

DEADHEADING

SHEARING BACK

bear great numbers of flowers and seeds simultaneously. In perennials, it's more common for the plants to send up their flowers for a short season, at the end of which they produce their seeds. Either way, if the faded flowers are cut from the plant, along with the seedpod that usually joins the flower to the stem, the plants' reproduction schedule is interrupted, and the production of seeds stopped. In truth, many new hybrids, particularly double-flowered types, are sterile and will flower without producing a single viable seed. These plants do not need to be deadheaded to prolong their flowering season. However, sterile hybrids are not often identified as such in garden literature. So the

smart gardener still maintains a vigilance over the garden, removing faded flowers before they wither completely. At the very least, this keeps the garden looking its best, and in many cases extends the flowering season by delaying the production of seed.

With some plants, gardeners have a tendency when deadheading to pull the petals from the plant without removing the seedpod. This does maintain the appearance of the garden, but does nothing to delay seed production. You have to be sure that the seedpod is removed. If the flowers are within or slightly above the foliage mass, all you need to do is use thumb and forefinger to snap the seedpod and flower off. If the flowers sit high above the foliage, remove the entire flower stem so that unattractive flower stalks are not left behind.

Many annuals lose steam in midsummer, but can be revived for more blossoms if they are cut back as they begin to look ragged (these are noted in the entries). Unless a plant produces clouds of wispy stems and flowers, I don't find that shearing the plant off produces good results, though it is one approach. Instead, I cut each flower stem individually, just above a leaf node, when the last flower is fading. This procedure is more work, but it leaves the plant looking better than if it were sheared.

In some plants, removing the faded flowers one by one is simply too much of a task. I put Swan River daisies, sweet alyssum, and lobelia in this category. The solution is to shear off the whole canopy of flowers in one clipping, when the flowers have gone by. The amount to shear depends on the plant (see the entries), but the general rule is to remove the flower heads and seedpods while leaving as much foliage on the plant as possible to help the plant reestablish itself.

Another alternative to either of these barbering techniques is simply to pull annuals from the ground when they are no longer attractive and replace them with healthy, young plants. This is one of the great advantages to maintaining a backup supply of seedlings, in pots or a nursery bed, that are at the ready to replace plants that have gone by; in this way the garden is always young and fresh and in flower.

Staking Many plants with a mature height over 18 inches need staking if they're to stand up straight. There are two kinds of staking that will take care of most plants in the garden. Peripheral staking surrounds a large plant with supports and holds the entire weight of the plant in bounds. Single staking supports an individual stem.

When in place, the stakes should be pushed or pounded at least 6 inches into the ground, and be 6 to 8 inches shorter than the height of the mature

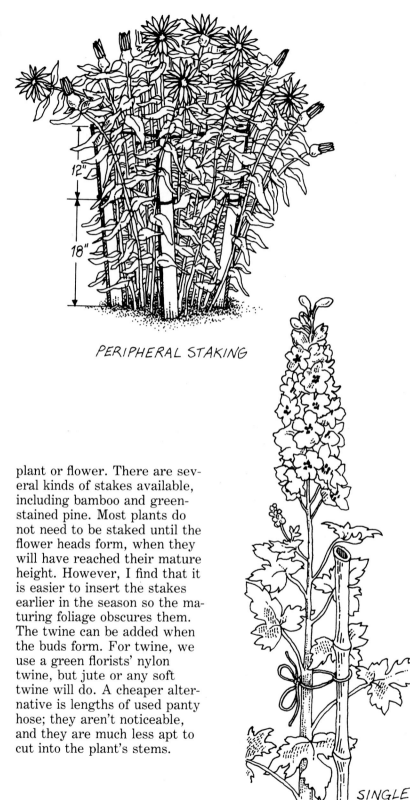

PERIPHERAL STAKING

SINGLE STAKING

plant or flower. There are several kinds of stakes available, including bamboo and green-stained pine. Most plants do not need to be staked until the flower heads form, when they will have reached their mature height. However, I find that it is easier to insert the stakes earlier in the season so the maturing foliage obscures them. The twine can be added when the buds form. For twine, we use a green florists' nylon twine, but jute or any soft twine will do. A cheaper alternative is lengths of used panty hose; they aren't noticeable, and they are much less apt to cut into the plant's stems.

MULCHING
YOUNG
PLANTS

Mulching By covering the soil, mulches serve several functions. Winter mulches (see After Frost) keep temperatures constant, and prevent the repeated freeze-thaw cycle that can heave unprotected plants out of the soil over the course of the winter. In summer, warm-weather mulches keep the soil moist and cool, conserve water, present a handsome appearance, and, in the bargain, cut down on weeds.

The oldest warm-weather mulch is the dust mulch, which is nothing more than the top ½ inch of topsoil cultivated and loosened with a hand weeder to dry out rapidly. While the rest of the soil stays moist and cool, this dry surface presents an inhospitable seed bed for weed seeds. It's neither expensive nor difficult to dust-mulch. It's also not as attractive as some of the mulching materials. And the soil has to be recultivated after every rain or watering.

In the Victory Garden, we add a mulching material to the surface of the soil. We use either wood chips, shredded pine bark, or nugget pine bark. For appearance, the shredded pine bark is a good choice because it's the most natural looking. Wood chips are the least expensive of the three, and also handsome. Nugget pine bark is the most expensive of these materials, but it has the advantage of being available in a variety of milled sizes, each package containing only nuggets of uniform size.

There are other mulching materials that are either readily available around the yard or inexpensive to purchase. These include salt marsh hay, pine needles, grass clippings, and black plastic. Some gardeners use one of these less-costly mulching materials for the annual garden, where the plants tend to fill in quickly and obscure the mulch anyway, and reserve the more expensive materials for the perennials, where the mulch is visible all season.

Regardless of the material selected, we wait until June, when the soil has had a chance to warm to 55 or 60 degrees, and then add a layer of mulch 2 to 3 inches thick. The important thing about applying the mulch is to keep it at least 2 inches from the plants' stems. At the end of the season, we remove these mulches when the garden is being cleaned out. The wood chips and pine bark can be saved to be used again. The coarser the material, the longer it will last.

Monthly Checklist

Artemisia
Chrysanthemum (Perennial)
Geranium
Impatiens
Lily
Oriental Poppy

Hardy chrysanthemum (see page 231)

AUGUST

It is during the hot, dry months of summer that gardeners most appreciate the annuals that can hold their own in heat, including Red Mound aster, gazania, gloriosa daisy, marigold, and vinca. These plants are particularly welcome now, when scorching weather proves to be too much for many annuals. If there are any that look seriously ragged, I just pull them out and replace them with one of the quick-growing plants sown in June. This not only rejuvenates the garden midseason, it also offers an opportunity to introduce another plant or two, and give the garden a new look for the fall.

The winding-down days of summer also spell the winding-down of some of our perennials, including bee balm and shasta daisies, which are two of the longest-flowering perennials available to the gardener, both blooming from June through August. But to make up for the loss, there are several new perennials coming in now, including garden phlox, some of the later varieties of lily, and purple loosestrife. And if they're treated properly after their first flowering season, there are some perennials that will make a second appearance this month, including painted daisies, baby's breath, and delphiniums. These second comings are never quite as showy as the first period of bloom, but they're a nice end-of-the-summer bonus.

In the Victory Garden, this is the time we move perennial seedlings, sown last month, to six-packs as soon as the true leaves appear. Aside from this, August is a fairly easy month in the flower garden, and a good time both to catch up on old jobs and to plan ahead for the fall. Daylilies can be divided now, rather than in September, as long as they've had a chance to conclude their flowering period. This is a good time to plan next spring's bulb garden. If you do this far enough in advance of your planting time, you will be able to read the bulb catalogues leisurely and order your bulbs by mail, taking advantage of the greater selection offered by the mail-order houses. (For more about bulb gardens, see the October feature.)

Rooted cuttings of Silver Mound artemisia

P **Artemisia** Artemisias are among the most trouble-free perennials available, but they do need a little attention in August to keep them looking their best.

In late summer, artemisias usually try to flower. If they're allowed to do this, the foliage often becomes coarse and the plant rank. So as soon as there's a sign of a flower (or early this month, even if there are no buds in sight), I cut the plant back by ⅓ of its height. The new growth that comes in for the fall will be fresh and young.

At the same time, as long as foliage is being cut anyway, you can start new plants from stem cuttings of non-flowering stems. This is the most practical way to propagate artemisias. The stem cuttings should be 3 to 4 inches long, and it's a good idea to remove all but the top 1 inch of foliage. If there are flower stems on the cutting, these should be removed, too. Dip the cutting in rooting hormone and set it into damp sand or perlite, and roots should form in about 2 weeks. At that point, the young plants should be moved to a pot of soil. In September, I add these cutting-grown artemisias to the nursery bed at 4- to 6-inch intervals, and from then on treat them as I do seed-grown perennials (see the September feature).

P **Chrysanthemum (Perennial)** It's the job of perennial chrysanthemums to help summer exit in style. These most familiar of garden plants blossom in the fall, in response to shorter periods of daylight. No variety blooms for more than 3 or 4 weeks, but by selecting several types it's possible to keep the garden in chrysanthemum flowers from late August through several fall frosts.

Chrysanthemums for the most part do not come true from seed. Mail-order catalogues do offer seeds, but these tend to be mixes of single-flowered plants only. For the best selection of named varieties, gardeners look to plants that have been propagated vegetatively, that is, by stem cutting or division. These include the full range of flower colors, shapes, and sizes. The least expensive way to begin a collection is to buy young plants, usually in 2½-inch pots, from garden centers in the spring. Most gardeners wait and buy potted plants in the fall, when garden centers carry little else. The plants will come on the market in August, and my advice is to buy early, and look for plants in bud but not yet in flower so you can enjoy their full blossoming season.

Most of the varieties available will be the cushion-type chrysanthemums that form mounded plants 10 to 15 inches all around; the flowers appear at the tips of each stem, making for a helmet of color over the leaves. (There is another type of chrysanthemum, known as upright, which is taller than most gardeners want, and not widely grown as a result.) There's almost no limit to how the plants can be used. I've put them into the perennial and annual beds for spots of color, grown them massed together by variety for a spectacular carpet effect, and I've seen them in window boxes and pots. As long as they're in full or half-day sunshine, and given a spot 12 to 15 inches across, there's no limit to their usefulness in the garden.

Perennial chrysanthemums (*Chrysanthemum x morifolium*) are known as hardy or garden chrysanthemums, but these words implying weather-tolerance stretch the point a little. While chrysanthemums are usually considered hardy in Zones 4 through 10, they are only winter-dependable in 6 through 10 (for a zone map, see the Appendix). In well over half the country, including the Victory Garden, chrysanthemums need special attention to see them through the winter. If you can spare the space, you can lift the plants after frost and set them into a cold frame. In our garden, all the perennials are treated to a thick blanket of mulch after the ground freezes (see After Frost), and the chrysanthemums are included here. They get no special attention beyond this, and we generally have a fairly good survival rate every year. Gardeners who live in Zones 3, 4, or 5 and who send their chrysanthemums into winter unprotected would be lucky indeed to see new growth every spring.

Chrysanthemums need regular division to keep them looking their best. They will go 2 years without this treatment and still produce handsome plants, but by the third season they will be so crowded that the flower show will be noticeably poorer. (See the April entry for division.)

A hardy spoon-type
chrysanthemum, so named
because of the petal shape

Potting geranium cuttings in perlite

By August, our wintered-over plants will have buds on them, so we move them out of their nursery beds and into flowering spots in the garden, spacing them about 1 foot apart. I usually give them some liquid fertilizer in the form of transplant solution at that point.

A **Geranium** Until fairly recently, the best way to maintain and increase a geranium collection was to take cuttings of garden plants in late summer and grow them indoors over winter. The improvements in seed propagation (see the February entry) have made this routine less critical to the geranium-loving gardener, but it is still an option if you can provide the indoor conditions they require to do well through the winter. They'll be healthy enough on 4 hours of sun daily, but they need 6 to 8 hours in order to flower indoors.

The cuttings should always come from young plants, not the same parent stock year after year. And of course the plant should be healthy if it is to produce another generation. The cuttings should be 3 or 4 inches long, and come from nonflowering stems. I always snap the cuttings from the branch by hand because cutting tools can spread disease and geraniums are rather disease-prone. Then, to save the cuttings unnecessary effort, I usually remove all but the top 2 or 3 leaves. After I dip the end of the stem in rooting hormone, I set it into a six-pack filled with sterile soilless mix. For the 3 weeks or so that the cutting takes to root, I keep the six-pack under plastic to conserve moisture. When the roots fill out the compartment, I transplant the cutting to potting soil and a 3-inch pot. Seed-grown geraniums and their cutting-grown offspring need no pinching, but plants that are vegetatively propagated should be pinched back 2 or 3 inches when they reach 6 to 9 inches in height. (Vegetatively propagated geraniums are still sold by garden centers. They can be identified by their double flowers and variegated foliage. Neither of these characteristics appears in seed-grown plants.) Indoors, geraniums should be watered thoroughly when the soil is slightly dry. If they're in bloom, they need a feeding twice a month; otherwise, once-monthly feedings will do. (For more about stem cuttings, see the August feature.)

If you have a potted plant, you can cut it back hard in the fall and bring it indoors before frost. It will probably live, but I wouldn't expect too much of it. The cutting-grown plants will be much better.

A **Impatiens** As is true of many tender perennials grown in the summer flower garden, impatiens can be grown as houseplants all year long. It's not a good idea to try to dig

New Guinea hybrids, varieties of impatiens that are propagated only by stem cuttings

up the whole plant from the garden — it's too much of a shock for them to do well indoors — but cuttings can be taken and rooted by the dozens, not only providing a full array of houseplants for the winter, but multiplying the collection for the following summer.

Flowering stems of impatiens do not make good choices for cuttings because they seem to produce poor or unbranched plants. I think the best idea is to cut the plants back, wait 3 weeks or so for new stems to develop, and then take those for cuttings before flower buds appear. (This same procedure applies to wax begonias.)

For more about rooting stem cuttings, see this month's feature.

B **Lily** Lilies are tall-growing bulbous perennials. I'm speaking here of true lilies, or garden lilies; the botanical name is *Lilium*. The range of choice is enormous, from fragrant Easter lilies (*L. longiflorum*) to exotic varieties available only from specialty houses. Some are 5 feet tall, others not much more than 1½ feet. Culturally they are all treated the same, so my advice is simply to select the height, flower color, and blossom season you want. They bloom for 4 to 6 weeks, some as early as June, others in July or August.

Lily bulbs come on the market in the spring, from garden centers, and in late summer from the mail-order houses. They are dug after they have flowered and their foliage has matured, when they are least stressed by the move, and either sold immediately or held in cold storage until the following spring. They aren't dormant when dug, though, or at any time in their cycle, so if not kept chilled they should be planted immediately, which we do in August. Once

A hardy lily, the variety Lilium speciosum rubrum

they're in the ground they're long-lived and dependable; each year they'll bear more flowers than the year before, all with just a minimum of attention.

The best site for lilies is one where the foliage receives full or half-day sunlight while the roots stay shaded and cool, and where the soil is well prepared and well drained. In the Victory Garden, our lilies are in the perennial border, where low-growing neighboring plants keep the soil moist and cool. If you are setting the bulbs into a new site, do them and yourselves a favor and work the bed carefully, following routine soil preparation. (See the September feature.) Lilies will spread a distance of 9 to 15 inches, depending on the species and variety. If you buy top-size bulbs, they will probably reach this spread their first year. The shorter the plant, the narrower. The bulbs should be planted 6 to 8 inches deep, with room enough to spread.

Lily bulbs divide every year. They can be left permanently in place until they become so crowded that flowering and growth decline; then they can be divided, after they have flowered but before the leaves yellow. It may take a season or two for the smaller bulbs to flower. Whether you divide or not, it's a good idea to add a dusting of 5-10-5 or 5-10-10 fertilizer (see the July feature) to the soil in the spring. Varieties more than 18 inches tall will need a single stake to help them support the weight of their flowers. When I do this, I put the stake at least 3 inches from the stem so I don't pierce the bulb when I push the stake down into the soil. I usually put the stakes in position when the plant reaches ½ to ⅔ of its projected height, or before this if the stems seem to require it.

P **Oriental Poppy** Oriental poppies (*Papaver orientale*) are unique in that the only time of the year when they can be safely handled without soil around their roots is after they've died down, usually in late July or early August. If they're jostled during their growth period, they die. If you want to propagate an Oriental poppy, you can either divide the roots or use a method called root cuttings. Division will produce the largest plants in the shortest length of time, but root cuttings will produce many more plants than division.

For a division, dig the whole clump up first. The entire root system will be vigorous, without the loss of strength seen in the centers of many perennials. The roots are not particularly tough, so you should be able to take several divisions, 4 to 6 inches across, and plant them in improved soil with a space 12 to 15 inches across to grow into. (There is no need to divide the plants unless you want to multiply your collection. They will stay within bounds for years.)

If you want more plants than is reasonable by division, then root cuttings will do the job. You can either use a spade to take a section of roots, leaving the main plant behind, or you can dig up the whole plant and then take the cuttings; in this case, some of the brittle roots are bound to break off and stay behind, which will result in natural root cuttings that will grow and maintain the clump. Oriental poppy roots are pencil-size, and each section of a root will produce a new plant. The only tricky part of this is making sure that you maintain the orientation of the roots — that you know which end was closest to the crown of the plant — because the tops of the root pieces will produce stems and

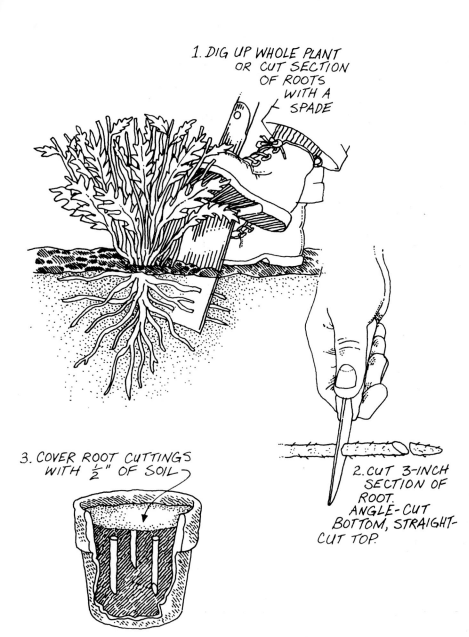

1. DIG UP WHOLE PLANT OR CUT SECTION OF ROOTS WITH A SPADE

3. COVER ROOT CUTTINGS WITH ½" OF SOIL

2. CUT 3-INCH SECTION OF ROOT. ANGLE-CUT BOTTOM, STRAIGHT-CUT TOP.

the bottoms will form roots. I usually keep tabs on this by cutting the tops of the roots squarely and the bottoms at an obvious angle; this way there's no confusing them.

The actual process (see the illustration) is simplicity itself: I place 3 or 4 pieces of root, each 3 inches long, top sides up, in a 4-inch pot filled with potting soil; the tops should be covered with about ½ inch of soil. Within a month new leaves will develop above the soil, at which point the cuttings can be unpotted, separated, and planted directly in the garden. Sometimes I leave the cuttings potted and set the pots in the cold frame for the winter. They'll be of flowering size in 2 years.

Opposite: The Oriental poppies in full command of the perennial border at the suburban site

PROPAGATION AND PLANTING

Starting Plants Indoors Established flowering plants, even young ones, are expensive because the buyer is paying for the nursery's materials, staff, and equipment. Most gardeners buy plants because it's so convenient, but I would like to encourage you to start plants yourself. There are a few species that are better bought because they are slow growers or difficult to manage without greenhouse equipment, but most can be propagated even by the novice. The basic choices are only two: either start the plant from seed, or take a stem cutting.

Sowing Seeds I don't recommend sowing flower seeds directly in the garden, though this is a popular way to start a bed of annuals. I'm against this route for two reasons. One is that the seeds cannot be sown until the weather is warm enough for the emerging plants to survive. The other is that there are always spots where germination fails, or plants develop poorly. I think it's better for home gardeners, as long as they can provide bright light, either natural or artificial, to sow seeds in pots indoors, and introduce only the best of the resulting seedlings to the garden.

Here's the routine I use to do this. For most plants, I start with a 4-inch pot which is big enough to give all the seeds room, at least for a while, but not so big that it occupies needed space unnecessarily.

SOW THINLY

SEED SOWING IN A POT OR SIX-PACK

However, some plants resent the transplant operation that is necessary to separate the seedlings later. These plants, identified in the entries, are better

sown 2 seeds to a compartment in six-packs. When the seedlings are a couple of inches tall, the weaker of the two in each compartment should be cut off at the soil line.

The germinating medium should be sterile, as emerging seedlings are very prone to damping-off fungus, which lurks in many nonsterilized soils. We use a packaged soilless mix, a blend of peat moss and vermiculite. Many of these mixes contain a great deal of peat, which tends to resist cold water when it's bone dry. I like to wet it before sowing so the newly planted seeds aren't flooded and moved about by watering. Because I usually use an entire bag of soilless mix at once, I water it with *warm* water while it's still in the bag, and then work with an already moistened medium. (If you are only using a little of the mix at a time, it's probably smarter to put the mix into the pot dry, sow the seeds, and then set the pot in 2 inches of warm-to-hot water for an hour or so; it will take this long for the medium to become thoroughly moistened.)

Next I fill the pot with moistened medium to within about ¼ inch of the rim of the pot; if the soil is too low, the seedlings are deprived of both light and air circulation. The soil must be firmed slightly before planting. I just put a same-size pot on the soil and press slightly. If the seeds are to be covered, I sow them directly on this surface, cover them with a loose layer of soilless mix, and then firm it down. If the seeds are not to be covered — some require light for germination, or are so small that they would be easily smothered — I put this thin layer of loose soilless mix on top of the firmed mix and sow the seeds on top, letting them nestle down into the loose mix. Then I firm the soil lightly.

The seeds should be sown as thinly as possible so the emerging seedlings have space to develop. This is easy enough with large seeds because you can see what you're doing, but some tiny seeds are hard to handle and hard to see when they land on the soil. One solution to this is to buy pelleted seeds if available. A less-expensive alternative is to mix the seeds with a little dry sand, and then sow both. The sand is easy to work with and quite visible.

Most seeds germinate best if the soil temperature is about 70 degrees. Normally, soil temperature is about 10 degrees below room temperature, which means that in most houses the soil is too cold for good, speedy germination. One solution is a heating cable, of which there are several on the market. Don't try to substitute a heating pad. Another possibility, though not quite so efficient, is to put the pots on a shelf near the source of house heat, such as on a mantel over the fireplace or near a radiator. Sometimes you can even set the pots on top of the refrigerator, as long as it's one with the heat vents close to the top; the only worry with this is that they'll be forgotten up there and allowed to dry.

Dryness is the major peril seeds face. Once the germinating process has begun, they cannot be allowed to dry out at all, or the tiny seedlings will die. Bottom heat, from whatever source, dries the soil more quickly than usual, so the moisture must be very carefully watched. It helps if the containers are covered with a transparent plastic material. If there are several pots together

on a heating cable, a sheet of plastic kitchen wrap will do. In other arrangements, you can wrap each pot in a plastic bag.

Germinating seeds, even those that need light to germinate, should not be put in the sunlight. They don't need it, and they will only dry out all the more quickly. If they're covered with plastic, the sun will actually bake the seeds in hot, trapped air.

The germination period for seeds is written on the seed packages. Generally it is a week or so. During this period, I keep an eye on the seeds, and when a few have sprouted, I remove the plastic covering and move the sun-lovers to a spot in the sun. Plants that prefer filtered light I put into bright, indirect light, but keep them out of the sun. The remaining seeds will probably have begun to germinate, and will break through in a day or two.

Stem Cuttings Many perennials can be started from stem cuttings, which are merely the tips of nonflowering stems of a healthy, growing

A HEALTHY STEM CUTTING READY FOR ROOTING

SEVERAL STEM CUTTINGS READY TO ROOT

plant. The cuttings should have at least 2 leaf nodes on the stem, so I generally take sections 3 to 6 inches long. The cuttings should be green and succulent, not old and woody. Most plants root fairly easily, but to be on the safe side, I usually take several cuttings, even if I am only interested in one mature plant.

The next step is to remove extra leaves so that the plant isn't overtaxed during the rooting period. At the very least, any leaves below the soil line should be removed. I usually remove even more than this, leaving only the top 2 or 3 leaves, or the top inch of foliage if the leaves are too small to count. Then I dip the cut ends of each stem into rooting hormone, a powder readily available from gardening centers. Finally, I set several cuttings together, 1½ to 2 inches apart, in a bulb pan filled with perlite, vermiculite, or coarse sand, making a hole in the rooting medium with a pencil before setting the stem in.

Then I firm the medium around the stem and water the pot thoroughly. Before I cover the pot with plastic kitchen wrap to conserve moisture, I mist the cuttings lightly and insert wooden plant labels into the rooting medium to keep the plastic from touching the leaves. Then I set the pot into bright light out of the sun.

The amount of time needed for roots to form will vary from plant to plant, from a week to a month or more. Bottom heat (see above) will hurry things along.

Growing On Whether young plants are started by seed or cutting, they need similar attention as they grow on toward maturity and planting time. They need to be transplanted to larger quarters as they increase in size. And depending on the plant being grown and the time of year, they need pinching to encourage bushiness and conditioning to acclimate them to weather changes.

Transplanting Seedlings are ready for transplant to larger quarters when they develop their true leaves. This will be the second set of leaves the plant grows, but the first to bear the characteristic leaf shape. On the average, true leaves form about 3 weeks after sowing. (There are a few exceptions to this rule that need more time before they can be moved. These are noted in the entries.) To transplant the seedlings, I just knock the soil ball from the pot and drop it onto a table from a height of 4 or 5 inches. After this gentle fall, the seedlings can be lifted easily from the medium.

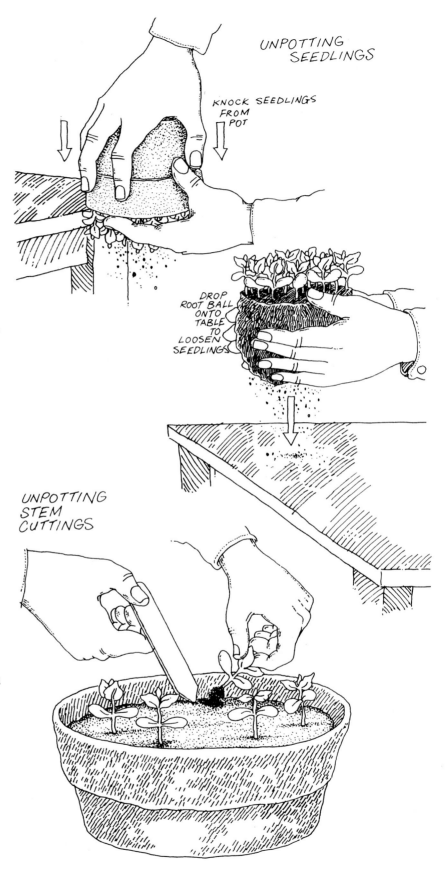

UNPOTTING SEEDLINGS

KNOCK SEEDLINGS FROM POT

DROP ROOT BALL ONTO TABLE TO LOOSEN SEEDLINGS

UNPOTTING STEM CUTTINGS

Stem cuttings should be moved when the roots are about 1 inch long. Although one knows roots are forming by the appearance of new leaves, there is no way to determine the length of the roots without looking. If I think they're ready, I use the thumb and forefinger of one hand to hold one of the plant's leaves, then with the other hand I prick the root ball gently free of the soil with the tip of a plant label. If the roots haven't grown enough, I firm them back into the soil and leave them for another few days.

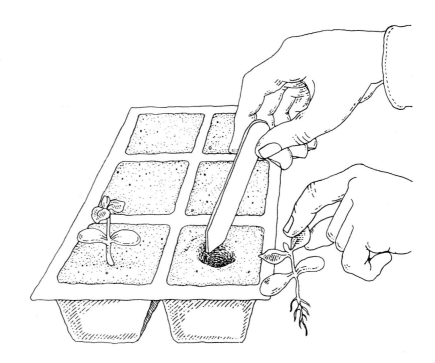

In the Victory Garden, seedlings go next into individual compartments in six-packs filled with packaged soil. Because cuttings are larger, I set these into individual 4-inch pots. Regardless of the container, the important aspect of this step is to be sure to set the plant in at the same level at which it grew previously.

If for some reason you hold your plants inside for long enough to become crowded in their second growing quarters, by all means move them on into 1-inch-larger containers. I often move my seedlings and cuttings 3 times or more before they're planted in the garden. Because the home gardener can rarely provide good growing conditions indoors, I think it's generally better for you to keep your plants indoors for as short a time as possible. In this book, seed-sowing of both annuals and perennials is timed to produce plants just filling out their six-packs by the time they're due to be planted outdoors.

Pinching Many plants are multibranched, and produce flowers only at the tips of these branches. Sometimes plants like these branch naturally. Sometimes varieties have been improved in this regard by breeders. And sometimes the plants' natural tendency to branch is not quite as pronounced as the gardener would like; these are the plants that can be helped by pinching.

Pinching is an extremely easy procedure. You simply remove the tip of the plant (see the illustration) with your thumb and finger, leaving about ¼ inch of stem above the leaf node. Even taking this tiny bit of the plant will force the subsequent growth outward, producing a plant that is shorter and bushier than it would otherwise have been. I generally take the first pinch when plants are 3 to 6 inches tall, and then pinch the resulting branches when they're 3 to 6 inches tall themselves. The important thing to keep in mind is that pinching delays flowering by 2 to 4 weeks, more in some species.

As helpful as pinching is in encouraging dense foliage, there are some plants that do not require it, and others are damaged by it. Among those that do not need pinching are

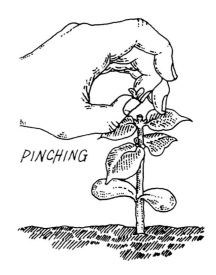

PINCHING

annual vines, such as morning glories and sweet peas, upright nasturtiums, and any plant that requires shearing, such as sweet alyssum and Swan River daisies. Among those that are damaged by pinching are baby's breath, celosia, cleome, gazania, globe amaranth, gloriosa daisy, annual hollyhock, trailing nasturtium, nicotiana, scabiosa, statice, and strawflower.

Conditioning To do their best, plants need bright, warm days and cool nights; this is nature's proviso. When plants are sown in the spring and grown indoors, where light levels are relatively low and temperatures are more constant than outside, they become leggy and weak. If they were moved directly into the full sun and changeable temperatures and humidity of the open garden, they would be extremely stressed, just as a pale-skinned person is on the first hot, sunny day at the beach. Even greenhouse plants, which have been in conditions close to

Seedlings becoming conditioned in the cold frame

those outdoors, will find the change a strain.

So before young plants can be set into the garden in the spring, they need to be conditioned to its harsh realities. There are several ways to do this. One is to cut down on the amount of water the plants receive, letting the soil dry out some between waterings. Another is to put them outside for gradually longer periods during the day and bring them in at night, which accustoms them to the light and temperature conditions outdoors. The third — and best — way to condition seedlings is to use a cold frame (for construction, see the March feature). We put most of our annual seedlings into the cold frame for 5 to 7 days before they are moved to the garden.

Plants sown or rooted in the summer do not need this treatment. They can be set outside as soon as they are moved to six-packs, as long as they're given a day or two indoors, out of the sun, after the transplant operation. Outdoors they should be kept in a spot where the light conditions are right for the plant — shade-

lovers do well in a lath-covered cold frame — and where they will not be overlooked at watering time. They are in very little soil, and will dry out quickly in hot summer weather. So keep an eye on them and water whenever the surface of the soil is dry.

Root Division This is a technique of vegetative propagation used with perennials. It involves taking a chunk of roots, usually 4 to 6 inches across, and planting it by itself in a fresh site. Many perennials can be treated in this way. And some must be, either because after a few years in the ground the roots will be so crowded that they begin to compete with one another, or because the plant's habit of growth is outward. These outward-growers are very common. After a few seasons, the original center of the plant is squeezed and exhausted while at the periphery the growth is young and vigorous. This is what I call the doughnut effect.

Sometimes, if you are interested more in producing a new plant than in revitalizing an old one, you can simply use a sharpened spade and perforate the root mass, loosening a 4- to 6-inch section of roots but leaving the main part of the plant intact. Not all plants lend themselves to this treatment; some roots are just so tough that you have to take the entire plant out so it's up where you can work with it. (See the individual entries.) Getting the

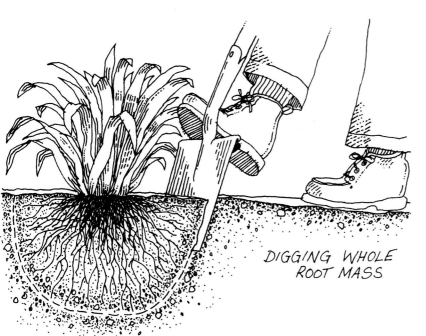

DIGGING WHOLE
ROOT MASS

DIGGING
SECTION OF
ROOT
MASS

plant out requires a well-sharpened spade to slice around the outer edges of the roots. The root mass doesn't usually show while it's still in the soil, so assume that the breadth of the roots corresponds to the breadth of the foliage. If it's a doughnut-plant, I cut the hole out with my spade, too. Regardless of the type of plant, I always cut the foliage back by a half to two-thirds to compensate for root loss during division.

Most roots can be severed, either with a spade or a very sharp knife. There are some, like daylilies, that need to be pried apart with 2 back-to-back spading forks. And there are others too tough even for this, requiring an axe or hatchet.

In the Victory Garden, we do most of our dividing in the spring so the plants have a long season of warm weather to become established. But many plants can also be divided in the fall, even as far north as we are.

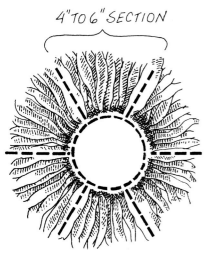

4" TO 6" SECTION

DIVIDING A
DOUGHNUT PLANT

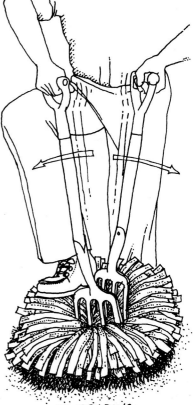

USING SPADING
FORKS TO DIVIDE
TOUGH ROOTS

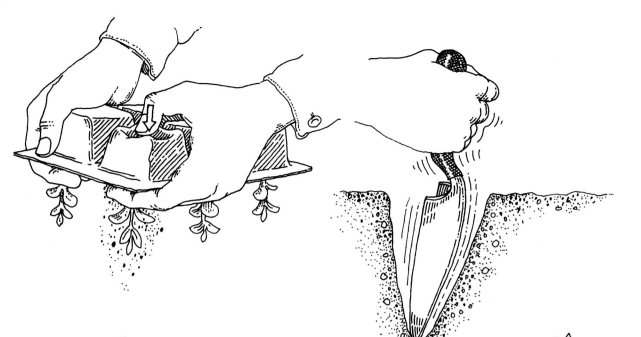

PLANTING SEEDLINGS
AND STEM CUTTINGS

Planting Whether a plant is large or small, there are some general rules about setting it into the ground.

First of all, I consider the most important step good soil preparation, especially for perennials (see After Frost).

Second, transplant is always a shock to a plant's system. I like to minimize this by working on a cloudy day if I can, to save the plants from the harshest rays of the sun. As an alternative, I would put them in late in the afternoon and then cover them with a very light mulch of salt marsh hay, pine needles, or a sheet of newspaper for a day or two. (This is not necessary with the spring perennial divisions.)

For a small plant, whether a seedling or a cutting, the planting procedure is very simple. First I mark the soil with bone meal so I know precisely where each plant is to go (for more, see the April feature). Then I unpot the plant, either by turning the rim of the pot upside down and tapping it

against the handle of my shovel, or, for plants in six-packs, by just pushing my thumb up through the bottom of the compartments, dislodging the plants. Then I use a trowel to make a good hole in the soil; there should be plenty of room for the whole root mass to fit in uncrowded. Then I set the root ball in the hole so that the plant sits at the same depth it grew in its container, and fill in around the roots with soil, firming lightly. Once the

plant is in place, I build up a small saucer of soil 2 or 3 inches out from the stem of the plant; this will trap water and direct it downward to the plant's roots.

For a large plant, by which I mean perennial divisions, either potted or bare-root, the procedure is somewhat different. First, the hole must be 18 inches deep and 24 inches across, or as close to these dimensions as your soil will allow. When I dig this hole, I

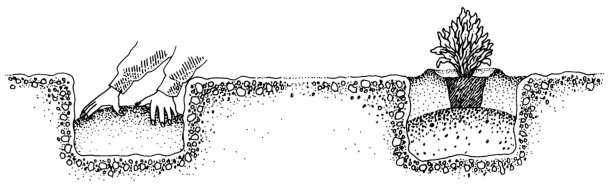

PLANTING POTTED DIVISIONS

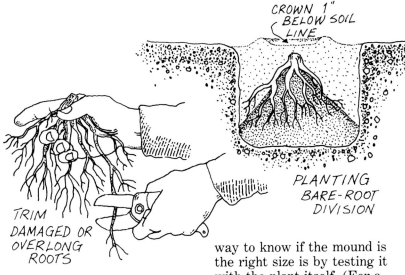

CROWN 1"
BELOW SOIL
LINE

PLANTING
BARE-ROOT
DIVISION

TRIM
DAMAGED OR
OVERLONG
ROOTS

have access to manure, you can make manure tea, which will serve the same function without adding chemicals to the garden. (See the July feature for more.) Finally, I water the plants in thoroughly by filling the saucers with water, letting them drain, and filling them again.

WATER
WITH
TRANSPLANT
SOLUTION

FILL
SAUCER
WITH WATER

put the rich topsoil, the top 2 inches of soil, into a wheelbarrow, and set the subsoil to one side. Then I improve the topsoil with a handful of bone meal and a couple of shovelfuls of organic matter, and use a spading fork to thoroughly mix the additives with the soil. Next, I mound this improved soil in the bottom of the planting hole, firming it with my hands to eliminate air pockets. The mound should be tall enough to bring the plant to the right depth; after transplant, a potted plant should be neither deeper nor shallower than it was in its pot; for a bare-root plant, the crown should be 1 inch below the soil line after planting. Trial and error are necessary here, as the only

way to know if the mound is the right size is by testing it with the plant itself. (For a potted plant, the mound of soil in the bottom of the hole should be just slightly mounded. For a bare-root plant, a more angled mound is better. See the illustrations.) When the plant is in place, I fill in around it with the rest of the improved soil, firming gently to eliminate air pockets. If there isn't enough improved topsoil to fill the hole, I finish off with the subsoil. The last step is to build a saucer of soil around the plants, a good 6 or 8 inches from the crown, so water is trapped and aimed downward toward the roots.

Once the plant is in, I give it a boost with transplant solution to get it off to a good start. My transplant solution is just a water-soluble fertilizer dissolved in water, but if you

248 **SEPTEMBER**

Monthly Checklist

Daylily
Narcissus
Oriental Poppy
Peony

*A naturalized bed of narcissus
(see page 252)*

SEPTEMBER

Our September weather is cool but not yet frosty — we don't usually have our first frost until October — these moderating temperatures, especially the cooler nights, will cause some of our annuals to slow down and send up fewer flowers. But there are other annuals that do very well in cool weather, and will revive for the first time since early summer. Among these are snapdragons and pinks, calendulas, annual phlox, and verbenas.

In the perennial border, we have many plants still in flower, including Carpathian harebell, gaillardia, pansies, purple loose-strife, coreopsis, dahlias, and Carolina phlox. And if the plants were cut back after the first flowering season, Maltese cross flowers will reappear this month for a second, less spectacular, show. And of course, the New England asters and perennial chrysanthemums all but own the garden this month. If you don't have hardy chrysanthemums of your own, you should be able to find them quite inexpensively in your neighborhood garden center; look for the ones that have the most buds, rather than open flowers, so you will be able to enjoy the plant's entire blossom period.

As for jobs that need doing, this is the month we move our young perennial plants, started from seed in July, to the nursery row for the winter (for more about this, see this month's feature). All the attention they need beyond this is a blanket of mulch later in the season (see After Frost) to protect them through their first winter. If you would prefer, there is no reason why these young perennials cannot be located in their permanent spot now, rather than in a nursery bed; for us, the nursery bed is a space saver.

If you have your spring-flowering bulbs, you can plant them outside this month. If you still have flowers doing well in your bulb site, you can hold all but the narcissus, which require a fairly long fall growing period, until next month. Though not spring-flowering, lily bulbs can be planted now, too, for next summer's flowers (see the August entry). And favored tender perennials growing outdoors can be grown for indoor plants if you take stem cuttings this month. Among the plants that respond well to this treatment are coleus, geraniums, impatiens, and wax begonias. Make sure, if you decide to do this, that you can provide the plants with the indoor light and heat conditions that will keep them happy.

P **Daylily** Daylilies have a well-deserved reputation for tolerating all sorts of woes and still flowering year after year. Unfortunately, I suspect that some gardeners interpret this as a license for neglect, forcing the plants to survive by their own resources. And I think that one of the most overlooked jobs is regular division, which keeps the plant youthful.

Daylilies usually need dividing every 3 or 4 years, after early summer flowering. Depending on the variety, this puts the division job into July, August, or September. In the Victory Garden, where our first expected fall frost is October 10, we can leave even the early-flowering varieties undivided until September, and still give them enough time to become established.

Like many perennials that grow in clumps, daylilies exhibit the doughnut effect after a few years in the ground: the center of the clump loses vigor while the outer edges thrive. At this point, division is the only way to revive the plant. The first step is to cut the foliage back by half. This is done partly for convenience and partly to compensate for

A single-flowered daylily

root loss. Daylilies are very tough-rooted, and it is often difficult to divide them while they're in the ground, as we can with so many other perennials. The only solution is to dig the plant up, and use two spading forks back to back to pry the roots apart. The center of the plant, which will be visibly weaker, should be discarded and the remaining growth divided into sections 6 to 8 inches across. Then they can be planted, either singly or in clusters, as described in the April entry. (For more about division, see the August feature.)

B **Narcissus** Most spring-flowering bulbs are planted in October in the Victory Garden, but narcissus do better if they're given a longer period of time to become rooted before cold weather. Those dug from your garden or a neighbor's can be planted as early as midsummer, but they're not available commercially until September.

There are several kinds of hardy narcissus. Some are called narcissus, some jonquils, some daffodils; once these terms indicated differences in the flower shape, but now they are used loosely and interchangeably. All are members of the genus *Narcissus*. Most varieties are 1 to 2 feet tall, with a spread of 6 to 8 inches. There are also miniatures, 6 to 8 inches tall and 2 to 3 inches across. Narcissus flower colors are mostly limited to white, yellow, and orange, but there are so many shades within these colors, such unusual bicolors, such a variety of flower shapes, that the selection at hand is enormous. All types are long-term and trouble-free; those that are particularly vigorous and multiply readily make good choices for naturalizing, and are usually so identified by the catalogues or garden center. The cluster-flowered varieties — those that bear several flowers to a stem — are sometimes less expensive than the types that send up one large single flower to each stem. The average blossom period is 2 weeks, but by selecting early-, mid-, and late-season varieties, it's possible to have 6 weeks of spring bloom. In the Victory Garden, narcissus come into flower in late March and continue until early May.

Narcissus can be planted in the garden bed with other bulbs, and left to grow for years and years. They'll divide and multiply every growing season. Personally, I prefer to see narcissus naturalized, growing wild through the grass or yard. (For more, see the October feature.) Either way, the foliage must be allowed to die back after flowering so the bulbs can draw all the nutrients from the green top growth. If the leaves are cut while they're still green, the bulbs are short-changed, and may die. The problem is that this foliage maturing takes 4 to 6 weeks, during which the leaves become progressively drier and browner. If you natu-

Opposite: Narcissus from a naturalizing mix

ralize narcissus — or any bulbs — in your lawn, you will either have to delay mowing the grass, or put them in an area that isn't mowed anyway. I have narcissus naturalized in a bed of pine needles under fir trees in my yard, where the mowing isn't a problem. Narcissus actually prefer full or half-day sunlight, but they've done well year after year in this site. They can also be planted under deciduous trees; even if they're heavily shaded in summer, they'll have enough spring sunshine to do very well.

Narcissus should be planted 3 times as deep in the soil as the bulb is tall from base to tip (see the October feature). If the bulbs are being naturalized, the distance between them will be random — they may be only 2 inches or so apart in some places — but if they're to be set in a garden bed, they should be 6 to 8 inches apart; the miniatures have less of a spread, and can be planted 2 to 3 inches apart.

Once planted, narcissus need very little attention. After they've flowered, I usually dust the soil with 5-10-5 fertilizer, and the maintenance job is done. If you want, you can propagate them after the foliage has died. Split the dividing bulbs apart and plant them all, even the small ones. In time they will grow to full-size bulbs bearing handsome flowers.

P **Oriental Poppy** A row of orange Oriental poppies lines the driveway at our suburban site. They're the kingpins and dominant members of the perennial border when they bloom for a month or so in June. The colors are white and brilliant shades of red and orange; the flowers themselves are very large, and held on tall stems. In the Victory Garden, these plants reach about 18 inches in height; most of this is in the floral canopy, as the foliage itself is only about 12 inches long and lies fairly flat. I usually put them in the front or intermediate row of the perennial border. The foliage isn't particularly good-looking. It also isn't particularly long-lasting, dying down completely, right to the soil, in midsummer. So I like to locate these plants next to large ones that will fill in the gap they leave; New England asters fit the bill perfectly, but a planting of new annuals makes another good choice.

Oriental poppies can be started from seed, but many of the best varieties do not breed true, so it is my custom to buy plants that have been grown vegetatively. Garden centers sell these plants in the spring, but mail-order houses ship them in the fall. The botanical name is *Papaver orientale*. My advice is to buy the color and height plants you want, as there are no other significant differences from variety to variety.

These plants are particularly hardy in cold weather. In fact, they're much better in the north than in the warmer climates; they're considered hardy in Zones 3 through 8 (see the Appendix). They would like full-day sunlight but they will grow in half-day sun, too. They need a site 12 to 15 inches across. It will take them a season or two to fill this area but once they do they will not spread beyond it.

Deadheading Oriental poppies

Peony Peonies are among the longest-lived flowering plants in the garden. They survive neglect, *very* cold weather (as low as −40°F), and still keep growing, year after year. In late May and June they send up large, often fragrant flowers in white, pink, red, or yellow.

Because peonies grow so slowly, breeding and testing new varieties is the work of a lifetime. So there is very little change in the market from year to year. The varieties offered for sale now are the same ones I remember from boyhood. Some types have smaller flowers than others; the large-flowered varieties, the doubles, are undoubtedly beautiful, but the flower heads are so heavy that they are often damaged by wind and rain. I lean toward the singles, the semidoubles, or anemone-flowered peonies; all have characteristically large peony blossoms that are still small enough to withstand weather.

A semidouble variety of peony

Peonies come on the market in garden centers in the spring. We usually buy from mail-order houses, which ship in the fall. Whether you buy from a catalogue or a garden center, my advice is to buy a single-flowered variety in the color you like. The plants themselves are all much the same size, regardless of the size of the flowers; an established plant is about 3 feet tall, and approximately the same distance across.

Peonies are extremely undemanding in most regards. They actually prefer full sunlight, but they'll grow very well in half-day sun as long as they are out from under the branch spread of trees so they don't suffer from root interference. Peonies are at their best if they're kept deadheaded, well watered, and fed with 5-10-5 fertilizer (see the July feature) in the spring, when the emerging shoots are 2 to 4 inches tall. But even if they're neglected, they keep growing and flowering. However, peonies are very fussy in one regard. They must be planted at the right depth — with their buds 1 to 2 inches below the soil surface. If the buds are too deep, the plants produce all foliage and no flowers.

Because peonies are such long-lived plants, I give them the best possible treatment when they go into the ground. First, I dig a hole 2 feet across and as deep as possible; the ideal depth is 1½ feet, but some soils are very hard to loosen this far down. An acceptable depth is 12 inches, which is manageable in most soils. Then I add either peat moss or leaf mold to the soil in the ratio of 2 parts soil to 1 part organic matter. (Manure, whether old or new, is not a good soil additive for peonies, as it fosters disease.) Then I add 2 handfuls of bone meal and lime if the pH is below 6.0. The best pH for peonies is 6.0–7.0.

The process of setting the plant in requires alternately adding and firming the soil, and testing the depth with the unpotted plant. I usually lay a stick across the opening of the hole so I can gauge soil level accurately. The tops of the pink buds must be 1 to 2 inches from the soil surface. Make sure the soil is firmed as you fill the hole; otherwise it will settle later and pull the plant down.

Peonies can be left indefinitely, but they can also be divided for new plants. This is most successful if it's done in September. The first step is to dig out the entire root system, then shake and wash the soil off so the pink buds are apparent. Each division should have 3 or 4 of these buds, or eyes. Sometimes peony roots are very tough, but a sharp knife should cut through. The new divisions can then be replanted as above. A 3- or 4-eye division will reach a spread of 12 inches or so after a year in the ground.

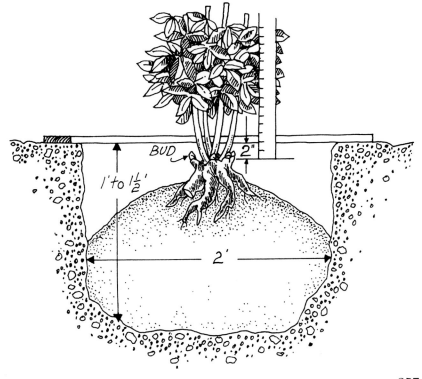

PERENNIALS AND BIENNIALS

I have a special fondness for perennials. I like their ruggedness, their ability to live through winter and send up green shoots through the lingering patches of ice and snow when the world still seems caught in winter's grasp. And I appreciate their ability to ward off most diseases and insects. To the degree that the word perennial implies permanence without much effort, these plants are misnamed. Perennials do have a great deal to recommend them, but like all plants they require regular care. Some are more tolerant of neglect than others, but all benefit from attention.

In the strictest sense, a perennial is any plant that can live 3 years or more in its native environment. By this definition, the number of the world's perennials is enormous and diverse, including most trees and weeds. Those grown in gardens, though, are usually herbaceous perennials, a particular type of perennial with non-woody stems that die back to the ground in winter during the plant's dormancy, to be triggered back into growth by warm spring weather. Herbaceous perennials live over because they die back; their roots are strong enough to survive frozen earth. The species is maintained because the individuals are maintained, and actually grow larger from year to year. (It's very different from

the life cycle of annuals, most of which is dedicated to producing quantities of seeds; with annuals it's the *next* generation that matters.) Perennials do produce flowers and seeds, but because seed reproduction is not the only means of survival, they generally produce fewer of both than do annuals. While perennials bloom for a relatively short period, the flowers themselves tend to be more interesting, more intricately shaped, more subtly colored. Think of the difference between a marigold and an iris.

The most commonly grown herbaceous perennials are reliably hardy throughout the country. Some are fussier, and not such good choices for very cold or very warm climates. (See the individual entries for hardiness ratings; there's a hardiness zone map in the Appendix.) Most herbaceous perennials require a period of cold-weather dormancy, so they are particularly popular in the areas of the country that have cold winters, but there is no part of the United States that is too warm for some perennial culture. (There are also tender perennials, which live over from year to year in their warm, native climate, but are treated as annuals in areas where winters are cold.)

Late spring in the perennial border at the suburban site

Biennials Biennials are a special category of plant. They flower one year on plants produced the previous year. For the winter between their two seasons, they are reliably hardy, but after they flower once, they have little future. There are 6 plants in this book that are biennials, or are treated as such: Canterbury bells, foxglove, and sweet Williams are hardy in Zones 4 through 10; English daisies, forget-me-nots, and pansies are hardy in 3 through 10.

Some biennials grow quickly enough that they can be sown in early spring for same-year flowers, but the home gardener is better advised to treat biennials as 2-year crops. In this book, I advise sowing biennials in July, moving them to nursery rows in September, mulching through the winter, and transplanting to their flowering site in April. Because biennials have a brief flowering season, they do not require the extensive soil preparation that perennials need. From the point of view of soil preparation, biennials can be considered as annuals.

Designing the Perennial Border There are many plants that fall within the category of herbaceous perennial, in all sizes and colors and shapes and textures. Some large, dramatic perennials, such as peonies, bee balm, New England asters, daylilies, and irises, can be planted individually in a site of their own and allowed to naturalize, that is, to grow unrestricted. But the general practice with perennials is to cluster several together in one bed. There are some good reasons for grouping them. One is that most perennials can be left in the ground for several years, which means a minimum of disturbance to the bed as a whole. The more important reason is that when grouped together, perennials provide a longer period of color than when they are planted separately. No single perennial blossoms for very long — 3 or 4 weeks is about average. By putting several perennials together, the gardener can orchestrate the time of bloom so that as some flowers are fading others are coming in.

Perennials seem to lend themselves to rectangular borders because this shape provides a stage for the changing and moving patterns of color. In the old days there was a firm if unspoken rule against mixing outsiders with the perennials, but customs are changing in favor of a mostly perennial garden with bulbs and annuals and biennials in small numbers. These additions — particularly annuals, which usually flower freely all summer long — provide constant and profuse color as the season progresses while the spotlight falls first on one dramatic perennial, then another. If the border were a musical, the annuals would be the chorus and the perennials the featured players. (And in my garden, Miss Lingard phlox would be the unquestioned star.)

Placing plants in the perennial border requires forethought, and a plan. There are no absolute rules about designing the border, but there are some tried-and-true approaches that will help you design a graceful garden with a long season of bloom.

First of all, most gardeners like to select plants that will combine to offer the longest season of bloom. This requires selecting quite a few plants, because so many perennials bloom for only 3 or 4 weeks. You may choose to schedule the blossoms differently. At our suburban site, for instance, most of the perennials bloom in the spring and fall. During the summer, the annuals and roses have center stage.

Another issue is height, both of foliage and flowers. As a general rule, the tall plants should be in the back and the shorter ones in the front, with an intermediate row between. The rows should be staggered occasionally, though, so that some intermediate plants come forward into the front row, or some short plants occupy both the front and intermediate positions. If the row setup is maintained absolutely, the border will look like a group graduation photograph.

Finally, the looks of the plants must be considered: the overall mass, the color and texture of the foliage, the color of the flowers. The rule here is variety. The perennial border is meant to be viewed as a whole. If several large, dramatic plants of different species are clustered together, the viewer's attention will be drawn to them, and the unity of the garden will be lost. In the same way, a grouping of vivid colors — several reds and oranges — will stand out.

Because it is traditional to design the perennial border to be in flower all season long, most are quite large. But I wouldn't want to see gardeners shy away from perennials because they don't have a space large enough for an all-season border. You can plant large perennials one to a site, or group a few in a cluster, with a wonderful effect. For instance, here are some beautiful combinations:

For early spring: alyssum (in front), intermediate-height sweet Williams (in the intermediate position), and foxglove (in the back).

For early summer: flax or pansies (in front), coreopsis (intermediate), and lupines (in the back).

For an early-summer cutting garden: white shasta daisies, Maltese cross, long-spurred columbine, gaillardia, and painted daisies.

For late summer and fall: hardy chrysanthemum, purple loose-strife, and New England aster.

Siting the Garden Perennials need freely circulating air and well-drained soil. Most do best in full sun but will grow and flower on half-day sunlight too. And there are several that actually prefer half-day or filtered sunlight. (Plumed bleeding hearts, long-spurred columbines, Siberian and Japanese irises, and day-lilies will grow in filtered-only light.) As long as they are given the light conditions they need, and ample air circulation to keep diseases to a minimum, perennials lend themselves to a number of sites. They can be planted as a free-standing hedge, or a border along a walk. Or they can be placed in front of a visual backdrop, such as a wall or fence. If you do this, keep in mind that the backdrop, especially a tall, solid one like the outer wall of a house, will interfere with moving air; you can compensate for this by leaving an air space of 12 to 18 inches between the plants and the wall. A living hedge used as a backdrop presents a different problem, which is root interference; you will have to leave a space

of 3 feet or so in order to clear the spread of the hedge roots.

Sowing Seeds Most people buy perennials as plants, either in the fall or spring. For some plants, such as those that grow slowly and reach flowering size only after several years, this is the best idea. But for many plants there is a much cheaper alternative in starting from seeds.

The seeds can be sown in early spring and the plants moved outdoors when the ground is workable; if the young plants are conditioned in a cold frame (see the August feature), they can withstand a light frost with no trouble. This is an increasingly popular procedure, one we often follow ourselves. As a rule, the plants will flower the first year.

An early spring sowing is a good idea for gardeners with a greenhouse, but for the home gardener, there are several strikes against this technique. Most important is that average indoor growing conditions are simply not good enough: rooms are too dark, even if they're sunny for several hours; humidity is too low. Even in these circumstances, the plants will live until the ground is workable and they can be set outside, but they've suffered as seedlings, and they aren't as vigorous as they should be. Space is another problem for many gardeners. Usually there are only so many windowsills available to hold young seedlings.

I think the better idea for home gardeners is to start perennials by seed in July, move them to six-packs when the true leaves develop, and then plant them outside for the winter. (For more about seed sowing, see the August feature.) They can be set directly into their flowering spot in Septem-

ber. However, because my gardens are still in bloom in September, and I don't want to pull out plants in flower to set in young plants that won't flower until the following summer, I usually set my seedlings into a nursery bed in September, to save garden space. The main advantage to midsummer sowing is that it produces sturdier plants that will bloom better the first summer, because they're older than plants sown in early spring. This is the schedule on which this book is organized. Most of the perennials are sown in July and moved to their permanent locations in April.

The nursery bed is home to the plants for several months, so it needs to provide the right light and soil conditions for the plants. For some gardeners, the best site for the nursery bed is a section of the vegetable garden. The young plants can be set in at intervals of 4 to 6 inches; this is much closer together than the plants could be put in their permanent spots, but they will be moved before they demand more room. In the Victory Garden no perennial will grow more than double its size between September and April. After the ground is frozen hard, the nursery row should be mulched to protect the plants through the winter (see After Frost).

There's only one caution about this routine, and that is to label the plants carefully with plastic or wood stakes, and then diagram the bed as a safety precaution. If you set in several plants and lose track of which is which, you'll have a real problem on your hands. After the plants have been set into the nursery bed, I water them with transplant solution, which will help them grow and

The early-summer perennial border at the Victory Garden, with phlox, roses, and daylilies

take root through the fall. (For more on planting and transplanting, see the August feature.)

Buying Plants Perennial plants are sold both by catalogue houses and garden centers. The plants may be divisions, seedlings, or rooted cuttings. If you buy from a local garden center, the plants will be potted in soil and actively growing. If you buy from a mail-order house, you are apt to receive a bare-root plant, which is an unpotted, dormant division. It will be wrapped in a moistened medium, and then wrapped again with plastic. Bare-root plants should be planted immediately; if you can't put them right into their permanent spot, unwrap the roots and heel them in in another part of the garden where there is worked soil available. (See the illustration.)

Soil Preparation If you are putting in a new perennial bed or border, the initial soil preparation has a great deal to do with the bed's longevity and health. By definition, perennials are in the ground for a long time, so they need nourishing soil. They are deep-rooted, so they need deeply dug soil. And they must withstand winter without suffering ice damage, so they need well-drained soil. Unless you're willing to empty an established bed of all plants and rework the soil, the only opportunity to prepare the bed is in the beginning, before a single plant is set in. Of course there are changes in a perennial border every year, as new plants are added and old ones divided, and this presents an opportunity to replenish the soil around the individual planting sites. The time to prepare the soil for a new perennial is in the fall (see After Frost). In the spring, simply level the bed with a steel rake. For planting, see the August feature.

Ongoing Care The most demanding maintenance routine with perennials is the routine division that many of them need to keep the clumps vigorous and growing in good soil. There are few perennials that need this treatment every year, but many require division every 3 to 5 years. The individual entries indicate which plants need division, and how frequently. (For division, see the August feature.)

Aside from this, perennials are little effort. In the spring, the first step is to remove the winter mulch (see After Frost). As soon as the shoots appear and mark the outlines of the plants, I ring the outer edges of the crowns — at least 2 inches from them — with a dusting of 5-10-5 and bone meal. Then I add a 1-inch layer of compost over the entire bed, making sure there's a 2-inch border of clear soil around the crown of each plant.

Finally, the perennial bed needs to be cleaned out in the fall. The stems of the plants should be cut back to 3 or 4 inches from the soil, and the old foliage removed from the bed entirely. This serves to keep diseases under control, as many fungi and bacteria can live over winter in the foliage. It is also good housekeeping; there's nothing worse than the looks of old leaves that have struggled through winter. They're also extremely hard to cut from the plant at that point because they will be tough and saturated with spring rain and ground water.

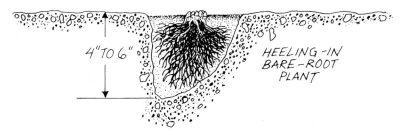

4" TO 6"

HEELING-IN BARE-ROOT PLANT

OCT

Monthly Checklist

Allium
Caladium
Chionodoxa
Crocus
Dahlia
Fritillaria
Fuchsia
Gladiolus
Grape Hyacinth
Hyacinth
Lily-of-the-Valley
Squill
Tuberous-Rooted Begonia
Tulip

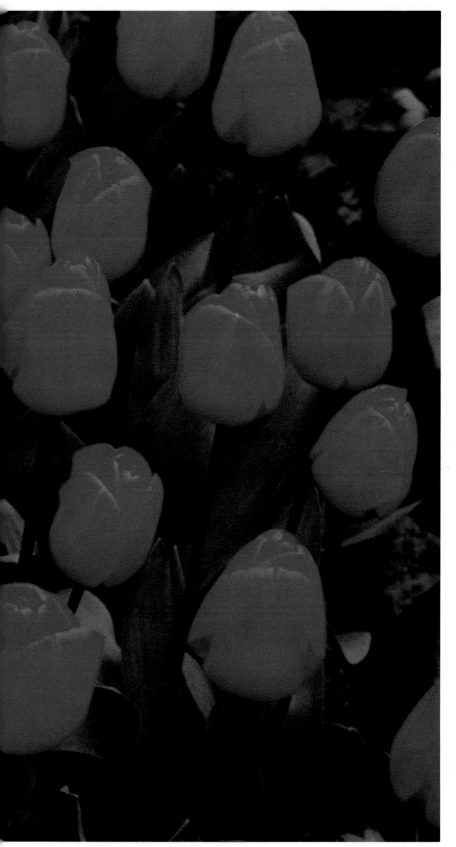

A bed of early single tulips (see page 278)

OCTOBER

This is the last month for flowers in the Victory Garden. We get our first killing frost this month — the average date is October 10 — which eliminates all but the most vigorous of our plants, such as petunias, snapdragons, and chrysanthemums. Even these, after the frost, will be pretty much over the hill. As soon as the frost hits, I usually pull out my annuals so I can prepare the soil and plant the spring-flowering bulbs. (The annual plants, broken or shredded into small pieces for faster decomposition, go right into the composter. See After Frost.) If your bulbs aren't going to the annual bed, there's no reason not to leave the still-flowering plants in for another few days.

The period after the first frost is also the time when I dig the tender tubers and prepare them for storage next year. This is an easy chore, and one that keeps a collection going and growing from year to year. If we act before the first frost, we can still take stem cuttings of tender perennials this month, too.

But most of the month is devoted to housecleaning and preparation for next spring. In the perennial garden, all the current year's foliage should be cut down to within a couple of inches of the soil line so there are no decomposing leaves or stems on the ground, creating a hospitable environment for diseases, many of which can survive winter. The perennial foliage can be added to the composter as well. (None of this material will decompose quickly over winter, but there will be some slow decay, and the process will pick up again in the spring warmth.) The only task remaining is to put the winter mulch on the perennial garden and the nursery bed — where the young perennials and biennials were planted in September — after the ground freezes solid. For us, this may not happen until December, but gardens in colder areas will probably need mulching sooner. Finally, the soil for new beds should be prepared in the fall, after the frost but before the ground freezes hard. (For instructions, see After Frost.)

All these jobs accomplished, we leave the flower garden for the winter, and turn our thoughts to plans for next spring.

B **Allium** The flower of a giant allium is like a fluffy purple ball balanced on a tall, stiff stem. It's like no other flower in the garden. It's only one of several species of allium on the market, but it is unquestionably the one that stands out, thanks partly to the fact that its flowers rise 3 to 5 feet above the foliage, which lies low to the ground. The giant allium (*Allium giganteum*) is a fascinating contrast to the dainty, white-flowered Neapolitan allium (*A. neapolitanum*), which rarely reaches more than 12 inches in height, with an 8-inch foliage spread. Both types, and others as well, are available through garden catalogues. They're sometimes known as flowering onions.

Giant allium in flower

Some allium are cold-tolerant, but both these species are a little sensitive to cold. They are reliably hardy in Zones 6 through 10 (see the Appendix). I've had no problems with either of them in the Victory Garden, but in the suburban site we've had some trouble wintering them over. Both gardens are in Zone 5, but the Victory Garden, being in the city and closer to the ocean, is noticeably warmer than the suburban site.

Giant allium bulbs are large, and they produce large plants. In the Victory Garden we cluster an odd number of bulbs together, but these are very costly bulbs, and planting in quantity is expensive. Because of the size, this is a plant that can be used singly as an accent without looking stranded. Like all bulbs, they propagate naturally, so by the second season, the single plant is no longer alone.

Because the bulbs of giant allium are so large, I dig them a hole with a spade. They should be planted so the top of the bulb is 4-6 inches below the surface of the soil. Each bulb needs an area 12 to 15 inches across, to allow for the foliage spread, and a site with at least half-day sunlight. They come into flower in early summer, usually June in the Victory Garden. After the flowers fade, the seed heads can be cut for a dried arrangement. Every 3 years, I dig and divide the clumps.

The Neapolitan allium is smaller, less expensive, and a week or two earlier to flower than the giant allium. It can be planted in clusters, and is particularly appealing in a rock garden. Clumps can be left indefinitely without dividing.

A **Caladium** Caladiums grow for 7 or 8 months, and then need a rest. Plants that have been growing outside all summer will start to decline in the shorter days and cooler nights of fall. This is all part of their natural cycle, so I just leave them in place until the foliage is killed in the first frost. The tuber isn't damaged by this at all. (Potted plants can be brought indoors for a night if an early freak frost is predicted, then set outside again for another few days of warm weather.)

After frost, I dig the tubers up and leave them in an airy, dry, frost-free spot for a few days, unpotting those that have spent the summer in containers plunged into the soil. Then I cut the foliage off, clean the dried soil from the tubers, sort them by variety, and bury them in dry peat moss, vermiculite, or perlite. Ideally, the temperature should be in the 40- to 50-degree range. If moisture is a problem in your storage area, it's probably smart to treat the tubers with a fungicide or bulb dust. Then I leave the tubers to enjoy their dormancy until March, when I start them growing again. (Sometimes they will start to sprout while in storage, so you should check them in late spring, and pot them if you see green shoots.)

B **Chionodoxa** Usually, common names of plants are far-fetched, but this beautiful little flowering bulb is described well when it is called glory-of-the-snow. It isn't the very first of the spring bulbs, but it does often come before

One of the widely available varieties of chionodoxa

the winter snows have melted. It seems to need cold temperatures; while it is hardy in Zones 3 through 10 (see the Appendix), it's better in cold weather than warm. The colors range from royal purple-blue to pale lilac, depending on the variety. The bulbs are sold by most of the mail-order bulb houses, but there is not usually much selection offered by any one house. In the Victory Garden we have the species *Chionodoxa gigantea*, an interesting name in view of the fact that the plants are never more than 5 or 6 inches tall and 2 to 3 inches across.

Chionodoxa is one of the minor bulbs (see this month's feature), so it's best planted in quantity under trees or near low shrubs and then allowed to naturalize. The plants are very tolerant of a range of light conditions, doing best in full sun but growing and spreading in half-day or filtered light, too. They should be planted as early as they become available, 3 inches deep, 2 to 3 inches apart. Wherever they're grown, their foliage must be allowed to ripen before it is mowed. If you want, you can dig and divide the bulbs in the fall. Or you can just let them go for years. They need no attention whatsoever, other than a feeding of 5-10-5 fertilizer every other spring. (See the July feature.)

B   **Crocus**   The sweetheart of the early spring flowers. Who can resist these brave, brightly colored flowers pushing through the snow? There are dozens of varieties of crocus on the market, both species and hybrid types, with their larger corms and flowers. The species crocus is a little smaller, but no crocus is taller than 6 inches or so. All do equally well in full, half-day, or filtered sunlight; the more shade they have, the later their 10-day blossom season, but there are early-,

Hybrid crocus, the variety Jeanne d'Arc

mid-, and late-season varieties for a longer flower period. As is true of many of the early-flowering spring bulbs, crocuses are better in cold temperatures than hot; they're hardy in Zones 3 through 10, but they're happiest from Zone 7 north.

Crocuses in fact grow from corms, but they are treated as bulbs and planted in October. They are too small to appear singly without looking like lost souls, so I like them either naturalized, or planted in one-variety clusters, 9 or 11 together, in the perennial bed or bulb garden. The large-flowered varieties are the best choice for naturalizing. Planting follows the basic formula for minor bulbs: they should be 3 times as deep as the corms are tall, and 2 to 4 inches apart. Crocuses can be divided in the fall, but they're best left undisturbed; if you want more, it's better to buy them. (For more about corms, see this month's feature.)

A **Dahlia** Tuberous dahlias are too tender to be left in the ground over winter, but they can be saved from year to year if they're dug out and brought inside. This applies not

One of the cactus-flowered types of tuberous dahlias

only to plants started from tubers in the spring, but to cuttings of those plants, which will have formed tubers over the course of the summer. (In the Victory Garden, annual dahlia plants are pulled and discarded after frost, but particularly nice selections can be dug, stored over winter, and saved for another year, as all annual dahlias form tubers during their first season of growth.)

This job can be done either before frost or after the foliage is killed in the first frost. I begin by cutting the stem back to about 4 inches from the ground. Each tuber is connected to the main stem by a thin neck, forming a circle of tubers no more than 12 inches across. These connecting necks are brittle and if broken the tuber is ruined, so the digging operation needs a light touch. I use a spading fork and work in a 12-inch circle around the outer edge of the plant, carefully loosening the mass of tubers from the soil. Once the clump is free, I remove it, wash the soil off the roots with a hose, and trim off the foliage and old roots. Then I turn the whole clump upside down and set it in a sheltered area out of the sun for a few hours.

The greatest danger to stored dahlia tubers is drying out — they shrivel very quickly. I usually store the clumps whole in peat moss, alternating a layer of peat, 2 or 3 inches thick, with a layer of tubers. The peat need not be moist, as it will insulate the moisture that comes from the tubers during storage. Another method, which allows the tubers to be stored on an open shelf, even in a basement not celebrated for its dry air, is to dip the tubers in melted paraffin. If you do this, you should divide the tubers now, in the fall, rather than wait for the spring. The fall division procedure is a little different from the spring (see the March entry) because in the fall the buds are not visible. The important thing is to make sure that each tuber, after division, is still attached to a small piece of the neck where the clump of tubers join. The piece need only be about an inch long. I usually just slice down through the neck so that all the tubers have an equal share; if there are 6 tubers in the clump, I give each 1/6 of the neck. (See the illustration.)

After division, each tuber is then dipped in melted paraffin. This is a dangerous job if not done carefully. I usually set a pan of hot water, with a layer of melted paraffin floating on the surface, over an outdoor grill; the heat from the coals keeps the paraffin liquid as I work. Then I hold each tuber with a pair of tongs, and dip them one by one into the water. Then I set them aside while the paraffin dries, and they're ready for the open shelf. I usually write the name of the variety on the tuber; a felt-tip permanent-ink pen will write clearly on the paraffin.

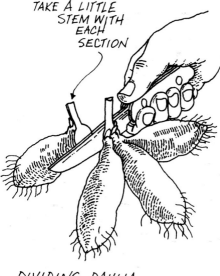

TAKE A LITTLE STEM WITH EACH SECTION

DIVIDING DAHLIA TUBERS

Imperial fritillaria in flower

B **Fritillaria** The most common species of this spring-flowering bulb is the imperial fritillaria (*Fritillaria imperialis*), and imperial it is. It stands as much as 3 feet tall, one straight flower stem rising over a low rosette of foliage. The flower head tops the stem and is unlike any other flower that grows. It blooms for 10 days or so toward the end of May, sending up yellow or red-orange flowers. The flowers give off a strong odor that I call musky; I've known others to say these plants smell like skunks. It's in the nose of the beholder, I guess. Imperial fritillaria is said to be hardy in Zones 5 through 10, but in my experience it's marginal in Zone 5; we've had trouble with this plant in both the Victory Garden and the suburban site, both of which are in Zone 5 (see the Appendix for a zone map).

There is a second, smaller species of fritillaria, known as the guinea-hen flower (*Fritillaria Meleagris*) because of its checkered petal design. This isn't quite so easy to find, but it has much to recommend it. It's smaller than the imperial type, 1 foot tall with a foliage spread of about 6 inches.

The flower head is more delicate than its imperial cousin's. It blooms earlier in the season — usually the end of April in the Victory Garden — and is hardy as far north as Zone 3. And the bulbs are much more reasonably priced than the large, expensive bulbs of the imperial type.

The leaves of imperial fritillaria disappear completely in midsummer, so the bulbs should be planted near other plants that will fill in the space; or they can be overplanted with annuals. They need a site with half-day or filtered sunlight, and it's good to protect them from the full force of the midday sun. The bulbs should be planted 6 inches deep and about 1 foot apart. They may need single-staking as they come into bud. As long as the flower production is good, they're best if they're allowed to grow season after season without dividing. They will reproduce very slowly. When the flowers begin to suffer, the bulbs can be dug, divided, and reset after the leaves have completely browned; the new bulbs will be visible at the base of the old.

The guinea-hen flower is also best in half-day light, tolerating either full or filtered light as an alternative. I plant the bulbs 3 inches deep and 6 inches apart. They don't spread rapidly, and can be left undivided for many seasons. You can simply divide them as you need more bulbs to start a collection in another location.

A **Fuchsia** I'm convinced that most gardeners consider fuchsias as one-season plants; when the cold weather comes in the fall, out they go. There is no reason to do this, as fuchsias can be kept over from year to year with very little bother. I have a plant in the Victory Garden that's been with us from the beginning.

Here is the way to save the plants. First, before the frosty weather comes — even before the night temperatures start dipping into the 30s — bring the plant indoors and cut the foliage back by about half; make the cuts in green growth so the new stems won't be forced to push their way through woody stems. Then unpot the plant. If you have a hanging-basket arrangement bought from a garden center (or one you potted yourself) you're apt to have 3 separate plants growing in the same pot. If so, separate them by cutting down through the soil with a knife. Then repot each plant in fresh soil.

At the same time, you can start a forest of new plants by rooting the stem tips of the pruned foliage. (See the August feature for instructions.) They will live through the winter indoors if given a spot in bright indirect light or winter sun. The soil should be kept constantly moist. They like a monthly dose of half-strength houseplant fertilizer.

A double-flowered hanging type of fuchsia

Fuchsias have a tendency toward extreme legginess, so they need regular pinching to encourage them to branch and form dense, well-shaped plants. I give rooted cuttings their first pinch when they have 3 to 5 new sets of leaves. From then on, I treat them as I do the parent, letting new branches develop 3 to 5 new sets of leaves, and then pinching back to the second set. I continue with this routine, pinching evenly all around the plant, until the specimen is bushy and the stems 9 to 12 inches long; then I stop and let the plant flower. By spring, I have several plants ready to flower.

[A]   **Gladiolus** Gladiolus corms can be dug as soon as their foliage has had a period of 4 to 6 weeks to ripen after flowering. So corms planted in April would be ready for digging in midsummer. In practice, however, most gardeners wait until the fall frost kills back the foliage, and then dig all the corms at once. I use a spading fork for this job, taking care not to puncture the corms as I dig. The corms need a chance to dry out some, so I just leave them on the soil for a couple of days after I dig them; they won't be damaged by a rainstorm during this period, but once out of the soil they will be nipped by frost, so if freezing temperatures are predicted, I bring the corms inside.

Then I cut back the foliage to about 1½ inches above the corm, and trim off dangling roots, both steps designed to reduce the bulk of the corms during storage. Then I give them another 2 or 3 weeks of drying time, either on a bench in the greenhouse or in a garage or unheated porch. After this time to dry, the old corm, shriveled now after its season of work, will snap away easily, leaving behind young corms and cormels for the next season. (If you try to remove the old corm prematurely, or if you wait too long, it won't come free without a struggle, and in the struggle you're apt to peel away the surface membrane of the young corms. Given a couple of weeks to dry, the corms will come apart without trouble, and the stump of the stem will twist off easily.)

In the Victory Garden, we don't save the cormels, as they are a season or two away from flowering size. The home gardener, though, may be inclined to hold on to them, which is certainly the thriftier move. I would store them by cormel size and variety in an onion bag or old nylon stocking, which is easily hung out of the reach of mice. They need a dark spot with 40- to 50-degree temperatures through their winter storage. Some large growers treat their corms with bulb dust to hold them over winter without disease problems, but in my opinion, this is not necessary for the home gardener.

B **Grape Hyacinth** This plant isn't a hyacinth at all but its flower spikes, while much smaller, are somewhat similar. Most varieties available from catalogues and garden centers are either blue or white flowered. The botanical name is *Muscari armeniacum*. They bloom for a week or so in April, and are hardy as far north as Zone 3 and as far south as Zone 10 (see the zone map in the Appendix).

Grape hyacinths are 6 to 8 inches tall; the leaves are narrow and grassy, and spread out about 3 inches. Like all the minor bulbs, they need to be planted in quantity to be noticeable; they multiply very rapidly, both by bulb division and by self-seeding, increasing by about one-quarter every year. In terms of sunlight, they're very easy to please. They do best in full sunlight, but grow in half-day or filtered light, too, and in fact are a good choice for shady bare spots under trees. Because they spread so quickly, they're less successful in the garden bed.

I plant grape hyacinths 3 inches deep and 3 inches apart. Generally I just plant them in a spot where I can let them go undisturbed, but if you care to, you can divide the bulbs after the foliage ripens. (For more about bulbs, see this month's feature.)

Grape hyacinths

Hyacinth Hyacinths have in their favor one of the sweetest spring fragrances known. They are also available in a wide range of colors, from soft to bright: blue, pink, purple, orange, yellow, red, and white. For a week or 10 days in April the flower heads are as dense and full as any of the early spring flowers; like tulips, they are more formal than most flowering bulbs. Most of the hyacinths on the market are known as Dutch hyacinths (*Hyacinthus orientalis*). Each bulb sends up one or two flowering spikes. These are hardy throughout the country, in Zones 4 through 10. (There is

Opposite: A naturalized bed of grape hyacinths and narcissus

another type of hyacinth, known as French-Roman, that has a looser, more casually formed flower, often several spikes to a bulb. These are considered hardy in Zones 6 through 10, but we have managed to pull them through in the Victory Garden, which is in a warm spot in Zone 5. See the Appendix for a zone map.)

Hyacinths are one of the best known of the spring-flowering bulbs, and they're very easy to find in the fall. Most reach heights of 6 to 8 inches. I've grown hyacinths in

Dutch hyacinths, the variety King of the Blues

small clusters here and there in the perennial border in the Victory Garden, but they also lend themselves to larger beds, where for a few days in the spring the bed is carpeted with these fragrant, colorful flowers. In any event they should be planted 6 to 8 inches apart, 5 inches deep.

These plants are amenable to a range of light conditions, preferring half-day sun but tolerating either full or filtered sunlight. They are somewhat more sensitive about other conditions. Rain and wind can damage their flowers. Ice can bruise the emerging shoot in the spring. So they appreciate an area that is somewhat protected from the elements during the spring, and I usually mulch their planting area in the fall to prevent ice damage to new spring growth.

I leave hyacinths in place for about 3 years, then dig the bulbs and divide them. This can be done anytime during the season as long as the foliage has had a chance to mature. Then I store the bulbs, marked by variety, in onion bags or nylon stockings hung from the joists in my basement. In the fall, I plant them out again.

For more about bulbs, see this month's feature.

Lily-of-the-valley

B **Lily-of-the-Valley** Though there is a fairly obscure pink-flowered variety, as far as most gardeners are concerned there is only one lily-of-the-valley, a spring-flowering bulb plant that sends up delicate, sweetly fragrant, white bell-shaped flowers along a stiff stem. Botanically, this plant is known as *Convallaria majalis*. It stands about 8 inches tall, and blooms for a week or two in May. It thrives in cool, moist, shady areas and spreads like wildfire; it's hardy in Zones 3 through 7 (see the Appendix). Because the leaves stay green all summer — an unusual trait for a bulb — lilies-of-the-valley are an excellent ground cover for that shady spot where grasses refuse to grow. They are less satisfactory in a garden bed, where they will forever be threatening to expand beyond the edges of the bed. They will tolerate a sunny spot, but their foliage is apt to look poor by the end of the summer. The ideal light conditions, in order of preference, are filtered light, half-day sun, and full sun. Lilies-of-the-valley are sold by most catalogue houses and garden centers. The small bulbs, known as pips, should be planted in the fall, 1 to 2 inches deep and 6 or 8 inches apart. Patches of bulbs in established plantings can also be moved easily to other sections of the garden (see this month's feature).

B **Squill** Squill is one of the minor bulbs (see this month's feature). It's a very early bloomer — with the crocuses in March — and one of the shortest of the flowering bulb plants, only 4 to 5 inches tall. As a rule, the flowers are

A naturalized planting of squill

blue; there are other colors as well, but the catalogues don't usually carry them. The best-known variety is *Scilla siberica*, which is often the only one offered for sale, unless you buy from a bulb specialty house. If you can find a wider variety of bulbs, you can select several for a longer flowering season.

Squill is much happier in cool climates than hot; it's considered hardy in Zones 3 through 7. It does equally well in full or half-day sun, and grows in filtered sunlight, too. Like all the minor bulbs, squill is best when planted in quantity; my own preference is to naturalize the bulbs, and let them go from year to year. I know a spot where they've been growing in short grass along a wooded path. There are hundreds of bulbs involved, but the overall effect is understated — a refreshing veil of tiny blue flowers appearing just above the spring grass.

Squill should be planted in the fall, 2 to 3 inches deep and 3 to 6 inches apart. At the narrower spacing the first and second season flowers will look dense; the 6-inch spacing will give the bulbs more room to spread, and the area will fill in completely in 3 to 5 years. Each bulb will send up 2 or 3 flowering stems that will last for a week or so.

Ⓐ **Tuberous-Rooted Begonia** If they're to be saved for another year, these tubers must be dug and stored in the fall. I leave them in the soil until the foliage is killed by frost, giving the plants the longest possible flowering season without in the least hurting the tuber, which can survive the first frost easily. After I dig the tubers up I rinse them off and let them dry for a few days; then I snap off the old growth. At that point I store the tubers in a container filled

A double-flowered bedding type tuberous-rooted begonia

with dry peat moss, perlite, or vermiculite, and keep them in a cool, dry spot all winter. Ideally, the temperatures should be constant within the range of 40 to 50 degrees. (If your storage area is a little damp, I suggest dusting the tubers with a fungicide before storage.) In the Victory Garden the tubers are started back into growth in March.

It is possible to propagate tuberous-rooted begonias by cuttings taken in late summer, but these are not easy plants for most people to carry over indoors. I think the better propagation technique, unless you have a greenhouse, is to start the tubers into growth in the spring, and then divide the tubers as soon as green shoots appear (see the March entry).

🅱 **Tulip** Tulips are the most regal of the spring-flowering bulbs. Partly because they're among the last to flower, partly because they are so tall and stately, they seem to be making a grand stage entrance when they come into flower.

Choosing tulip varieties is a matter of preference, and there are many types available. In the Victory Garden,

we like the early singles and doubles. The doubles bloom
just a little later than the singles, presenting a good 2 or 3
weeks of color in April, when it is most appreciated. (There
are earlier tulips on the market: species types and Kaufman-
niana tulips will blossom in early April, or even late March.)
Some years we give the whole strip at the base of the greenhouse over to the majestic Darwin hybrids, which blossom
through April and May. This is only a sampling of the varieties available. Some are much taller than others, some have
simple one-color flowers while others are striped or frilled.

*Tulip season in the Victory
Garden bulb bed*

My suggestion is to sit with a catalogue and survey the
choices. No matter what you select, it's hard to go wrong.

Culturally, tulips are very much alike. They want a
site with full or half-day sunlight, and cool temperatures.
They will grow in Zones 3 through 10, but they're best in 3
through 7 (see the Appendix); in warmer climates the winters aren't cold enough to trigger the dormancy period they
need. The flowers themselves are best in cool weather, too.
Most varieties will bloom for a week or two at most, but
they will fade earlier if the temperatures soar.

As is true of all flowering bulbs, tulip foliage must be
allowed to ripen, that is, to turn brown and wither and die,
before it is cut from the plant. This will take a month to 6
weeks, during which there are only progressively uglier
leaves and no flowers.

As is also true of other flowering bulbs, tulip bulbs
divide every year. But unlike other bulbs, tulips are not able
to send up as large a flower once the bulb has divided, and
given the favored position tulips hold in most gardens, the
loss is noticeable. After 2 or 3 years in the ground, some of

the divided bulbs will send up leaves only, and no flowers.

For both these reasons — the ripening foliage and the dividing bulbs — tulips need special treatment. Actually there are three ways to handle them, each with its advantages. The first method is a money-saver, and makes use of all the divided bulbs. It involves digging and replanting the bulbs every year. The second method is simpler but more extravagant: the bulbs are pulled after flowering and discarded before the withering leaves have a chance to ruin the looks of the garden. (For more about this, see the May entry.) In both these methods, the bulbs are planted 5 or 6 inches deep and 5 or 6 inches apart. As a third choice, the bulbs can be planted 10 inches deep, and 5 or 6 inches apart. This deep planting delays division so that the bulbs can be left for 5 years or so, and still produce a handsome bed. After this length of time, they would need to be dug and divided.

In the Victory Garden itself, we employ one of the first two methods. If we decide to save the bulbs, we dig them when the foliage begins to look unpresentable and heel-in the bulbs in another spot in the garden (see the May entry). Our spring bulb garden is also our annuals garden, so we need to clear the tulips out, one way or another.

In our suburban site, we have used the third approach with good results. We have small clusters of tulips deep-planted along the front and middle rows of the perennial border. After they flower in the spring, their browning leaves are camouflaged by developing foliage around them. Even if the withering leaves are apparent, the planting isn't large enough to ruin the looks of the garden. (For more about bulbs, see this month's feature.)

Top, opposite: Mixed tall Darwin hybrid tulips

Bottom, opposite: A profusion of tulips, massed for maximum effect

BULBS

Bulbs are responsible for some of the most dramatic flowers in the garden. In most, a few low-lying leaves surround a tall, strong stem at the top of which sits either a single flower or a small cluster. Most bulbous flowers are simple of shape and exquisite of color. While there are bulbous plants that flower in summer and fall, the most common ones are spring bloomers, and these are the ones that are easiest to find in the catalogues. No bulbous flower has a particularly long life; a week or two is about average. But there are so many choices, so many types available, that by selecting carefully the gardener can have a great deal of variety over a fairly long season. In the Victory Garden, the bulbs come into flower in early March (some years even in late February) and continue into June. Most bulbs are very long-lived, and multiply well on their own; most will also flower in a range of light conditions, from full sun to filtered sunlight only.

Bulbous plants range in height from 3 or 4 inches to 2 feet or more. The larger ones include tulips, narcissus, hyacinths, giant alliums, and fritillarias. These are flowers with presence, noticeable from a distance. The smaller bulbs, called the minor bulbs, need to be planted in quantity to make an impact. They are so small that they seem to disappear otherwise.

Spring-flowering bulbs come on the market in the late summer and fall. The earlier they're planted, the more time the roots have to become established before the onslaught of cold weather. Some bulbs, such as narcissus, should be planted as soon as they are purchased because they benefit from a long period of root development. In the Victory Garden, where our bulb garden is occupied by summer annuals, we wait until October to plant other bulbs, which gives them plenty of time to take root without abbreviating the annual season. Bulbs are sold in great numbers through garden centers and most of the major seed houses. In addition, there are specialty bulb catalogues that offer enormous variety. When I can, I buy bulbs designated as top-size; these are enjoying their last season of bloom before they split into two or more small bulbs. Because the bulb is large, the flower is large. Top-size bulbs are usually expensive. The smaller ones will grow to top-size in a season or two, so they're good buys, also.

Siting Bulbs are very adaptable to different locations. They can be planted in the perennial border, and treated like other perennials. They can be grown in a separate bulb bed — a spectacular site. Many types can be put right in the lawn and allowed to spread and naturalize. Each way, they will bloom dependably year after year. I've planted bulbs in each of these ways in the Victory Garden and the suburban site, and I like them all. The perennial-bed approach is easy. And the naturalized planting is casual and charming. The separate bed is dazzling and space-efficient as well if the site is turned over to summer-flowering annuals after the bulbs have gone by.

One of the factors determining the site is the period of foliage ripening that follows

A spring bulb garden in flower with a red azalea

There are many kinds of plants that are known as bulbous, but not all rightly deserve the title. What they have in common is a thick growth at or below the soil line. However, they differ in the function of those growths, and as a result, they are cared for, stored, and propagated differently.

TUBERS

BEGONIA

A tuber, unlike a corm or bulb, has several eyes from which roots and stems develop. A tuberous plant, as opposed to a tuberous-rooted plant, bears only one tuber, which increases in size, slightly, with age. It does not divide of its own accord, but new tubers can be propagated by cutting the tuber into sections. Caladiums and tuberous-rooted begonias, which are misnamed, are both grown from tubers.

CORMS

CROCUS

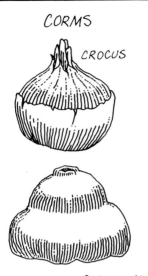

GLADIOLUS

There are two major differences between a corm and a bulb. A corm has a bud at its tip, whereas a bulb contains within its structure an entire flower in embryonic form. A parent corm dies after propagation, at the end of one flowering season, leaving behind several corms and cormels; by contrast, a bulb continues to live after it divides. Gladioluses and crocuses grow from corms.

BULBS

DAFFODIL

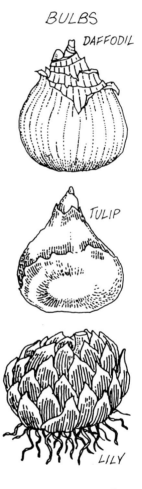

TULIP

LILY

A true bulb is an underground stem that stores the next season's flowers. Roots and new bulbs develop from the plate at the base of the bulb. Daffodils and tulips are both true bulbs.

TUBEROUS ROOTS

DAHLIA

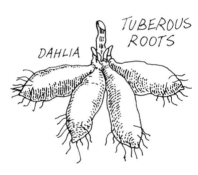

These are similar to tubers, the main difference being that tuberous-rooted plants develop several tubers during one growing season. These may be joined at a main stem, as are dahlias, or they may develop along the roots, like potatoes. These plants are propagated by separating the individual tubers.

RHIZOMES

BEARDED IRIS

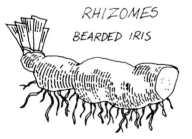

A rhizome is a thick, underground stem that grows horizontally, at or very near the surface of the soil. These plants, of which the bearded iris is a prime example, can be divided by cutting the rhizome into sections.

flowering. During this time, the bulbs draw strength from the leaves and put it in storage for another season. If the bulb is denied this part of the process, it suffers, and may die. So while the browning foliage isn't much to look at, it's necessary. During this time, the foliage of bulbs planted in a perennial border can be obscured with other, fresh plants (like annuals) and won't show much. But if a variety of bulbs is planted together in a separate bed, the garden will, from very early in the season, have a few browning leaves. In the Victory Garden our bulb garden is mostly tulips, and we get around this by lifting the bulbs after flowering, and either throwing them away or heeling them in elsewhere to ripen out of sight. (Tulips need special attention anyway. See this month's entry.)

Design I never put in a bulb garden without a good design on paper. These plants are so orderly in appearance that misplacement tends to be very obvious.

Regardless of the site where they're planted, the essential principle is always the same: plant masses of color. Even if you have only a dozen bulbs, put them all together for a handsome cluster. If you space them here and there they're just not as effective.

The Victory Garden bulb bed is a long rectangular site at the base of the greenhouse. Given its shape, I tend to plant in rectangular clusters, rather than the rounded ones that would be more appropriate in a more naturally shaped garden. I generally put the tallest-growing flowers toward the back, and the shorter ones in the front. As for the actual shape of the clusters, I've tried

A formal bulb garden, set out and ready for planting

two approaches, one quite formal and one more relaxed. The more formal planting is the square one, where the sides of the cluster are either parallel or perpendicular to the edges of the bed. The more casual effect is produced if the clusters are situated on the bias, that is, diagonally.

Season of bloom is another important consideration in designing a bulb garden. In general, the smaller the bulb the earlier the flower, but there are enough exceptions to this rule that the gardener should plan the season carefully. The actual blooming time varies from year to year, depending on the weather. It also depends on the site where the bulbs are planted. Most bulbs will flower with only filtered sunshine, but they'll be later than those with full-day sun.

Planting the Bulb Garden If I'm planting a full bulb garden in the fall, my first step is to transfer my paper plan to the garden site. This takes some measurement, but it's not difficult. I mark the periphery

of each single-variety cluster with bone meal until the entire design of the bed is visible on the soil. I label each cluster with a wooden plant label and indelible ink. Then I set the bulbs into place on the prepared soil (see After Frost).

As a rule, bulbs should be planted at a depth 3 times as great as their height from tip to base. For many of the smaller bulbs, a trowel is all that is needed to make a hole of the right depth. For larger plants that need to be 5 or 6 inches under the surface, either a trowel or a bulb planter will work. A bulb planter is a tapered metal cylinder with a handle at one end; the bottom of the cylinder has a serrated edge that will cut through any soil, even sodded soil. For even larger bulbs, such as giant allium, the bulb planter will not make a deep enough hole, so a spade is called for.

Regardless of how the hole is made or how deep it is, the treatment is the same once the soil is excavated: the soil at the bottom of the hole is loosened, a teaspoon of bone meal is added, and the bulb is set in; then the soil is replaced and firmed.

Naturalizing This is one of my favorite ways to handle bulbs. I have masses of narcissus naturalized in my yard, and while they're in fairly deep shade, under a pine tree, they come up year after year, always more of them than the year before. The planting is fairly easy, and as long as the foliage is allowed to mature, the yield is rewarding. (If bulbs are naturalized in the lawn, the mowing of that area must be postponed until the foliage is completely brown.)

Naturalized bulbs should look as if nature were responsible, not the gardener. For this reason, there should be no appearance of a "design." The placement should look random so that as the bulbs reproduce and the masses of bulbs increase, they form clumps in a natural, nongeometric pattern. For this reason, I advise against any sort of placement that is conscious; no matter how much you try to avoid a pattern, one tends to emerge. So what I do is toss the bulbs on the ground as I walk around the area I want to naturalize. Then I plant them where they land, moving the bulbs a couple of inches apart if they're touching.

The best bulbs for naturalizing are hardy and usually small. I put into this group crocus, grape hyacinth, squill, lily-of-the-valley, chionodoxa, and, while not as small as the rest, narcissus. (Tulips and hyacinths are not good choices because they're too formal.) Large-area plantings are a must. Some of the smaller bulbs will practically disappear if they're planted in insufficient numbers, and small plantings of narcissus look isolated and awkward. With the minor bulbs, I like to plant an area 2

or 3 feet in all directions, which means that many bulbs will be planted. With the minor bulbs, I skip the tossing routine, and just plant them 2 to 4 inches apart.

Whether they're planted in sod or in a garden bed, bulbs should be set in at a depth that is equal to 3 times their height from base to tip. A step-on bulb planter (one operated by foot) will work to cut through sod, but I often find it just as easy to use a sharpened spade. First of all, I dig down to the right depth and remove the sod. Then I loosen the soil at the base of the hole, scratch in a teaspoon or so of bone meal, and set the bulb in, tip up. Then I replace the sod and firm it with my foot. That's all there is to it.

Ongoing Care Bulbs are probably the easiest of all types of flowers to maintain. (Tulips are an exception here. See this month's entry.) In the spring, I cultivate the soil lightly with a hand-weeding tool to control weeds and loosen the soil. When the flowers begin to fade, I deadhead them, flower stem and all, leaving the foliage behind to ripen. (I only deadhead the larger bulbs; there's no practical way to deadhead the minor bulbs unless there are very few of them.) When all the flowers have gone by, I put a ring of 5-10-5 fertilizer (see the July feature) around the plants, at least 2 inches from the stem; this will nourish the plants through the important growing stage that follows flowering. The only remaining job is to clear away the foliage after it has lost all trace of green.

Reproduction Most bulbs can be left for years without being divided. (Tulips

and hyacinths are exceptions. See the October entries.) The bulbs will multiply underground. While it is better to leave the bulbs undisturbed if possible, they can be divided after their foliage has withered almost entirely. Two or more distinct bulbs are often connected at the basal plate. So, all that is involved is waiting until the foliage has turned brown, then digging them up carefully so they're not punctured in the process, and pulling them apart. Usually there are some large bulbs and some smaller ones. All will produce flowers eventually, so I suggest sorting them by size, and saving them all until the fall. For the months or weeks between digging and replanting, I store the dry bulbs in a cool spot where they have good air circulation. Old nylon stockings are an excellent container for them. (If your storage area is damp, I recommend coating them before storage with bulb dust or ground sulfur — both available from garden centers — to prevent rotting.)

If you already have patches of the minor bulbs growing on your property, you can propagate them very easily in the early spring or fall: just dig up several 4-inch squares of sod, 4 inches deep, and move them to the new location at 8- to 12-inch intervals. This avoids handling the individual bulbs — several are contained in those chunks of sod — and fills the area in very quickly. The leaves will die back if the sods are moved in the fall, but the plants will revive. If you want to control the area the bulbs occupy, you can keep them in bounds with a metal edging ribbon.

AFTER FROST

AFTER FROST

There are several weather factors that make autumn autumn — shorter days, dimmer light, drier soil and air — and all affect growing plants. But it is the first frost, when the temperature dips to 32°F or less, that can change the garden overnight. Not all plants die in the first frost; there are a few, including some annuals, that will continue to grow and even to flower after a light frost, to 30 degrees. A few flowering plants can even withstand temperatures into the mid-20s, though this is generally considered a hard, or killing, frost. Despite these survivors' instincts, most plants are noticeably poorer as the weather cools in the fall.

From the garden's point of view, autumn is much more than the end of summer. It is also an important period of preparation, both for the cold months ahead and for the spring that follows. In an established garden where plants are wintering over, the autumn jobs are to clear away old growth and mulch the bed for the winter. For a new garden, or for one that is empty of plants through winter, this is the time to prepare the soil.

Clearing the Garden Good housekeeping is a gardening must, for the sake of both health and appearance. One season's foliage does not decompose and disappear in the course of a single winter; if old stems and leaves are left in the garden, they will still be there in the spring, made tough and stringy by exposure to the elements. In that state, the foliage is very hard to remove — scissors just turn it to mush. So the time to clear old growth away is in the fall, when it is dry and easily cut, and when there are no emerging shoots underfoot to worry about.

Annuals can simply be pulled out, roots and all. With perennials, I just cut the foliage from the plant with clippers or hedge shears, leaving a stub 3 or 4 inches tall; I don't like to come any closer to the soil for fear of cutting into the crown and jeopardizing the future life of the plant. As a rule, the foliage of spring-flowering bulbs is removed as soon as it has withered completely, usually in early summer, but if this hasn't been done yet, it should be attended to now. All of this old foliage can be added to the compost pile (see below).

Roses are woody perennials that should *not* be pruned more than necessary. For more about mulching roses, see below.

Winter Mulching Winter can be very hard on plants, but the problem is not, as you might think, the long months of deep freeze. If the plants you're growing are hardy in your area (see the zone map in the Appendix), normal low tem-

peratures won't bother them at all. The threat comes instead
from mild winter days when the sun is warm enough to thaw
bare ground, which then freezes again when temperatures
drop at night. The freeze-and-thaw cycle causes the ground
to expand and contract, and this movement dislodges plants,
heaving them out of the soil into cold, dry air that will kill
them almost immediately.

A winter mulch prevents this problem by shading the
soil so that it remains frozen all winter, while at the same
time allowing air and moisture to penetrate. Nature's mulch
is snow, and in areas that can count on a snow cover of 4 or
5 inches all winter long, no further mulching is necessary.
Here in the Victory Garden we have many winters when the
snowfall is scant, and these open, cold periods are torture
for plants. So we faithfully mulch our perennials and biennials, both established plants and youngsters in nursery beds,
every fall. Ordinarily bulbs don't need mulching, but because
ours are in a raised bed and often planted rather close to the
edge where they are more exposed to the elements than

*Raised beds in the Victory Garden
with a winter mulch of salt marsh
hay*

usual, we mulch the bulbs too. We also mulch the walkways between the beds to cut off channels where cold air could whip through.

A good mulch is an organic material that has not been treated with weed killer; that has an open texture that blocks sunshine but allows air and water to reach the soil; and that has substance enough to retain this texture fairly well — they all mat down some — through a season of ice and snow. In the Victory Garden we use salt marsh hay; it's a particularly good choice because the weed seeds it carries are unable to sprout outside the briny environment of the marsh. This material is easy to come by in coastal regions like ours, but most areas of the country have some locally available material that is widely used as a mulch; these include buckwheat hulls, ground tobacco stems, and peanut shells, among many others. And some good mulches are available throughout the country: hay, straw, pine needles, the branches of discarded Christmas trees. Half-decomposed compost is chunky enough to make a good mulch, and it provides nourishment as well. The leaves of deciduous trees are another choice; they tend to mat down quite a bit over the course of the winter, but you can prevent this by mixing twigs in with the leaves to create air spaces. Decorative mulches commonly associated with warm weather, such as wood chips and bark, can also be used as a winter mulch, but if you need a fair amount of mulch you may find this an expensive choice.

Adding Mulch Winter mulches should always be applied after the ground has frozen solid, which may be as much as 2 months after the first fall frost. Don't put the mulch on prematurely, while the ground is still soft, as rodents are apt to nest in the mulch and burrow down to feed on your planted bulbs and roots. If you wait until the ground is hard, the rodents will have found other nesting places. Most mulches should be applied in a layer 4 to 6 inches deep; the warm-weather mulches are so coarse that a 2-inch layer is probably enough. The mulch should completely blanket the surface of the soil, including the crowns of the plants.

Removing Mulch If the mulch is half-decomposed compost, the only spring job is to pull the mulch away from the crowns of the plants so new growth can emerge easily. I usually arrange it in a saucer around the crowns to help trap and direct water toward the roots. All other mulches must be removed after winter. I do this by hand, wearing gloves and working carefully. I don't touch any sort of tool to the ground at this time of the year as there's too much danger of nicking the top of some tiny shoot just breaking through the soil.

I don't like to remove all the mulch at once because after months of dense shade, bright spring sunlight can easily burn new growth. Instead, I remove the mulch in two stages. First I take off the top half of the layer, which allows more light to reach the soil so the plants can start greening but still protects the new shoots from the full intensity of the sun. After about a week, I remove the rest of the mulch. The plants will have no trouble weathering a frost, but temperatures into the low 20s wouldn't help them along much, so I keep the mulching material on hand for another few weeks, and cover the plants for the night if a blast of cold is predicted. Once we're reliably into warm spring weather, I add the mulch to the composter. (If they make it through winter without reducing to a soggy mess, mulches can be used again. After removing them from the soil, I leave them in the sun until they're dry. Then I either put them back on the garden as a summer mulch in a 2- or 3-inch layer — see the July feature — or store them dry until the following fall.)

It's important to remove the mulch early enough in the spring so the plants do not grow more than 1 or 2 inches in height under the darkness of the mulch; plants develop weak stems if they're forced to reach for light. For perennials and biennials, whether established plants or yearlings in the nursery bed, I like to have all the mulch removed by 3 weeks before the last expected frost, which is April 20 in the Victory Garden. So I begin the two-stage operation the last week of March.

Mulched roses at the suburban site, the tree roses given the additional protection of straw and burlap

Mulching Roses Two factors affect the ability of grafted roses to survive winter: good drainage and protection from bitter, penetrating cold and drying winds. Without sufficient drainage, water accumulates in the soil, freezes in the cold weather, and causes ice damage to the roots. Without protection from cold temperatures, the top growth of the plant is in jeopardy, and often some or all of the canes die back. Roots can usually recover from severe cane loss, but if the bud union itself is killed, the hybrid scion that produces the lovely flowers is dead; the hardy understock may send up a few flowers, but they won't be very appealing. (Ungrafted roses are not a worry in regard to winter. Most, including the old roses and climbers, are very hardy and can survive well into Zone 4, even without protection. For more about the grafting process, see the April entry.)

Providing good drainage is a once-only opportunity, and must be done at planting (see the April entry). Protecting the plant's top growth is a yearly job done every fall, after the first hard frost. This blast of subfreezing weather will help to harden the wood, better preparing the plants for winter; it's not enough to harm the bud union, which can survive unprotected to around 10°F.

Throughout about half the country, from Zone 6 southward, it is enough to treat roses as equal members of the perennial garden and give them only the protection afforded the other perennials (see above). The Victory Garden, while technically in Zone 5, is so close to Zone 6 that this is all we need to do. But for most gardeners in Zones 3 through 5, the 4- to 6-inch layer of mulch that blankets the perennials will not be enough to see grafted roses through the winter.

One way to increase the amount of protection is by using a thicker layer of mulch, up to 12 inches or so, hilled up in a pyramid around the plant's stem. The function of the rose mulch is somewhat different from the function of a perennial mulch; in addition to shading the soil in order to prevent the repeated cycle of freeze and thaw, it must also act as a barrier to bitter cold and piercing winds. For this reason, the hilling-up materials are denser than those suggested for perennials; usually either soil or peat moss is used. If soil, it should be brought in from another section of the garden, not pulled in from right around the plant, as this can expose the root system even as it protects the crown. This hilling-up with an extra quantity of mulch is probably enough to protect roses through most of Zone 5.

There are devices on the market that provide more protection than hilling up by holding a larger amount of soil in place around the stem. They are collars, made of nylon screening and available in several diameters; they are all 12 inches tall. The collar should be large enough around so it is not in contact with the canes. It is slipped around the plant, and filled with a mulching material; then additional mulch is hilled up around the outside of the collar.

For those in the coldest areas of the country, the ultimate winter rose protection is the complete enclosure, with each plant individually wrapped or covered. You can do this yourself by putting stakes in the ground, and wrapping burlap or wire mesh around the outer periphery of the stakes. When I use this arrangement, I prune the bushes back to 2 feet tall, and build a structure that tops the plant by 2 or 3 inches. Then I fill in the enclosure with mulch, and hill up around the outside with 6 to 8 inches of additional mulch (again, brought in from another part of the garden). I've rarely lost more than the tips of the canes with this approach, even in much colder areas than the Victory Garden. This gives the plants a 2-foot head start on the growing season in the spring, and produces large plants for the summer.

Another option is to buy one of the styrofoam snow cones on the market. These are more expensive than the do-it-yourself approach, and they're not particularly good looking. In addition, the bush must be pruned so the cone fits over without touching. On the plus side, the cones provide complete enclosure, they're reusable from year to year, and they stack together for compact storage. They're also easy to use. After pruning, just slip the cone over and weight it down with a brick or heavy stone. Then hill up around the bottom with 6 to 8 inches of mulch to close off any air pockets that may be left where the cone meets the ground. If the temperatures rise about 60°F, make sure to open the tops to provide ventilation.

Winter rose protection should be removed on the same schedule as the perennial mulch (see above). For more, see the April entry.

Soil Preparation Gardeners are faced with a whole range of unalterable conditions: temperature, rainfall, sunlight, frost dates. The nature of the soil does not belong in this list. It is one variable that gardeners can and should do something about. In fact, I consider thorough soil preparation an absolute must for a good garden. It loosens the soil so air and water can move through. It nourishes the soil so that the soil can in turn nourish the plants. I'd stop shy of saying that soil preparation can work miracles, but it can bring almost any soil to near-optimum conditions.

The process described here is overall soil preparation, including adding materials to improve the soil and turning it over to a depth of several inches. This can only be done in a new garden, or in one where the plants are removed at the end of the season. (For the ongoing care that replenishes established beds, see the September and October features.) I like to do this job in the fall because it gives the added ingredients time to work thoroughly into the soil. However, if you are planting annuals only, and if you do not have sod to contend with, you can leave the soil preparation until spring (see the May feature).

Removing Sod If grass now covers the site where you want your garden to be, you will have to remove the sod. I strongly recommend that this be done in the fall.

It is possible to till sod into the soil with a rotary tilling machine, but I don't find that this works particularly well. For one thing, it's a big job for the average tilling machine designed for home use. For another, it leaves bits of severed roots throughout the soil, which may be able to regenerate if they are within a couple of inches of the surface.

LIFTING SOD

3" TO 4" THICK

This means that grass tilled in the fall can easily reappear in the spring.

My preference is to separate the sod from the soil in layers 3 to 4 inches deep. In the case of some shallow-rooted grasses, this will remove the entire plant. Some roots of deeper-rooted grasses may be left behind, but it is difficult to take a layer of sod thicker than 3 or 4 inches. Depending on the variety of the grass grown, the sod may or may not come up easily. I suggest starting with a grub hoe to remove patches of sod about 3 or 4 inches across. If the grub hoe isn't up to the job, try a spade. You can begin the spading process by cutting out a square of sod about 6 inches to each side. Once this piece is removed, you should be able to slide the spade under the roots and pry up the sod.

The sod should not be discarded. It's a valuable source of organic matter, and it has its grip on your best topsoil, which you don't want to lose. You have three options for putting the sod to use:

The first is to bury the sod, upside down, under 12 inches of soil and scatter 5-10-5 fertilizer over it to help it decompose quickly. From this depth, there is no likelihood that the grasses will be able to sprout. This is a good method, and it will allow you to complete soil preparation in the fall because the sod is so deep. But it's very hard work.

Another option, and the one I've used in our suburban site, is to shake the topsoil from the patches of sod into the garden, and then add the clumps of grass to the compost pile (see below). This also leaves the garden free for complete fall soil preparation while it saves valuable organic matter. And it is much easier than the first method.

The third option is one I recommend only if you intend to plant annuals the following season. Simply remove the sod and flip it over, scattering 5-10-5 and lime or sulfur to correct the pH (see below). Then leave the rest of the job of preparing the soil for the spring. The sod won't decay completely over winter, but it will be far enough along by spring for you to work it in easily, especially with a tiller. The exposed roots will probably die in the winter cold, so they shouldn't sprout again.

Correcting pH The pH scale measures the level of acidity or alkalinity in the soil. This is an important aspect of soil chemistry because it affects the availability of certain needed chemicals to growing plants. There are even pH levels at which plants will not grow. The scale runs from 0 to 14, 0 being completely acidic, 14 being completely alkaline, and 7.0 being neutral. For most growing plants, slightly acid soil is best, with a pH of 6.0 to 6.8. Few soils enjoy this level naturally, so adjusting the pH is a regular part of soil preparation.

The only way to determine the pH reading of your soil is with a soil test. You can either do this yourself with a kit you buy from a garden center — the simple ones are inexpensive and will do the job — or you can send soil samples to your county agricultural service for analysis. If you decide on the latter, you will receive a report detailing not only the pH of the soil, but its nutrient content and the steps you should take to bring the soil to optimum growing conditions. (For more about the nutrients necessary in gardening, see the July feature.)

In the Victory Garden, our soil runs toward acid, so we add ground dolomite limestone to raise the pH. Ground agricultural sulfur will correct for alkalinity. To change the pH by one whole point, spread 5 to 6 pounds of the appropriate material over 100 square feet of soil. I usually add enough limestone to bring the pH close to 6.8, because over the course of the winter, as it seeps into the soil, some will be lost. By correcting to the maximum, I know that I will still have a pH reading within the acceptable range by spring. All I do is spread the limestone over the soil surface in as fine and even a layer as possible — a spreader isn't really necessary — and then lightly rake it in so that it begins to work into the soil with the next rain.

Correcting the soil pH is one job that really must be done in the fall. Lime and sulfur both leach through slowly, and the long months of winter give them time to blend thoroughly with the soil. This is an extremely simple job that takes practically no time. I recommend taking care of it in the fall, even if you plan to grow only annuals the next year.

In sandy soils, it may be necessary to correct the pH of the soil every year. In bulkier soil, where limestone and sulfur should both be fairly stable, a soil test every 3 years is probably sufficient. This is important not only for new gardens, but for established perennial or bulb beds; if additional limestone or sulfur is indicated, it can be added to the soil surface in the fall, after the past season's foliage is cleared away, and before the winter mulch is added.

Adding Organic Matter Organic matter is plant or animal material in the process of decay. It is hard to overstate the role it plays in soil improvement. It gives the soil substance; it creates air spaces so water and nutrients can circulate to the plants' roots; and it holds water, almost like a sponge, so that roots may absorb moisture gradually between waterings or rainfall. While I don't recommend organic matter as the only source of nutrients for soil, it does add needed elements to the soil's chemistry, and contributes to the release of soil-held nutrients.

I add organic matter to the soil whenever I have the opportunity. A thin, 1-inch layer spread over the soil of an established perennial border in the spring will supply nutrients to the soil and, through earthworm activity, will gradually work down to blend with the soil. When I put a new plant in the perennial border in place of an older one, I add organic matter to the excavated soil. And when I prepare a new garden bed, especially one where bulbs or perennials will grow, I add a layer of 2 to 4 inches of organic matter when the soil is prepared in the fall.

There are several types of organic matter that can be added to the garden. Because it replicates nature's blend of many kinds of plant life, compost is best. Leaf mold, which is compost made exclusively of leaves, is an excellent material but it is extremely slow to decay, requiring 2 to 3 years to break down before it can be put on the garden. I prefer to add leaf rakings to the compost pile, which speeds their decay.

The composter that we use in the Victory Garden is one we designed and built ourselves. It's slightly more elaborate than other designs I've seen, but it works like a charm. (For directions, see the illustrations.) It has 3 separate bins so that as the material begins to break down, it can be

Building the Composter

1. Lay the bottom members on a flat section of ground: put two 9-foot lengths of 2″ × 4″ lumber 33 inches apart from outer edge to outer edge.

2. Cut 4 of the 12-foot lengths of lumber into 4 pieces each. Two of the pieces should be 32 inches long to form the sides of each of the bin dividers. The other two pieces should be 36 inches long, for the top and bottom of each divider. (Assembled in this way, the joints are protected from the elements.)

3. Staple a 3-foot square of wire fencing to one side of each divider. Drill and bolt the dividers to the bottom members, making sure that the wire on the end dividers faces outward.

4. Brace the back of the composter with a 9-foot strip of 2″ × 4″ lumber across the top of the dividers.

5. Cut a 9-foot length of wire and fasten it to the back of the composter with galvanized poultry-wire staples.

6. The front end of each bin is closed off as the bins are filled. We use 6 1″ × 6″ boards for each bin, with staples or nails partially driven into the long edges to allow for ventilation space. The boards slide into position along grooved strips nailed to the front of each divider. The two outside strips are L-shaped, and the inside strips are T-shaped; both are cut on a table saw from 2″ × 4″ lumber.

Materials

2" × 4" framing lumber, treated with a good wood preservative (do not use creosote)	3 9-foot lengths (for bottom members and top brace) 5 12-foot lengths (for dividers and grooved strips)
1" × 6" common pine	18 3-foot lengths (for front slats)
2" × 2" welded, galvanized 36" dog-wire or wire fencing	21-foot length (for dividers and back section)
⅝" galvanized carriage bolts, 4 inches long	12 (to secure dividers to bottom members and top brace)
16-penny galvanized spikes	5 pounds (to fasten the sides of the dividers)
Galvanized poultry-wire staples	250 (to secure wire fencing to dividers and back section)

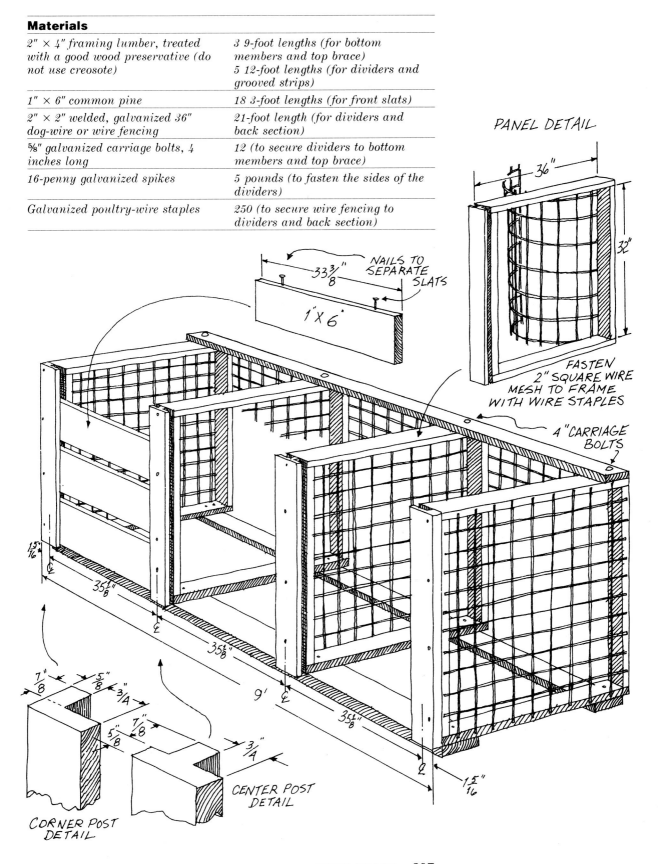

PANEL DETAIL

36"

32"

FASTEN 2" SQUARE WIRE MESH TO FRAME WITH WIRE STAPLES

4" CARRIAGE BOLTS

NAILS TO SEPARATE SLATS

33⅜"

1" X 6"

15/16"

35⅛"

35⅛"

35⅛"

9'

CORNER POST DETAIL

7/8" 5/8" 3/4"

CENTER POST DETAIL

7/8" 5/8" 3/4"

15/16"

moved from one bin to another. The process of turning the material over speeds its decay, and this 3-bin setup makes it possible to separate piles of compost in different stages, some old and ready to use, some new and only beginning to decay, and some in between.

I don't recommend adding animal scraps or fat to compost, as they tend to smell and attract pests. But any kind of plant life is fine, including grass clippings (if no weed killer has been used on the lawn), flowers, stems, apple cores, overgrown zucchinis. I put this kind of material in the bottom of one bin of the composter; it decays more quickly if it's chopped or shredded first, but it can be added whole. When this layer is 5 to 10 inches deep, I add 10-10-10 or 5-10-5 fertilizer or a layer of horse manure to speed decay. Then another 5 to 10 inches of plant material, topped with a dusting of ground limestone and a couple of inches of soil. Actually, the sequencing of these layers is not important, so long as these proportions are followed.

I always build up the sides of the layers somewhat, so there's a bowl in the center to hold water. If there's a dry spell that lasts a few days, I water the pile to keep the decay process going. During the hottest part of the summer, I often cover the pile with plastic, hay, or grass clippings to hold moisture in. (The compost will decay fastest in the shade, because the material will dry out less quickly.) When the material has decayed to the point where it is all a uniform color and its structure is clearly breaking down, I fork the contents of the first bin into the second, and begin a new pile in the first. When the material in the second bin is a dark crumbly brown, having lost nearly all of its original structure, I fork it into the third bin, and use it as I need it to improve the soil before planting.

If you don't have space for a composter, you might contact your municipal government to see if there is a town composting program. If not, you will have to turn to other sources of organic matter. Manure is excellent, if you can get it. Cow manure is best, but horse manure is more available these days. In the fall, fresh manure can be put on the garden, but if you are doing soil preparation in the spring, the manure must be at least 6 months old or it will be so caustic that it will burn the roots of spring plantings.

If you can't get compost or manure, you can also buy organic material from garden centers. The best choices are peat moss and composted cow manure. Be sure you do not buy dehydrated cow manure for this purpose; it is much more concentrated than the composted material, and must be used in small portions, as a fertilizer. (For more, see the July feature.)

Improving Drainage In the Victory Garden, where we add organic matter to our soil regularly, and where our beds are raised above ground level, drainage is not much of a problem. But in some soils, especially those with a great deal of clay, something must be added to lighten the texture so that air and water can circulate. This is particularly important in perennial and bulb beds, as poor drainage will result in overly wet soil and winter ice damage. To test the drainage of your soil, dig a little depression, an inch or so deep and 8 or 10 inches across, and fill it with water. If the water doesn't drain away in an hour, you've got drainage problems, and I suggest working in a 2-inch layer of builder's sand to correct this poor state of affairs. If the soil is so light that water drains through very quickly, add organic matter to give the soil more body. This can be done either in the fall or spring, with general soil preparation.

Adding Bone Meal This is one of the best natural fertilizers available. It contains negligible amounts of nitrogen, but it is very rich in phosphorus, which helps plants develop strong root systems, so it is a valuable soil addition in perennial and bulb beds. Most fertilizers should be added in the spring because they move so quickly through the soil, but bone meal, if applied to the soil surface, moves down to the root zone extremely slowly. For this reason, I always try to put it into soil that I can mix by hand, either at the time of overall soil preparation, or when perennial-bed soil is excavated to make ready for a new plant. When it is applied with general soil preparation, I add it at the rate of 3 to 6 pounds per 100 square feet. For a single-site excavation I'd add a good handful of bone meal for a bushel-basket-size hole.

Turning the Soil Once all the necessary additions are layered on the surface of the soil, the next step is to turn them in, which also has the effect of opening and loosening the soil. This can be done with a rotary tilling machine, but most flower gardens are small enough to warrant doing the whole thing by hand, with a spading fork. To avoid digging and redigging the same soil, see the procedure suggested in the illustrations.

In the Victory Garden, we dig all our beds to a depth of 8 to 12 inches. (A bed where only annuals are to be grown need be dug only to a depth of 4 to 6 inches.) Then we leave the grade rough over winter. In the spring, when the soil has dried out enough to work — it's ready if a ball of soil, squeezed together, breaks apart with the flick of a finger — I rake the bed smooth with a steel rake. Then I'm ready for planting.

ZONE MAP

This is the zone map for the United States and Canada, based on the U.S. Department of Agriculture's survey. It divides the area into 10 zones, the lines of demarcation being based on the expected minimum winter temperature. As you can see from the chart, each zone represents a ten-degree differential.

In the perennial and bulb entries in this book, I have indicated the zones where the plants can be expected to do well. However, these zones are based on averages over large geographical areas, and there will be important variations within each zone. For instance, the Victory Garden and the suburban site are both in Zone 5, and only a few miles apart. But the Victory Garden is very close to the border of Zone 6, and noticeably warmer; some plants that do well here are marginal at best in the suburban garden. So if I were you, I would talk to neighbors who garden, and ask them about the subtleties of the local weather. Even this is not foolproof, as differences in air circulation and moisture, even over a very short distance, can affect the miniclimate of one individual garden. The best gauge of all is your own record; once you've been gardening in one site for a few years, you will know what you can expect in the way of weather.

Please note that this map does not indicate the dates for last spring and first fall frost. These dates vary dramatically over a small area, so your county agricultural agent and neighbors who garden are your best sources of information.

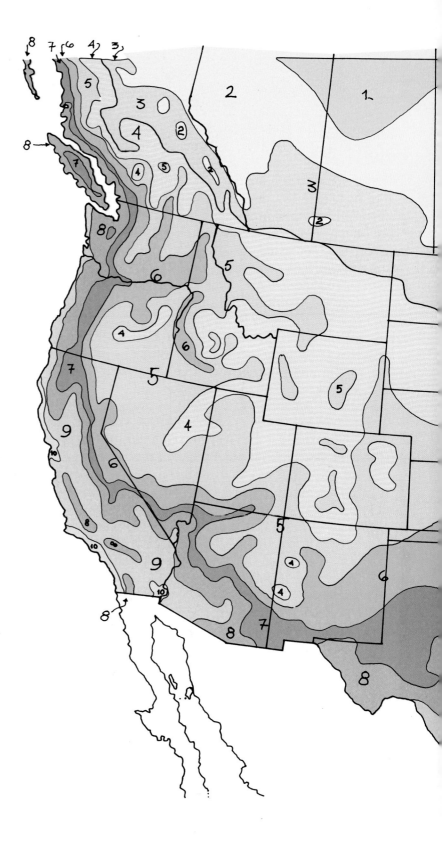

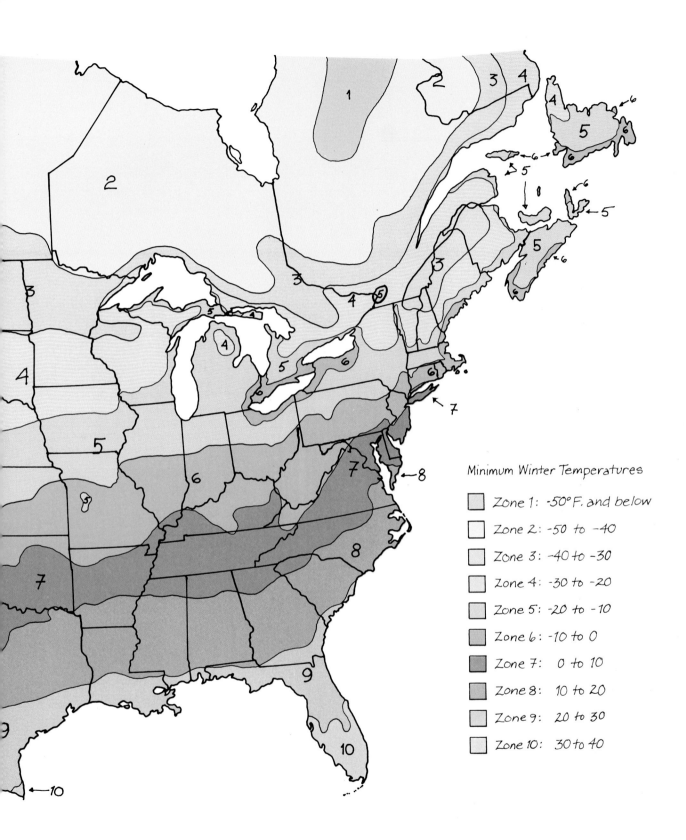

Minimum Winter Temperatures

☐	Zone 1: -50°F. and below
☐	Zone 2: -50 to -40
☐	Zone 3: -40 to -30
☐	Zone 4: -30 to -20
☐	Zone 5: -20 to -10
☐	Zone 6: -10 to 0
☐	Zone 7: 0 to 10
☐	Zone 8: 10 to 20
☐	Zone 9: 20 to 30
☐	Zone 10: 30 to 40

INDEX

Numbers in italics indicate an illustration or photograph of the subject.

A

abrasion, of rose canes, 124
accent plants, 140, 259, 265
acidity, soil, 295–296; for bearded iris, 186; for Japanese iris, 104
aeration of soil, 191, 293, 296, 299
African marigold. *See* marigold, African
ageratum, *39, 40*; sowing seeds, 39–40; thinning, 40; transplanting, 40; hardening off, 40; setting out, *133*–134; starting new seedlings, 134 (also 182); shearing back, 134; growing in containers, 190; lead time of, 175; replacing, 194; varieties of, 39 (also *133*)
Ageratum houstonianum. See ageratum
agricultural agent, 161, 175, 224
agricultural extension service, 295
air circulation, 128–129 (also 299); for bulb storage, 285; for disease prevention, 45, 102, 147, 148–149, 172, 197; in perennial border, 260; providing, for clematis, 91; providing, for roses, 120, 160
Alcea rosea. See hollyhock
alkalinity, soil, 295–296
All-America Winners, 176. *See also entries for individual plants*
allium, giant: planting, 265; blossoming period of, 265 (also 182); propagation of, 265; dividing, 265; drying seed heads, 265; as accent flower, 282
allium, Neapolitan: planting, 265; blossoming period of, 265
Allium giganteum. See allium, giant
A. neapolitanum. See allium, Neapolitan
Althaea rosea. See hollyhock
alyssum, perennial, *81*, 167–168, 260; sowing seeds, 195 (also 16); transplanting, 195 (also 81);

hardening off, 195; wintering over, 195 (also 81); mulching, 195; setting out, 195 (also 81); shearing back, 82; dividing, 82; propagating, 82
alyssum, sweet. *See* sweet alyssum
Alyssum saxatile. See alyssum, perennial
amaranth, globe. *See* globe amaranth
annual bed, *176, 177*; biennials in, 97, 127, 198; bulbs in, 282; perennials in, 218, 232; planning, 33, 34, 174; planting, *178, 179*
annuals: soil preparation for, 177 (also 295, 299); sowing seeds, 175, 176 (also 38, 240); transplanting, 242 (also 80); pinching back, 243–244; hardening off, 244 (also 80, 175); setting out, 246 (also 132, 175); fertilizing, 177 (also 194); staking, 177; flowering period of, 174, 194, 259; watering, 220–221 (also 194); deadheading, 177; cutting back, 194; mulching, 227; sowing seeds outdoors, 240; replacing, 194, 230; pulling out, 264, 288; growing in containers, 190–191; lead time of, 38, *chart 175*; life cycle of, 258; in perennial border, 174, 259; seed production of, 174, 224, 225; tuberous, 175; uses for, 174
annuals, perennials treated as, 174, 175, 258; blue salvia, 60; browallia, 136; gazania, 49; geranium, 22; nierembergia, 56; sweet alyssum, 67; verbena, 70
Antirrhinum majus. See snapdragon
aphids, 98, 153, *160*, 161; hosing off, 147, 224
Aquilegia flabellata. See columbine
A. x hybrida. See columbine
artemisia, *82*; soil preparation for, 82–83; setting out, 83; cutting back, 83, 231; taking cuttings, 83, 231; transplanting, 231; mulching, 83; varieties of, 83
Artemisia Schmidtiana. See artemisia
aster, New England, *111*; setting out, 111–112; flowering period of, 111, 250; pinching back, 111; dividing, 112; naturalizing, 259; in perennial border, 260; varieties of, 111

aster (annual): sowing seeds of, 40–41; hardening off, 41; setting out, 135; diseases and pests of, 40, 134–135; as cut flowers, 40, 135, 174; as hot weather plant, 230; lead time of, 175; varieties of, 135, 230
Aster novae-angliae. See aster, New England
aster (perennial). *See* aster, New England
aster-yellows, 40, 134, 135
Aurinia saxatilis. See alyssum, perennial
autumn. *See* fall
axe, 106, 245
azalea, *282*

B

baby's breath: setting out, 83–84; cutting back, 84; drying, 217; dividing, 84; propagation of, 84
bachelor's buttons. *See* cornflower
balloonflower: sowing seeds of, 195–196; transplanting, 80; wintering over, 196; setting out, 85, 196; flowering season of, 195; varieties of, 85, 195–196
balloonflower, Marie's: propagation of, 196; taking stem cuttings, 194, 195, 196. *See also* balloonflower
bamboo stakes, 226
bare-root plants: planting, 96, 247, *261*
bare-root roses, 120; planting, *121*, 122
basal offshoots, 99, 101
bedding plants: annuals, 50, 51, 56, 58, 133, 141, 174; biennials, 211, 259; perennials, 19, 20, 26, 29, 149, 259
bee balm, *86, 196*; sowing seeds, 196–197 (also 16); pinching back, 197; wintering over, 197; setting out, 86, 196–197; diseases of, 86, 197; propagation of, 85; dividing, 85, 197; taking stem cuttings, 197 (also 194); cutting back, 86; naturalizing, 259; varieties of, 197
bees, plants attractive to, 85, 159, 196
Begonia x semperflorens-cultorum. See wax begonia
Begonia tuberhybrida. See tuberous-rooted begonia
bellflower, peach-leafed: sowing seed, 212–213; transplanting, 213; wintering over, 213; setting out, 114; dividing, 114, 213
Bellis perennis. See English daisy

Design and art direction by Dianne Schaefer/Designworks
Color separation and film by Black Dot
Typesetting by DEKR
Printing and binding by W. A. Krueger
Paper: 70 lb. Warrenflo by S. D. Warren